Passenger on the Pearl

Passenger on the Pearl

The True Story of Emily Edmonson's Flight from Slavery

WINIFRED CONKLING

ALGONQUIN YOUNG READERS
2015

Published by
ALGONQUIN YOUNG READERS
An imprint of Algonquin Books of Chapel Hill
Post Office Box 2225
Chapel Hill, North Carolina 27515-2225

a division of
WORKMAN PUBLISHING
225 Varick Street
New York, New York 10014

PHOTO CREDITS
Getty Museum: Page 116; Library of Congress: Pages 2, 4, 5, 7, 12, 18, 21, 25, 27,
36–37, 40, 42, 48, 50, 64, 68, 69, 81, 82, 83, 86, 87, 89, 90, 101, 103, 111, 114, 121, 127,
128, 133, 138, 149; Louisiana State Museum: Page 67; National Archives: Page 58;
New York Public Library: Page 91; Onondaga Historical Society: Page 109;
Wikipedia Commons: 75, 108, 140.

Library of Congress Cataloging-in-Publication Data
Conkling, Winifred.
Passenger on the Pearl : the true story of Emily Edmonson's flight
from slavery / Winifred Conkling.—First edition.
pages cm
Includes bibliographical references.
ISBN 978-1-61620-196-8
1. Edmonson, Emily, 1835–1895—Juvenile literature. 2. Pearl (Schooner)—
Juvenile literature. 3. Fugitive slaves—Washington Region—Biography—Juvenile
literature. 4. Fugitive slaves—Washington Region—History—19th century—Juvenile
literature. 5. Antislavery movements—Washington Region—History—19th century—
Juvenile literature. 6. Antislavery movements—United States—History—19th century—
Juvenile literature. 7. Underground Railroad—Washington Region—Juvenile literature.
8. Washington Region—History—19th century—Juvenile literature.
9. Edmondson family—Juvenile literature. I. Title.
E445.D6C66 2015
306.3'62092—dc23
[B]   2014029246

10 9 8 7 6 5 4 3 2 1
First Edition

Contents

No man can tell the intense agony which is felt by the slave when wavering on the point of making his escape. All that he has is at stake; and even that which he has not is at stake also. The life which he has may be lost, and the liberty which he seeks, may not be gained.

FREDERICK DOUGLASS
My Bondage and My Freedom, 1855

ONE

A Mother's Sorrow

W HEN AMELIA CULVER met Paul Edmonson, she had no intention of ever marrying. Milly, as she was known, enjoyed spending time with Paul at church on Sundays, and the more she learned about him the more she cared for him, but she did not want to be his wife. She realized that she had fallen in love, but she was not concerned about love. Milly knew the truth: She was enslaved, and in Montgomery County, Maryland, in the early 19th century, her future did not belong to her.

At the time, Paul was enslaved on a nearby farm. They would not be able to live together as man and wife because they had different owners; but if they married, Milly and Paul would be able to see each other from time to time. Any children they might have would be born into bondage, owned by Milly's master. Milly understood that the joy of marriage and family would end in heartbreak when her children—her babies—grew old enough to be torn away from her to work or to be sold in the slave market.

Despite what seemed like inevitable sadness, Paul asked Milly to marry him. She turned him down. Milly longed for love and family, but still more, she longed for liberty. "I loved Paul very much," Milly said. "But I thought it wasn't right to bring children into the world to be slaves."

Milly's family and others at Asbury Methodist Church in Washington, D.C., urged her to reconsider Paul's offer, arguing that Paul was a good man and it was her Christian duty to marry and have children.

Paul proposed again, and this time she accepted.

The copper plate used to make this engraving was discovered by workmen clearing the ruins of Pennsylvania Hall in Philadelphia, which was built by the Pennsylvania Anti-Slavery Society. After it was completed, the building stood for only three days before it was burned to the ground by anti-black rioters on May 17, 1838.

"THIS CHILD ISN'T OURS"

As Milly had predicted, the painful realities of love within slavery soon followed. "Well, Paul and me, we was married, and we was happy enough," Milly said. "But when our first child was born I says to him, 'There 'tis now, Paul, our troubles is begun. This child isn't ours.

"'Oh, Paul,' says I, 'what a thing it is to have children that isn't ours!'

"Paul, he says to me, 'Milly, my dear, if they be God's children, it ain't so much matter whether they be ours or no; they may be heirs of the kingdom.'" Milly tried to find peace in his words, but she still worried.

In the early years of her marriage, Milly and her young children lived with her mistress, Rebecca Culver, and Culver's married sister in Colesville, Maryland. It was not uncommon for an enslaved person to be freed when his owner died, and in 1821, Paul's owner freed him in her will. While many owners did not recognize slave marriages, Culver allowed Milly to work as a seamstress and live with Paul and their children on a local farm. Milly and Paul continued to have children, increasing Culver's wealth significantly.

"I had mostly sewing," Milly said. "Sometimes a shirt to make in a day—it was coarse like, you know—or a pair of sheets or some such, but whatever 'twas, I always got it done. Then I had all my housework and babies to take care of and many's the time after ten o'clock I've took my children's clothes and washed 'em all out and ironed 'em late in the night 'cause I couldn't never bear to see my children dirty. Always wanted to see 'em sweet and clean. I brought 'em up and taught 'em the very best ways I was able."

Culver was mentally challenged and she was never able to manage her finances on her own. In 1827, Culver's brother petitioned the court in Montgomery County to have her ruled legally incompetent. The judge agreed and named her brother-in-law, Francis Valdenar, as guardian of her business affairs, which included oversight of Milly and her children.

By the mid-1830s, Milly had given birth to fourteen children, eight girls and six boys. She lived in constant fear that they would be taken from her. "I never seen a white man come onto the place that I didn't think, There, now, he's coming to look at my children," Milly said. "And when I saw any white man going by, I've called in my children and hid 'em for fear he'd see 'em and want to buy 'em."

In time, Milly's fears were realized. As was common practice at the time, when any of her children reached age 12 or 13, he or she was taken from home and hired out to families in the Washington, D.C., area to live and work as domestic slaves. Their wages were sent back to Culver, who depended on this income.

Heartbroken, Milly begged her girls not to marry until they were free so that they would not become mothers of children born into slavery. She said, "Now, girls, don't you never come to the sorrows that I have. Don't you never marry till you get your liberty. Don't you marry to be mothers to children that ain't your own." Each of the Edmonson children, both the boys and the girls, shared their mother's belief that aside from their duty to God, nothing was more important than freedom.

In 1863, Henry Louis Stephens (1824–1882) created this lithograph titled "The Sale." The image is the third in a 12-part series of antislavery trading cards titled "Journey of a Slave from the Plantation to the Battlefield." Abolitionists distributed the cards as a means of spreading their message.

AN UNCERTAIN FUTURE

Over the years, Valdenar had allowed the five oldest Edmonson sisters—Elizabeth, Martha, Eveline, Henrietta, and Eliza—to buy their freedom. They raised the money by taking on extra work and keeping a portion of their earnings, or by accepting money from family and friends. By 1848, Culver was in poor health, and she faced growing debts. Six of the Edmonson children were hired out at the time. There were no plans for their imminent sale, but the siblings realized that their futures were far from secure. Slave owners prized the Edmonson children for their honesty, intelligence, and morality; slave dealers prized them because they could demand a high price on the auction block. Would Valdenar sell one or more of them to pay Culver's expenses?

If they were sold, they could end up in fine homes working as domestics and butlers or they could end up in the Lower South, working as field hands or, worse yet, as "fancy girls" in the New Orleans sex trade. The two hired-out Edmonson sisters, Mary

PICKING COTTON ON A GEORGIA PLANTATION.

The Edmonson siblings feared being sold south to work in the fields as shown in this 1858 wood engraving of cotton picking on a Georgia plantation.

and Emily, had pale complexions and fine features, which meant that they could fetch a high price in the southern market. They were only 15 and 13 years old, respectively—a bit young to be sold into this line of work even by the standards of the time, but their true age did not matter. In such circumstances, slave traders were known to falsify documents and add a year or more to the reported age of their young female slaves.

All of the enslaved Edmonson children had discussed with their parents the possibility of running away. They faced difficult choices: If they stayed, they risked being sold south at their owner's convenience. If they ran away and were caught, they faced the likelihood that they would be sold to harsher owners in the South.

While she had not experienced such hardships herself, Emily had seen coffles of slaves shuffling down the streets of the city, men and women walking with shackles around their ankles and handcuffs on their wrists, paired together and linked by long metal chains. These human herds were driven like cattle or swine down Pennsylvania Avenue and the streets of Washington, D.C., chained together so that they could not flee while being moved from one place to another. Most coffles were bound for the Deep South to labor as field slaves on cotton and sugar plantations. Field slaves performed backbreaking work from sunrise to sunset, often under the watchful eye of an overseer with a bullwhip; house slaves spent their days cooking and cleaning and watching children.

The only option Emily and her enslaved brothers and sisters saw to ensure their freedom and safety was to flee—and to pray that they could avoid getting caught. When the Edmonson family learned of a bold escape planned for a spring night in April, they decided to take the chance. A lifetime of freedom was worth the risk of capture, they reasoned.

A woman outside a slave pen in Alexandria, Virginia. Her attire—a long skirt or dress made of an inexpensive, coarse fabric known as "slave cloth"—was typical of enslaved women in the mid-19th century.

⤞ TWO ⤝

Escape: April 15, 1848

EMILY EDMONSON WAITED in darkness. Some time near 9 p.m. she heard a handful of dirt scatter across her bedroom window. That was it: the signal.

She peeked outside and saw her older brother Samuel looking up from the shadows. She grabbed a small bag, snuffed out the candle by her bed, and tiptoed through the silent house. She slipped out the back door, leaving the house for the last time.

Emily walked along the dark streets, her brother by her side. She wore a plain, ankle-length dress with a wool shawl wrapped around her shoulders to protect against the chill. She had pulled her hair into a neat bun at the nape of her neck. Nothing about her appearance drew attention, but still her heart pounded, fast and steady.

When they were out of earshot, she asked Samuel, "What will Mother think?"

"Don't stop to think of her," Samuel said, not slowing his pace. "She would rather we'd be free than to spend time to talk about her."

Emily hurried to keep up. He was right. Of course he was right. Samuel was 21, a grown man, and she trusted him to keep her safe, as safe as possible. This was what Mother wanted; this was what they all wanted—to be free.

Emily and Samuel walked down Pennsylvania Avenue, past the north entrance to the Executive Mansion, the building later renamed the White House. Horse-drawn carriages passed them on the unpaved street, and they kept on, heads down to avoid

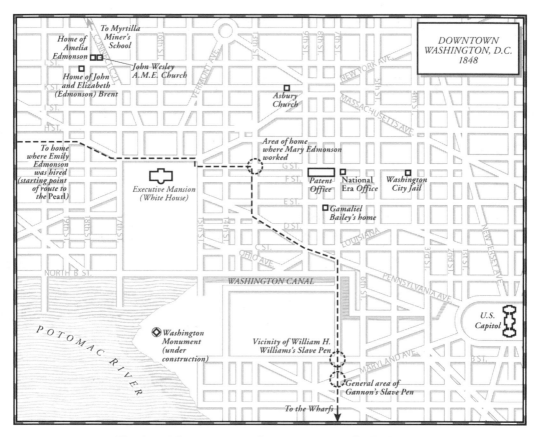

The dotted line represents the probable route Emily, Mary, and Samuel Edmonson took to get to the *Pearl*.

notice. They walked quickly, but not so fast that they appeared hurried or guilty; they preferred not to be noticed at all.

They kept a steady pace, block after block, until they approached the house at the intersection of Thirteenth and G Streets where their sister Mary worked. Emily could see her older sister standing at an upstairs window, waiting and watching for them. Mary's silhouette disappeared, and a moment later she stepped barefoot out the door. She slipped on her shoes and joined Emily and Samuel.

The three runaways made a quick stop at a bakery on F Street. Inside, Emily inhaled the yeasty, sweet aroma of freshly baked bread. A friend on the late shift sold Samuel five dozen rolls—no questions asked; then they continued on their way. Many in the black community knew about the plan, but they knew not to talk about it in public: They didn't want to risk being overheard.

A drizzly rain began to fall by the time Emily, Samuel, and Mary passed near the homes of slave trader Joseph Gannon and William H. Williams, a slave trader who ran one of the most fearsome slave pens in Washington, D.C. Williams's house looked like an ordinary residence, except for the high brick wall that surrounded the backyard. That wall hid the truth, a reality that genteel white residents of the nation's capital didn't want to see and enslaved people didn't want to be reminded of. Behind that wall, the yard was lined with prison cells, shackles, whips, and, of course, men, women, and children held in bondage to be sold as slaves. Emily knew that if she and her siblings were caught trying to escape, they could easily end up in a slave pen just like that.

It had to be well past 9 p.m. by now, dangerously close to the "colored curfew." Keep moving, keep moving. Emily listened for the sound of the bell at the Perseverance Fire Company signaling the hour. When the ten o'clock bell rang, all black people—both free and enslaved—had to be off the streets or they could be arrested, fined, and flogged or beaten.

They walked a little faster, marching down Seventh Street and across the Washington City Canal, which smelled of rotting fish and discarded produce. They hurried on in the direction of

Discrimination: A Matter of Law

If you were black and you lived in the nation's capital in 1848, you had more to worry about than simply a 10 p.m. curfew. A group of regulations known as the Black Code established a legal system of discrimination against black residents. The law, spelled out in The Black Code of the District of Columbia, stated that among other infractions, it was illegal for blacks, whether free or enslaved, to vote, hold elective office, testify against whites in court, serve on juries, own firearms, bathe in certain waters, stay out past 10 p.m., hold dances, or fly kites.

Black people who could not present documentation of their free status could be imprisoned in slave pens such as this one in Alexandria, Virginia, shown in a photo from the early 1860s.

In addition, blacks were considered enslaved unless they could document their free status. In an absurd miscarriage of justice, some free black people who did not have their papers when they were stopped were falsely accused of being slaves and imprisoned because they could not prove their status. They were then responsible for paying their jail fees; if they could not afford to pay, they were sold as slaves. One of the most notorious examples of this practice was the capture of Solomon Northup, a free man who was sold into slavery because he did not have his free papers with him. His story was documented in his 1853 autobiography, *Twelve Years a Slave*.

the Potomac River, then turned east on a secluded path toward White House Wharf, named for the single white house perched on the bluff overlooking the river. The dampness of the grass soaked her feet and weighed down the hem of her skirt as Emily crossed a field. As she approached the landing down by the river, she first saw two lights marking the bow and stern of a ship. Eventually, the fog and mist thinned enough for her to make out the shape of a two-masted vessel. That was it, her passage to freedom: the *Pearl*.

Escape on the *Pearl*

When the Edmonsons boarded the *Pearl*, they were unaware that they were about to take part in the largest and most ambitious slave escape attempt in United States history. They knew only the basic plan: The *Pearl* was to sail about 225 miles down the Potomac River and up the Chesapeake Bay to Frenchtown Wharf, Maryland. This was one of the few ports deep enough for a ship of that size to dock. After the journey on the water, which was expected to take three to five days, depending on the weather, the fugitives planned to travel to Philadelphia, most likely making the 16-mile journey along the New Castle and Frenchtown Turnpike on foot or in carriages.

The original plan had been modest in scale, but the abolitionist organizers allowed the plot to expand, ultimately inviting 76 runaways to take part. They hoped that the size and scope of the escape would draw nationwide attention to the debate over slavery in the nation's capital. At the time, the existence of slavery was a matter left to the states, but Washington, D.C., was different. Congress had the authority to abolish slavery in the District, if it chose to do so. The presence of slavery in the District of Columbia had become the center of an increasingly serious nationwide conflict between abolitionists and advocates of slavery.

BOARDING THE *PEARL*

Emily paused at the edge of the wharf, aware that when she boarded the boat she was going to change her life in ways she could not predict: She had never disobeyed her owner's wishes before; she had never broken the law before; she had never done anything so dangerous before. She drew a deep breath and moved forward.

On board, a nervous young white man flashed a lantern in Emily's face and looked her over, head to toe. Without speaking, he opened the hatch, permitting Emily and her siblings to go below deck. She glanced back toward the city, toward the life she was leaving behind, and she followed her sister and brother down a wooden ladder to the hold below.

Two small lanterns illuminated the crowded space inside the belly of the ship, leaving much of the cabin in darkness. Everywhere Emily looked she saw the anxious faces of neighbors and friends, people she knew well and some she did not recognize at all. Young and old, men, women, and children, all jammed into the small, low-ceilinged space. At five feet, two inches tall, Emily could stand straight, but the taller runaways had to crouch, since the hold had less than six feet of headroom.

A moment later, Emily saw three of her other brothers—Ephraim, Richard, and John—who waved from the back of the boat. Emily followed Samuel and Mary through the crowd, toward a small cleared space where her older brothers had placed two boxes for their sisters to sit so that they might get a little extra fresh air from the two portholes. Emily greeted her brothers and then took a seat.

There was no turning back: They were fugitives now.

Captain Drayton's Change of Heart

As a young man, Daniel Drayton had little sympathy for slaves. Enslaved people often asked him, as the captain of a small bay craft, if he would help them make their way to freedom by allowing them to board his ship as stowaways. For years, Drayton ignored their pleas. "At that time, I had regarded the negroes as only fit to be slaves," Drayton wrote in his 1853 memoir.

But Drayton's opinions about slavery changed after he converted to Christianity. "I no longer considered myself as living for myself alone," he wrote. "I regarded myself as bound to do unto others as I would that they should do to me. . . . Why had not these black people, so anxious to escape from their masters, as good a right to their liberty as I had to mine?"

Drayton first helped with a slave escape in 1847, a year before his experience with the *Pearl*. He docked a ship loaded with oysters at the Seventh Street Wharf in the District of Columbia. Not long after Drayton arrived, a free black man approached him and offered to pay him to smuggle his wife and five children to the North. The desperate man explained that his wife had already paid for her freedom but her owner refused to release her. If Drayton didn't help him, slave traders would send the man's family south and he would likely never see them again.

Drayton sympathized with the family's situation. He hid the woman and her five children and a niece onboard his ship and took them to the northern end of the Chesapeake Bay, where the woman's husband met them and escorted them to freedom in Pennsylvania, a state that had outlawed slavery. Pleased with the outcome of the first escape, Drayton agreed to repeat the plan, this time on a boat called the *Pearl*.

⪜ THREE ⪛

Against the Tide

JUDSON DIGGS, A free man of color, made his living driving passengers in his carriage. He pulled the reins and his mule, Caesar, halted down by the water just east of the Seventh Street Wharf. Diggs climbed down from the driver's seat, then helped his two female passengers exit the carriage with their bundles.

Diggs almost certainly knew that his passengers were runaway slaves. Many people in the black community had heard whispers about arrangements being made for a large-scale escape. When they were unloaded at the wharf, he asked the women for his fare: 25 cents.

The women apologized, explaining that they did not have the money, but they promised to pay him when they reached freedom.

Diggs may have sympathized with their desire for freedom, but he did not give free rides and he did not like feeling duped. Diggs did not expect to ever receive payment. Angry, he left the women at the wharf, turned toward the city, and urged his mule back up the wet and muddy path.

Sometime after ten o'clock, Emily heard the sound of shuffling feet and the noise of heavy ropes and chains dragging and dropping on the deck above. Not much later, the boat rocked gently and

This horse-drawn wagon may have been similar to the one used by Judson Diggs in 1848.

the hull creaked and groaned as the ship drifted from the wharf to the middle of the Potomac River. The *Pearl* had eased its way only about a half mile downriver when it stalled completely. Emily stared out of the small porthole, but the scenery did not change. Where was the wind?

Those below deck may have been able to hear the anchor being thrown overboard and splashing into the water. With so little wind to combat the tide, the ship needed to anchor to avoid being pushed back up the river toward Washington. At that point, they were trapped midstream, waiting for the winds to stir and the tides to change. The water was dead calm, stagnant. If the wind didn't pick up soon, the ship would be a helpless target for slave owners eager to recapture and reclaim their runaways.

Throughout the night, those on board prayed for stronger winds to complete their escape or for compassion from their captors if they made it no farther. After dawn on Sunday morning, the sun began to dissolve the fog and stir the air. They heard chains rattling on the deck as someone raised the anchor and the ship began to drift. A middle-aged white man with a thin, weathered face and long, wavy hair uncovered the hatches, allowing a rush of fresh air to flood the cabin below deck. The man distributed bread and removed the bulkhead between the hold and the cabin so that those who wanted to could get into the cabin to cook.

At last, the wind began to grow stronger and the boat hurried along, trying to make up for lost time. The sound of water sloshing against the hull and the bounce of the ship in the waves reassured those on board that they were, at last, on their way.

SUNDAY WORSHIP

No one knows what scripture was read or what prayers were shared aloud, but it is known that the runaways staged an impromptu church service in the dark cabin below deck on Sunday morning. Several people rummaged through their belongings and pulled out the Bibles that they had brought with them, and they took turns reading aloud. At home, Emily and Mary had worshiped regularly at the Asbury Methodist Church on the corner of Eleventh and K Streets, so they would have found comfort in the familiar words and affirming messages. Emily remained frightened and expected the journey to freedom to be difficult, but she believed the promise that salvation would follow their time of trial. Mary, always poised and pious, was a source of strength with her faith and steadfast belief in the Divine. Mary may have been only 15 years old, but sitting next to her made Emily feel safer.

Emily listened intently. When someone near her held out the Bible and offered to pass it to her for a turn at reading, Emily smiled and shook her head. She and Mary could neither take a turn reading aloud nor follow the words in the text because neither of them knew how to read. Instead, Emily listened and prayed—for safe passage, for steady winds, for family left behind, for freedom. She felt grateful that she and her brothers and sister and all those on board had made it through their first night as fugitives.

During the service, Emily may have thought about her mother and the family she had left behind. On the afternoon of their escape, Emily, Mary, and Samuel had visited their parents and older sisters. When it was time to say good-bye, Emily's mother had held each of her children and said, as she did each time they parted, "Be good children and the blessed Lord will take care of you." Her mother's final words were the same she always said, but those words now took on special meaning.

All around her, voices rose up, singing familiar hymns. Emily added her voice to Mary's and the others', letting the words and melodies fill the stale, dark cabin and transform it into a holy place.

The blessed Lord will take care of you. Please, yes, please.

Slavery and Literacy

Laws against educating enslaved people are older than the Declaration of Independence. As far back as 1740, the South Carolina General Assembly had enacted a law that made it illegal to teach someone in bondage to write. Writing was considered a sign of status and deemed unnecessary for black Americans, free or enslaved. Reading, on the other hand, was encouraged during the colonial period, so that slaves could become familiar with the Bible.

The watercolor "Black man reading newspaper by candlelight" was painted in 1863 by Henry Louis Stephens. The headline of the newspaper he is reading says, "Presidential Proclamation, Slavery."

The literacy laws that made it illegal for slaves to both read and write came almost 100 years later, in reaction to Nat Turner's 1831 rebellion, in which he and his supporters killed 60 white people while attempting to launch a revolution against slavery. After that event, slave owners feared that their slaves would learn to read and write passes (letters of permission for travel) and antislavery materials and that with these skills they could more easily prepare an organized uprising.

Despite the laws, some enslaved people became literate. Instruction was done in secret because in the South, those who were caught teaching black people to read could be fined, beaten, or imprisoned. Slaves learning to read were often beaten, and some had their fingers and toes amputated. Still, reading offered intellectual freedom, and for many, the desire to read and write overshadowed the risks of punishment.

❧ FOUR ❧

Chasing the *Pearl*

ON SUNDAY, APRIL 16, 1848, in Washington, D.C., dozens of white families woke up to find that their morning fires had not been lit, their livestock had not been fed, and their breakfast had not been prepared. Where were their slaves?

They soon learned that other owners' slaves were missing, too. Joseph Downing discovered that his slave, John Brooke, was missing; former first lady Dolley Madison's slave Mary Stewart could not be found; John Stull learned that his slave, Mary Ann, and two of her sons were gone. During the course of the morning, word of the escapes traveled from house to house; the total number of known missing slaves grew by the hour. Runaway slaves were fairly common, but they usually fled alone or in pairs or small family groups. Could scores of enslaved people have been so bold and reckless as to escape together?

There was no time to waste. Major Hampton C. Williams, justice of the peace, rang the church and fire bells, calling the men in the surrounding neighborhoods into action. Within the hour, Williams and a half dozen other men had formed a search party, mounted their horses, and started toward the roads leading north out of the city, the most common escape routes used by fleeing slaves.

Williams slowed his horse when, on the outskirts of town, he encountered Judson Diggs, the carriage driver who had been cheated out of his 25-cent fare the night before. He asked Diggs what he knew about the escape.

Diggs could have said he knew nothing. He could have encouraged the posse to explore the roads out of town or steered them onto another false path. Instead, Diggs told Williams that he and his men were headed the wrong way and to look down at the Seventh Street Wharf.

Williams sized up his informant: Could Diggs be trusted? Williams hadn't considered an escape on the water, and he wasn't confident about the accuracy of the information.

With no time to waste, Williams divided the search party, and one group continued toward the main roads while he and several others circled back toward the wharf. Williams went down to the water and learned that a schooner known as the *Pearl* had been docked there but left in the middle of the night. Williams knew that Diggs had been telling the truth.

One of the men in the posse, Francis Dodge Jr., offered the use of his steamboat so that they could continue the search on the water. Dodge, a wealthy tobacco trader from Georgetown, owned three of the runaway slaves. By noon, Williams, Dodge, and about 30 other men set out on Dodge's steamboat, the *Salem*.

Williams and his men knew that the *Pearl* had a big head start, but they didn't know how far ahead the runaways might be. The weather had turned windy, which made sea travel unsafe, but they had no choice except to ignore the approaching storm. When they met a passenger steamboat making its way north up the Potomac River, Samuel Baker, the captain of the *Salem*, flagged down the boat and asked the captain if he had seen a schooner headed down the Potomac toward the Chesapeake Bay. He learned that the *Pearl* wasn't far ahead.

ONE STEP AHEAD

By Sunday afternoon, the wind kicked up another notch. The *Pearl* began to rock and sway—back and forth, back and forth—the rhythm occasionally broken by the jolt of an unexpected wave. Emily's stomach soured and she felt cold sweat develop across her brow. Her queasy stomach left her shaky and faint. She tried to breathe steadily to calm her stomach, but the damp, stale air below deck offered no relief. Mary could not console her because she, too, suffered from seasickness.

The girls wanted to go up on deck for a breath of fresh air, but they had to wait until after sundown so that they would not be seen by passing boats. When it was finally dark enough to

The Edmonsons boarded the *Pearl*, a ship that resembled this two-masted schooner. These bay craft boats transported coal, wood, and other cargo in the waters of the Chesapeake Bay.

climb on deck, Emily was so weak from hours of illness that she could not lift herself, so her brothers had to carry her. Emily was not as tall and slender as her sister, but her brothers did not struggle to move either one of them. Once on deck, Emily breathed the fresh air and let the wind blow across her face until she began to feel like herself again.

By nightfall, the wind had gone from gusty to gale force in strength. The *Pearl* creaked and moaned as the waves thrashed it back and forth. Could the boat survive a journey on the rough waters of the Chesapeake Bay?

On the deck, two men quarreled as the wind and rain battered the *Pearl*. One argued that they should change the route and travel to Delaware by way of the outside passage in the Atlantic Ocean; the other insisted that the ship was not seaworthy and no one would ever survive the journey. At that point, some on board may have asked themselves whether it would be worse to drown at sea or return to a brutal beating and the ongoing cruelty of slavery.

They finally settled the argument and decided to anchor the *Pearl* in Cornfield Harbor, a deepwater shelter used by ships facing dangerous winds. They would go on when the winds calmed, but until then, all they could do was rest and wait out the storm.

IN THE SHADOWS

The *Salem* sped through the night, hoping to capture the *Pearl* before it entered the bay, where it would be much more difficult to find. Wind and waves rocked the steamship, which powered on through the storm.

Just after midnight, the *Salem* reached the mouth of the Potomac River, near the Chesapeake Bay. The winds whipped around the ship and limited visibility. Their 140-mile journey had

The Slave Ship, painted by Joseph Mallord William Turner (1775–1851), shows a schooner caught in a violent storm. The *Pearl* was not built to withstand the intense conditions of open waters in a storm.

ended; they could go no farther because Dodge's steamship had not been insured for travel on the more tumultuous open waters of the bay.

Williams prepared to turn back, assuming he had lost the chase. Unwilling to accept defeat, the crew continued to scan the darkness, searching for signs of the *Pearl*.

One of the men noticed something unusual near the shoreline. Was it real or a figment of his wishful thinking? The crew studied the shadows in the marshes of Cornfield Harbor and one by one they made out a shape in the darkness, a shape that looked quite a bit like the silhouette of the missing schooner.

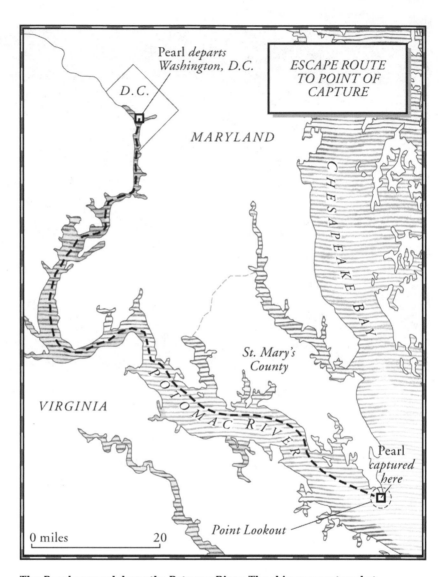

The *Pearl* escaped down the Potomac River. The ship was captured at
Point Lookout before it was able to travel north into the Chesapeake Bay.

⮞ FIVE ⮜

Capture

EMILY WOKE FROM a fitful sleep when she heard the whistle and hiss of a steamboat blowing off air nearby. Startled, she sat up and listened. Was that noise a trick of the wind? Or had they been discovered? She strained to hear more. A moment later, footsteps thundered on the deck above them and muffled voices mixed with the noise of the pummeling rain. No! It couldn't be. They had been free for scarcely 24 hours.

The runaways must have turned to one another, eyes wide, unsure of what to do. Mothers put their arms around their children and held them close. Some of the men searched for objects that could be used in self-defense, if necessary, but resistance would be futile; they had no guns, no knives, no weapons of any kind.

Emily and Mary joined their brothers and a group of other young fugitives to consider the essential question: Should they fight or surrender peacefully?

Samuel searched the cargo hold for something—anything—that he could use as a weapon. He found nothing suitable. He understood that he would be defeated, but the thought of being put in chains and having his sisters sent to New Orleans was too much to accept without a fight.

Emily and Richard urged Samuel to surrender peacefully to avoid bloodshed. If they fought, they would die. A moment later, an angry white man lifted the hatch and looked down at the frightened faces of the fugitives below. Emily stared up at him, unsure what to do. The cabin buzzed with frenzy and fright. Children cried and clung to their mothers' skirts; some of the women wailed, some called out for mercy, and some lowered their heads in silent defeat.

Emily watched Richard and Samuel and several of the other men bound up the stairs and onto the deck of the ship without warning. In a loud voice, Richard said, "Do yourselves no harm, gentlemen, for we are here!"

Rather than reassure the nervous posse, the sudden appearance of the muscular young runaways startled their captors. Were the men surrendering or about to put up a fight? In the rain and dim lantern light, the situation became confusing. While Emily may not have been able to discern clearly what was happening in the chaos on deck, she may have been able to see a jittery member of the posse try to throw a punch in Samuel's direction. Luckily for Samuel, at that moment, a wave crashed into the boat and the *Pearl* lurched, causing the blow to glance off the side of Samuel's head and strike someone else in the back.

Above the noise of the scuffle that followed, Emily heard the voice of the captain of the *Pearl*, urging everyone to stay calm. He pointed out that the slaves were not resisting, so there was no need for violence. No doubt the captain's appeal helped maintain peace and prevent an all-out brawl, which almost certainly would have ended in injury or death for many of the fugitives.

When order was restored, the four Edmonson brothers and the other male slaves were chained together, wrist to wrist, and moved onto the *Salem*, where they could be supervised and controlled more easily. Emily and the other women and children remained on the *Pearl*, locked below deck. They were once again enslaved, their short-lived freedom stolen from them by angry slaveholders intent on revenge.

⇒ SIX ⇒

Back to Washington

MORNING DAWNED, THE waters calmed, and the *Pearl* began its voyage back to the nation's capital, towed behind the steamship *Salem*. This time their progress proved steady and predictable, leaving the runaways plenty of opportunity to agonize over what would happen when they reached Washington, D.C.

Just after sunrise the following morning, the *Salem* arrived at Alexandria, Virginia, where Emily saw a mob of angry citizens gathered on the wharves. When the passengers were in sight of the shore, their captors ordered up on deck the white men who had helped with the escape and many of the male runaways, exhibiting them like trophies after a hunting expedition, the winnings after a day of slave-hunting as sport.

At the sight of the fugitives, the crowd went wild, yelling and cheering for their captors. If people were this worked up outside the city, what kind of angry mob would be waiting for them in Washington?

Not long after, the *Salem* docked at a steamboat wharf on the Potomac River in Washington, D.C. The passengers were forced to leave the ships in an orderly procession: first, the three white men, followed by the male slaves chained together, two by two, then the female slaves—many with babies in their arms—followed by the older children. Altogether there were 77 enslaved people: 38 men and older boys, 26 women and older girls, and 13 children.

Emily paired with Mary, of course. The two Edmonson sisters stood tall and marched toward the city with as much poise and dignity as they could muster. Each wore her long hair parted in the middle and braided into ropes that were twisted into buns. They knew they could not flee, so they trudged steadily forward, their arms around each other's waist for comfort and support.

As they made their way up Seventh Street, the crowd of spectators grew denser and more hostile. The runaways were surrounded prey in the sights of a pack of wolves, hungry for revenge. People yelled and taunted the girls as they passed. At one point someone in the mob yelled to Emily: "Aren't you ashamed to run away and make all this trouble for everybody?"

"No, sir," she replied. "We are not and if we had to go through it again, we'd do the same thing."

The man turned to the person next to him and said, "Ain't she got good spunk?"

Tears streaked the faces of many black people watching the procession, stunned and powerless, no doubt thinking about the harsh treatment that awaited the recaptured runaways. One of the faces in the crowd belonged to their brother-in-law John Brent, who watched the line of fugitives, looking for members of the family. When he saw Emily and her siblings marching toward the jail, Brent fainted; his greatest fear about the escape attempt had come to pass.

Ahead of Emily, people in the mob jeered and pushed and threatened the prisoners, especially the white men who had

The Release of Chester English

While they were being marched toward the Washington City Jail, the captain of the *Pearl*, Daniel Drayton, urged his captors to release crew member Chester English. English was a young married father, probably in his early twenties, and he had been told nothing about the escape plan. Drayton didn't want to take English on the journey in the first place, but the captain who owned the boat insisted because he had already hired English as cook and crew, and he wanted to keep him.

Drayton told English that they would be transporting a load of timber to the nation's capital. On their way to Washington they did, in fact, stop in Machodock, Virginia, to buy about 20 cords of wood, but that was not the purpose of their journey. On the night of the escape, Drayton said that a number of black people planned to join them for a trip down the bay, and that all English had to do was lift up the hatch and let them enter the hold. English was baffled by the instructions, but he promised to do what he was told. According to Drayton, English never understood that the passengers were escaping; he thought they were going on a pleasure cruise.

English had not been charged with a crime and it was clear that he was confused about what was happening. When it came time to move Drayton and the other white man into the carriage to get them away from the surrounding mob, one of the police officers released English.

Once freed, English turned and walked through the crowd, all but unnoticed. He wandered back down to the steamboat wharf, the only landmark he recognized in the city. When he arrived, the steamer *Salem* was gone.

Alone in a strange place, English was not sure what to do. Before his voyage on the *Pearl*, he had never been more than 30 miles from his home in Philadelphia. He approached a man near the wharf and rather than simply asking for help returning home, he told his entire story, including information about helping the runaways on the *Pearl*. In response, the stranger secured him in a hack and sent him back to the jail. English remained imprisoned there until the trials were held, when charges against him were dropped in exchange for his testimony against Drayton and Edward Sayres, the second captain of the *Pearl*.

JA
WASHI

SUNDAY

Senator Morton's Washerwoman,
Gateway of Corridor.

SECRETS OF THE PRISON-HOUSE—THE BLACK HOLE OF WASHINGTON,

This wood engraving titled "Secrets of the prison-house" by Arthur Lumley appeared in Frank Leslie's illustrated newspaper in 1861.

helped with the escape. Members of the posse flanked them as human shields, holding back the hostile crowd. Their captors had become their guardians, their only defense against assault from the irate mob.

As the prisoners marched, the size of the mob continued to increase. When they passed Joseph Gannon's slave pen—the same pen they had passed on the first night of their escape—the slave trader, armed with a bowie knife, rushed out, reached around the police escorts, and stabbed in the direction of one of the white captains. The blade nicked the captain's ear, causing blood to run down the man's neck as he continued to march toward the jail.

A lawman told the slave trader that the captain was in the hands of the law.

"Damn the law!" Gannon said. "I have three Negroes and I will give them all for one thrust at this scoundrel!"

The procession kept moving forward, and he followed, waiting for an opportunity to attack again. Eventually, the would-be attacker fell back in the crowd, but there were plenty of others to yell and wave fists in his place.

By this time, the crowd had grown to several thousand people. When the prisoners had almost reached Pennsylvania Avenue, the mob began to chant: "Lynch them! Lynch them!"

The lawmen had lost control of the crowd. If the mob moved to hang the accused, nothing could be done to stop them. Not long after, one of the police officers hired a carriage and shoved the white men into it. The mob surrounded the carriage and followed as it made its way toward the jail. The white men were safer in jail than they would have been on the street.

BEHIND BARS

Emily and the other runaways kept marching and eventually arrived at the Washington City Jail, more commonly known as the Blue Jug because of the garish shade of blue paint covering the three-story stone building with iron bars on the windows. When they arrived at the jail, most of the fugitives were forced into the cold, damp basement cells, but Emily and Mary were directed to the women's quarters upstairs. Their cell had no bed or chairs or other furnishings, just a single blanket to protect them from the hard, cold floor, but they found comfort in being together.

The haunting and mournful voices and cries of the prisoners bounced off the walls. Although they had been enslaved all their lives, until they heard the clang of the cell door lock behind them that day, Emily and Mary had never been caged.

The Abolitionist Press

Abolitionists used the press to change public opinion and promote their antislavery agenda. Starting around 1820, abolitionists published a steady stream of newspapers, children's books, sermons, speeches, broadsides, memoirs of former slaves, and other documents that helped to present their case. In the mid-19th century, more than 40 newspapers promoted the emancipation of slaves, including William Lloyd Garrison's *The Liberator* (1831–1865), Frederick Douglass's *North Star* (1838–1851), and the *National Anti-Slavery Standard* (1840–1870), the official newspaper of the American Anti-Slavery Society.

Showdown at the *National Era*

On the day the fugitives from the *Pearl* marched through Washington, D.C., the mob followed them all the way to the front of the Washington City Jail. After the prisoners were secured inside, the mob continued to grow. Someone suggested that they move several blocks down the street to the office of the *National Era*, an antislavery newspaper edited by abolitionist Gamaliel Bailey. No one in the crowd had any evidence that the newspaper had anything to do with the escape on the *Pearl*, but many of the protesters assumed that the press and its editor were at least sympathetic to the cause.

Gamaliel Bailey (1807–1859) used journalism to promote the abolitionist cause. Before editing the *National Era*, he worked at the Cincinnati *Philanthropist*, the first antislavery newspaper in the west.

The mob moved down the street to the newspaper building across from the U.S. Patent Office, on Seventh Street. As the evening wore on, the crowd became increasingly excited and belligerent—louder, bigger, angrier. At one point, someone picked up a stone and hurled it toward the building. Someone else grabbed a brick and broke a window and a door, adding the sound of shattering glass to the din of the night.

Captain John H. Goddard, a leader in the city's Auxiliary Guard, tried to calm the crowd, attempting to convince the agitators that they didn't want to give the sympathizers in the North any more reason to become involved in District business.

Someone else in the crowd defended the right of a free press, even an abolitionist press.

The mob had reached a pivotal moment—that turning point at which it must decide whether to press on with violence or settle down and act with civility. Suddenly, a strong wind stirred and brought with it an unexpected downpour. The energy shifted; the rain dampened the enthusiasm of the rioters. The crowd cleared around ten o'clock, but not before agreeing to meet again the following night.

The second night, a crowd of several thousand people, most from Maryland and Virginia rather than the District, gathered once again outside the *National Era* building, threatening to destroy the press and run its editor, 40-year-old Gamaliel Bailey, out of town. From the steps of the Patent Office, across from the *Era*, Daniel Radcliffe, a prominent Washington lawyer, tried to convince the members of the crowd to go home, but they grew more agitated. When it became clear that the crowd would not leave without some action, Radcliffe negotiated a compromise in which a committee of 50, five men from each ward in the city plus Georgetown and Tenleytown, agreed to present their case to Bailey.

Members of the committee assembled outside Bailey's home, a block away from the *Era* offices. The newspaper editor opened his door and stood on his front porch to address the crowd. A spokesman for the group tried to convince Bailey to shut down the press voluntarily: "This community is satisfied that the existence of your press among us is endangering the public peace." He told Bailey that he had until 10 a.m. the following day to close the *Era* or face the consequences.

Bailey listened to his critics' complaints. He could hear the shouting and chanting of the angry crowd a block away. When the members of the committee finished, Bailey addressed the mob: "Let me say to you that I am a peace-man. I have taken no measures to defend my office, my house or myself. I appeal to the good sense and intelligence

of the community, and stand upon my rights as an American citizen, looking to the law alone for protection."

The protesters urged him to reconsider his position: "We advise you to
be out of the way! The people think that your press endangers their property and their lives; and they have appointed us to tell you so, and ask you
to remove it tomorrow. If you say that you will do so, they will retire satisfied. If you refuse, they say they will tear it down."

The discussion continued, but they had reached an impasse.

Finally, Bailey, whose previous abolitionist press had been destroyed
three times by mob violence, said: "I cannot surrender my rights. Were I
to die for it, I cannot surrender my rights! Tell those who sent you hither

This 1859 photograph shows the view from the *National Era*
building, including the front of the U.S. Patent Office Building
on Seventh Street and the U.S. Post Office on the right. The
angry mob gathered in the open space, and those addressing
the crowd stood on the stairs of the Patent Office in front of
the pillars.

that my press and my house are undefended. They must do as they see proper. I maintain my rights and I make no resistance!"

Bailey went inside his home and closed the door.

Outside, the crowd chanted, "Down with the *Era*!" "Gut the office!"

The mob retreated and regrouped at the newspaper offices a block away. Once they left, Bailey woke his six young children and moved them to the safety of his next-door neighbor's house just in case the protesters returned to attack his home and family.

When the gang arrived at the *Era* offices, they found that city police had been stationed to guard the building. Rather than challenging the officers, the mob passed a resolution "to pull it down the next day at ten o'clock if the press was not meanwhile removed."

In the morning, ten o'clock came—and went—without violence. The press remained intact and Bailey published the regular weekly edition of the *National Era*. In it he described the attacks against him, calling them an outrage against freedom. He also denied any involvement in the escape on the *Pearl* and pledged that he would never "take part in any movement that would involve treachery of any kind."

Other newspapers also called for an end to the violence. On April 20, 1848, the board of aldermen and Auxiliary Guard published handbills promoting peace and stating that "events have transpired within the last few days deeply affecting the peace and character of our community." The notices warned that "fearful acts of lawless and irresponsible violence can only aggregate the evil."

Whether the crowds found the arguments persuasive or they lost interest in the cause can't be known, but after three days of turmoil and tension, the city grew quiet again.

⪻ SEVEN ⪼

Sold

AFTER A RESTLESS night in jail, Emily, Mary, and the other runaways were taken downstairs. The justices of the peace called the prisoners forward one by one so that they could be identified by their owners and reclaimed. Some of the runaways stared at the floor in submission; others looked at their captors with contempt. Some wept; others stood silent, resigned to their future and too physically and emotionally exhausted to protest.

During the proceedings, Emily listened as one female slave who tried to run away with her child was given the chance to repent and return to her owner rather than risk being sold south. She refused. When a newspaper reporter covering the event asked the woman why she had rejected her owner's offer, she said: "Have I not the same right to my freedom that you have, and could you have neglected a chance of gaining it had you been a slave?"

Moments later, another woman stepped forward when she heard her name called and said: "Here I am, sir, once free, again a slave."

Emily recognized Valdenar, the man who managed Culver's business affairs. When their names were called by the judge, Emily and the other Edmonson runaways stepped forward. As they passed the two white captains, one of the girls (probably Mary) said: "God bless you, sirs. You did all you could. It is not your fault that we are not free."

Valdenar did not take the Edmonsons with him. Instead, he went outside the jail to speak with the slave dealers who had come to negotiate with owners who were willing to sell their runaways at a discount rather than take the chance that they would escape again. How much could he get if he sold all six of the Edmonsons on the spot?

Acting on behalf of the family, John Brent, Elizabeth's husband, came down to the jail and asked Valdenar what it would cost to buy his family's freedom. Brent explained to Valdenar that he did not have all the money he needed on hand, but he begged the agent to give him time to raise the necessary funds from sympathetic family and friends.

The cost to buy six slaves was enormous. Strong, able-bodied men and youthful, attractive women—especially those like Emily and Mary with pale complexions—routinely sold for $800 to $1,000 apiece, sometimes more. Paul Edmonson, father of the runaways, was freed when his owner died and emancipated him in her will, and he worked to save money to buy a 40-acre farm in Montgomery County. He grew oats, corn, and potatoes; he also owned several cows, pigs, and horses. If he sold everything he had, the farm and everything on it, he would not have enough money to buy back a *single one* of his children.

Valdenar considered the offer and told Brent that he could have one day, 24 hours, to raise a good-faith deposit. Brent hurried away, grateful for the chance to ransom his family but daunted by the task that lay ahead.

The following morning, Brent went to Valdenar's home to negotiate a final price. Instead of naming a figure, Valdenar told Brent that he had already sold the six Edmonson siblings to Bruin & Hill, slave dealers from Alexandria and Baltimore, for $4,500.

It would do no good for Brent to protest; the sale had been

completed. Now that a slave dealer was involved, the price would be even higher, making it much more difficult to ransom them. How could he ever raise enough money to buy their freedom?

Although the cause seemed hopeless, Brent went to Alexandria, Virginia, to beg the slave trader, 39-year-old Joseph Bruin, to let him buy back his wife's brothers and sisters. Bruin refused to consider selling them, explaining that he had had his eyes on the family for years and could get twice what he had paid for them in the New Orleans market. Brent's pleading had no impact on Bruin. Hopeless and distraught, Brent had to leave, knowing he might never see Emily and the other runaway members of his family again.

INTO THE NIGHT

Back at the jail, Emily watched in anguish as, all around her, families were being destroyed, divided, and sold apart: Children were torn from their parents, wives from their husbands, brothers from their sisters.

Emily and Mary returned to their jail cell, uncertain of their fate. Emily could not imagine being forced to go on without her family, especially her beloved sister. She tried to settle in for the night, turning and shifting position until she made herself as comfortable as possible on the stone floor. She heard Mary breathing next to her, slow and steady. Not much later, one of the jailers appeared outside the cell and told the girls to get up and follow him. It was past ten o'clock. Why would they be asked to move in the middle of the night?

Emily looked at Mary. She could not help but hope that members of their family had been able to come up with the money necessary to buy their freedom. Were they being sent home to their mother's house, no longer enslaved but free?

This broadside was produced as part of a petition campaign to convince Congress to outlaw slavery in the nation's capital. The text and images portray the horrors and injustice of slavery. The text notes that on February 8, 1836, the House of Representatives rejected the petition to abolish slavery in Washington, D.C., by a vote of 163 to 47.

Trying not to wake the others resting in their cells, Emily and Mary went down the stone staircase to the main level of the jail. Their hopes of liberty were lost as soon as they saw their four brothers, their wrists bound by handcuffs.

Outside the jail, they were loaded into a carriage and taken through the streets of the sleeping city, across the bridge to Alexandria, Virginia. The horses slowed and the carriage stopped at 1707 Duke Street. From the road, the building looked like a comfortable Federal-style brick home, but the high walls around the yard revealed the truth: They had arrived at a slave pen.

CAPTIVE AT BRUIN & HILL

Once they were in the backyard, Emily and Mary were separated from their brothers and taken to a large, dark cell without a bed or blanket. Emily could hear the sounds of the night—sleeping, snoring, stirring in the darkness—but she was unsure how many other people were held in the surrounding cells. Emily tried to keep quiet and settle down for the few hours of quiet before morning; she was exhausted and afraid, and she knew it would do no good to make noise now.

In the morning, Emily saw her brothers eating breakfast and learned that the men were kept together in a lower-level cell. She and Mary were assigned the unpleasant jobs of dumping and cleaning out the chamber pots and doing the laundry for the 13 men also held at Bruin & Hill.

She learned that Bruin had said that he would not sell any of the Edmonsons, but it was understood that he would do so if enough money was offered. Time was the enemy: Family and friends were collecting money for the girls' ransom, but where would they find the nearly $5,000 needed to prevent a trip to the New Orleans market?

Slave Pen, *Alexandria, Va.*

The 1861 photograph shows a slave pen in Alexandria, Virginia, similar to Bruin & Hill.

Samuel wept and apologized to his sisters, begging them to forgive him for leading them into trouble. He said that he would gladly die for them, if that would save them from the fate he feared. Emily tried to reassure her brother and put his heart at peace, but there was nothing any of them could do but wait and pray.

As the days wore on, Bruin moved Emily and Mary inside his house to work as housekeepers and babysitters. Bruin told Emily that he admired her family; they stood tall, spoke gently, and enjoyed a confidence exhibited by few others in his pen. They were poised, proud, and pious. Bruin observed that they had clearly been raised in a home that promoted strong moral and religious values.

Although he was a slave trader, Bruin made an effort to present himself as an honorable and upstanding businessman and gentleman, even to the men and women who were considered his property. Bruin waited days and then weeks to see if the Edmonson family could raise the money necessary for their ransom. If they did, he could avoid the expense and risk of sending them south. Profits to be made selling slaves were higher in the South, but so was the risk of losing his valuable property to disease.

The longer the Edmonsons stayed in Virginia, the less likely it was that they would be sent south. In late May, the slave-trading "season" in New Orleans ended, because traders didn't want to expose their property to yellow fever and other infectious diseases, which were widespread in the hot, mosquito-filled summer months. By late April, with the end of the slave-selling season fast approaching, Bruin wanted to sell the Edmonsons quickly, either to the family or to the highest bidder in the South.

Bruin had met with Paul Edmonson, but Paul was unable to come up with the money to ransom his children. They were out of time.

Since the family had not been able to come up with any money, Bruin made up his mind: As soon as possible he would send the six Edmonson runaways, along with about 40 other enslaved people, by steamship to Baltimore, where they would catch a second ship to New Orleans.

What Happened to Judson Diggs?

In the days that followed the capture of the *Pearl*, the families of the runaways tried to figure out how the plot had been discovered. No one knows how Judson Diggs's betrayal was revealed, but members of the black community blamed him for the failed plan. Diggs was one of them—he knew the sting of slavery and the satisfaction of finding freedom—so many considered his act of denying liberty to others to be unforgivable.

Taking the law into their own hands, a group of young black men sought revenge by pulling Diggs from his carriage, beating him up, and throwing him into a stream that ran along the north side of the old John Wesley Church in Washington, D.C. Diggs survived and fully recovered from his physical injuries. He was considered an outcast—"despised and avoided"—until he died in his late sixties.

~ EIGHT ~

Baltimore

WHEN THEY ARRIVED in Baltimore, Emily, Mary, and about a dozen other enslaved people walked from the steamboat landing to 11 Camden Street, a slave pen run by Joseph S. Donovan, a partner of Bruin & Hill. At first, Emily found the slave trader's unapologetically crass and vulgar language startling, but she did her best not to listen to his profanity or obscene and insulting remarks, especially those targeting the female slaves.

Emily forced herself to tolerate his rudeness, but when he forbade the women to pray together, she and Mary decided to disobey. They began waking up very early in the morning so that they could meet with four or five other women and worship without interruption. The girls were devout Methodists; their faith defined who they were and they refused to abandon their religion to appease a godless slave trader.

Other women joined in their prayer circle, including one known as Aunt Rachel, a middle-aged woman with a strong faith who had been sold away from her husband. Emily's heart ached when she heard Aunt Rachel tell how her poor husband often used to come to the prison and beg the trader to sell her to his owners, who he thought were willing to purchase her, if the price was not too high.

The trader repeatedly ran him off the lot with brutal threats and curses.

Emily longed for her parents and family back in Washington; she understood Aunt Rachel's sorrow. Most enslaved people knew that sorrow, either from experience or from the threat of losing a loved one. Emily prayed for Aunt Rachel to be reunited with her husband and for their ultimate freedom. That was all she could do, and she would not allow a vicious slave trader to stop her from making her appeal to God.

Of course, they prayed for their ransom, but this prayer seemed to go unanswered. Emily and her siblings were told to pack their things and prepare to leave for New Orleans. The day before they were to sail out of Baltimore Harbor, they finally received word that a messenger would arrive on the morning train, ready to negotiate with the slave trader for the purchase of the family. All night, Emily dreamed that she was just hours away from freedom. She imagined that the messenger would arrive, cash in hand, ready to take them home to Washington as free women.

In the morning, Joseph Donovan forced Emily and the others to march down to the wharf. They begged for more time: Their representative was on his way, but his train would not arrive for another hour.

The slave trader felt he had waited long enough. Apparently unconcerned about the Edmonsons' plight, he had the crew of the *Union* continue to get ready for their departure. Once the Edmonsons boarded the ship, a two-masted, square-rigged brig, there was little chance that they would ever return or see their family again.

LAST-MINUTE NEGOTIATIONS

Emily waited aboard the *Union*, unaware that on shore the train from Washington had arrived. William Chaplin, a well-dressed, 52-year-old Harvard-educated abolitionist, arrived at the slave pen as a representative of the Edmonson family. Donovan soon learned that Chaplin had with him only $900, a great deal of money, but not nearly enough to buy all six family members. Chaplin wanted to use the cash—donated by a grandson of John Jacob Astor, a German-American businessman who had made a fortune in the fur trade—as a down payment on all six of the Edmonsons, but the slave trader refused.

Instead, after some discussion, Donovan said that he would consider selling one of the men, but he refused to sell the girls at any price. Chaplin pressed for a more advantageous arrangement, but ultimately he agreed to buy Richard Edmonson, whose wife and children were said to be suffering without him. Chaplin handed over the $900 in exchange for the paperwork granting Richard his freedom.

By the time they had finished their business, the inspector of the Port of Baltimore had already checked over the Manifest of Negroes, Mulattos, and Persons of Color. In that document, Mary was listed as 17 and Emily as 15; their ages were increased to make them more desirable to men in the New Orleans market. The *Union* had pulled away from the wharf. The slave trader refused to call back the ship to allow Richard to disembark. Even though he was a free man, Richard would have to sail to New Orleans, then sail back to Washington to rejoin his family at some future date. When the *Union* drifted out of Baltimore's Inner Harbor, Richard had no idea that he was, in fact, free.

What Happened to the Other Fugitives
of the *Pearl*?

Hope Slatter, a slave trader from Baltimore, bought most of the fugitives from the *Pearl*. At sunset on the Friday after the escape, Slatter marched nearly 50 people through the streets of Washington, D.C., to the Baltimore and Ohio railroad depot, where they were to be sent to the southern slave market. The following letter, published in several northern newspapers, provides an eyewitness account of the events that evening:

Washington, April 22, 1848

Last evening, as I was passing the railroad depot, I saw a large number of colored people gathered round one of the cars, and from manifestations of grief among some of them, I was induced to draw near and ascertain the cause of it. I found in the car towards which they were so eagerly gazing about fifty color [*sic*] people, some of whom were nearly as white as myself. . . . About half of them were females, a few of whom had but a slight tinge of African blood in their veins, and were finely formed and beautiful. The men were ironed together, and the whole group looked sad and dejected. At each end of the car stood two ruffianly-looking personages, with large canes in their hands, and, if their countenances were an index of their hearts, they were the very impersonation of hardened villainy itself.

In the middle of the car stood the notorious slave dealer of Baltimore, Slatter, who . . . had purchased the men and women around him and was taking his departure for Georgia. While observing this old, gray-headed villain—this dealer in the bodies and souls of men—the chaplain of the Senate [Chaplain Henry Slicer] entered the car and took his brother Slatter by the hand, chatted with him for some time and seemed to view the heart-rending scene before him with as little concern as we should look upon cattle. . . .

Some of the colored people outside, as well as in the car, were weeping most bitterly. I learned that many families were separated. Wives were there to take leave of their husbands, and husbands of their wives, children of their parents, brothers and sisters shaking hands perhaps for the last time, friends parting with friends, and the tenderest ties of humanity sundered at the single bid of the inhuman slave broker before them. A husband, in the meridian of life, begged to see the partner of his bosom. He protested that she was free—that she had free papers and was torn from him and shut up in the jail. He clambered up to one of the windows of the car to see his wife, and, as she was reaching forward her hand to him, the black-hearted villain, Slatter, ordered him down. He did not obey. The husband and wife, with tears streaming down their cheeks, besought him to let them converse for a moment.

But no! A monster more hideous, hardened and savage, than the blackest spirit of the pit, knocked them down from the car and ordered him away. The bystanders could hardly restrain themselves from laying violent hands upon the brutes. This is but a faint description of that scene, which took place within a few rods of the capitol, under enactments recognized by Congress. O! what a revolting scene to a feeling heart.

—John Slingerland, Albany, New York

MANIFEST of NEGROES, MULATTOS, and PERSONS OF COLOR, taken on board the *Brig Alo* — whereof *Saml Fooks* is Master, burthen *2 3 6* tons, to be transported to the port of *Mobile* — in the district of *Alabama* — for the purpose of being sold or disposed of as slaves, or to be held to service or labor.

NUMBER OF ENTRY.	NAMES.	SEX. MALE.	SEX. FEMALE.	AGE.	HEIGHT. FEET.	HEIGHT. INCHES.	Whether Negro, Mulatto, or Person of Color.	OWNER OR SHIPPER'S NAME.	RESIDENCE.
1	Hinson Thomas	"		45	5	9	Black	B McCampbell	Baltimore
2	Charles Hopkins	"		23	5	11	"		
3	Samuel Matthews	"		40	5	10	Mulatto		
4	George Brooks	"		18	5	10½	Do		
5	Elisha Frost	"		20	5	10	Black		
6	Joseph Roach	"		23	5	7½	"		
7	Eli Gordon	"		30	5	8	"		
8	William Hess	"		20	5	6	"		
9	Nicolas Lemmy	"		19	5	7	Mulatto		
10	Edward Woods	"		45	5	6	Brown		
11	George Neil	"		26	5	5	Black		
12	Peter Rance	"		25	5	4	Do		
13	Daniel Best	"		22	5	4	Mulatto		
14	Frank Harrison	"		18	5	6½	Black		
15	Charles Smith	"		18	5	8	"		
16	Aaron Harrison	"		17	5	6	"		
17	William Thomas	"		22	5	3	"		
18	Aaron Joy	"		20	5	3½	"		
19	George B Curtis	"		19	5	3½	Brown		
20	John Stewart	"		17	5	3	"		
21	Aaron Hawkins	"		14	4	9	Black		
22	John Campbell	"		11	4	6	"		
23	Lorenzo Hopkins	"		10	4	2	"		
24	William Sill	"		8	3	10	"		
25	John Little	"		5	3	4	"		
26	Sarah Robinson + Child		"	25	5	3	"		
27	Jane Anderson		"	20	5	7	Brown		
28	Mary Gray		"	18	5	5	Black		
29	Jane Hawkins		"	20	5	8	Mulatto		
30	Celia Leninburg		"	17	5	5	Brown		
31	Leah Clark + Child		"	28	5	3	Black		
32	Mary Hagerson + child		"	20	5	4	"		
33	Jane Joy + child		"	20	5	3	"		
34	Harry Vinson + child		"	23	5	2	"		
35	Louisa Elliott		"	18	5	1	Mulatto		
36	Phoebe Burton		"	34	4	11½	Brown		
37	Eliza Butler + child		"	37	4	11	Black		
38	Phillis Chester		"	23	5	1½	"		
39	Dolly Martin		"	20	4	11½	"		
40	Charlotte Green		"	11	4	7	"		
41	Rachael Griggs		"	11	4	7	"		
42	Sarah Johnson		"	11	4	6	"		

District of Baltimore, Port of Baltimore,   day of   184

B M Campbell, Shipper of the persons named, and particularly described in the *above* manifest of *Slaves*
Samy Fooks Master of the *Brig Alo* — do solemnly, sincerely, and truly swear, each of us to the best of our knowledge and belief
that *the above named Slaves* *have* not been imported into the United State since the first day of January, one thousand
eight hundred and eight; and that under the Laws of the State of Maryland *are* held to service or labor as Slaves and *are* not entitled to
freedom under these laws, at a certain time and after a known period of service.—SO HELP GOD.
Sworn-to this *4* day of *Octr* 184   before   B M Campbell
N. F. Williams COLLECTOR.   S Fooks

This manifest is similar to the Manifest of Negroes, Mulattos, and Persons of
Color used to document the enslaved people aboard the *Union*.

Sold South: The Second Middle Passage

The United States had an uncomfortable relationship with slavery from its earliest days. As early as the Constitutional Convention of 1787, legislators disagreed about the question of whether slavery should be allowed. As part of a compromise to keep the young country united, Congress agreed to phase out the international slave trade after 20 years. As of January 1, 1808, it became illegal to import slaves from overseas, although it remained legal to buy and sell enslaved people already in the country.

At the same time that Congress banned the transatlantic slave trade, there was an increase in demand for slave labor in the South. The Louisiana Purchase of 1803 expanded the land available for agricultural development, and

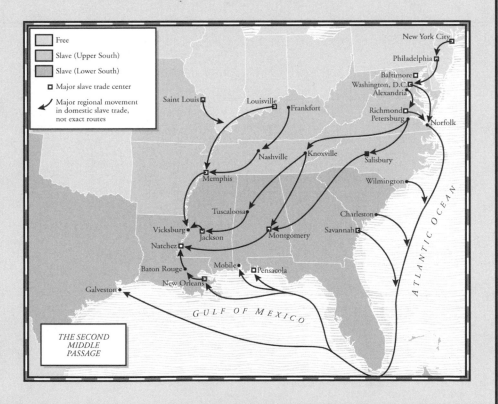

cotton and sugar, two of the most popular crops, were also very labor intensive. While there were too few slaves in the Lower South, there were too many in the Upper South. Maryland and Virginia had a surplus of slaves because of natural population increases and because farmers were planting their fields with wheat and other crops that required less labor to produce.

The result: a domestic slave trade from the Upper South to the Lower South that became known as the Second Middle Passage. (The original Middle Passage involved the transportation of enslaved people from Africa to North America.) At least one million slaves, including six members of the Edmonson family, were part of this forced migration between 1790 and 1860.

NINE

New Orleans

ONCE AGAIN, EMILY and the others sent south had to endure travel in the dark, poorly ventilated spaces below deck, in the cargo hold of the *Union*. And, not surprisingly, once again Emily and Mary suffered from severe seasickness, this time much worse than the episode on the *Pearl*. By the time the *Union* reached the Carolina coast, the winds had begun to gust from the south, pounding and rocking the ship in the ocean waves. Emily could not keep fluids down and her lips became dry and cracked. She was dangerously dehydrated, her skin wrinkled like crumpled paper, her eyes sunken into their sockets. Her breathing grew fast and shallow. Mary's condition was not much better.

How long could they hold on like that? Their brothers carried them up on deck for fresh air whenever they could do so safely, but most of the time they could do little more than sit with Emily and Mary, wipe their faces, and tell them that things were going to get better. In time, the situation did improve: The winds died down and the girls began to recover. They remained weak, but they were able to hold down fluids, giving their bodies the chance to regain strength.

Emily and the other people aboard the *Union* faced another challenge when they reached the dangerously shallow waters around Key West, Florida. Unfamiliar with the sandbars, reefs, and other hazards hidden just beneath the surface of the water, the captain of the *Union* raised a flag to signal a pilot-boat captain to guide them through the area. Before the smaller boat approached, the captain of the *Union* hid the slaves below deck, perhaps thinking that he could negotiate a lower fee if the other captain didn't know about the valuable cargo he was carrying. To conceal the slaves, the captain placed a heavy canvas cover over the grated hatchway door, blocking the air circulation in the overheated, stuffy cargo hold below.

It did not take long for the air to grow stagnant and stale. Emily felt faint and struggled to breathe while the captain and pilot up on deck squabbled about the price. The men and women had been separated into two cargo areas. One of the men took a stick and punctured a hole through the canvas on their side, introducing some fresh air. The women were unable to break the seal; they shouted for help, but no one responded. Emily breathed the hot, used air, but she was growing weaker by the minute.

After what felt like enough time to sail all the way around the world, a member of the crew pulled back the canvas, allowing air back into the hold below deck. Emily gasped to fill her lungs with as much air as they could hold. Then, one after another, as they caught their breath, the captives began to crawl out onto the deck. When they could safely move to the fresh air, Mary and Emily were too weak to stand, so once again their brothers had to carry them into the open.

The captains had not been able to agree on terms, so the pilot-boat captain refused to help them. Without a guide, the captain of the *Union* could not navigate the treacherous waters, so he had to turn back and sail the long way around Key West to remain in safer waters. That, along with foul weather, extended the length of the trip by several days. As a result, supplies of food and water began to run low. The captain rationed water, providing the crew with one quart of water a day and limiting the enslaved to just a gill a day, or about five ounces each. Emily sipped her ration slowly, but when she finished, her mouth still felt dry. She tried to deny her thirst, but she longed for fresh water. In an expression of kindness, some of the sailors shared a pint of their water supply with Emily and Mary, who, in turn, shared with the other women.

When the *Union* finally approached New Orleans on June 14, 1848, the weather turned against them again. As they arrived at the mouth of the Mississippi River, another violent storm battered the ship. The waves rolled the ship so severely that when a pilot boat approached to guide them on the journey upriver to New Orleans, it would sometimes disappear from sight as if swallowed by the waves, only to rise up and appear again when the wave passed by. Emily may have feared what awaited them in the South, but she was grateful to reach land after an exhausting 20-day journey.

TO THE SHOWROOM

The following morning, at about ten o'clock, Emily and the other 34 enslaved people left the *Union* and walked about six blocks through the city to a slave pen run by another partner of Bruin & Hill. Trembling and terrified, Emily began to cry. Without warning, an overseer approached and struck her on the chin, saying: "Stop crying or I'll give you something to cry about." He followed with another threat: "There is the calaboose [a public place for flogging slaves], where they whip those who do not behave themselves!"

As soon as the man stepped away, a woman she did not know whispered to Emily that she needed to force herself to look as cheerful as possible or she would be beaten. Emily wondered if she would ever be able to master such a false face. One of her brothers approached a moment later and asked what the woman had said; when she told him, he encouraged Emily to follow the advice.

Later that afternoon, Emily watched as her brothers were taken away. When she saw them a few hours later, she barely recognized them: Their hair had been cut short, their mustaches shaved off, and their fine butler's clothing had been exchanged for blue jackets and pants made of coarse fabric, the clothing of field slaves. Not long afterward, an overseer presented Emily and Mary with their uniforms—plain calico-print dresses and kerchiefs for their hair.

Detail from an illustration, "Slaves for Sale: A Scene in New Orleans," published in *The Illustrated London News* April 6, 1861. *Harper's Weekly* printed it with the title "A Slave Pen at New Orleans Before the Auction" on January 24, 1863.

Once they had been properly outfitted, some of the slaves were forced to stand on an open porch facing the street and display themselves to people walking by. The porch served as a store window—an outdoor show-room—and they were the merchandise. Emily and the others waited inside; and when buyers called, they paraded across the auction floor in rows. Emily tried to smile and look pleasant, but there was no joy in her expression. Some of the men in the crowd told vulgar jokes and taunted the girls as they passed, but Emily had figured out that she had to tolerate and ignore their behavior.

A man took a liking to one of the girls near Emily. He called the girl to him, then demanded that she open her mouth so that he could look at her teeth, as if he were inspecting livestock. He touched her as he pleased, and the young girl had to stand and bear it without resistance.

While no one knows the details of what Emily and Mary were forced to endure in the showroom, in many cases prospective buyers took slaves into back rooms for a closer, private inspection. A buyer interested in purchasing a particular slave could make a detailed examination of the property, demanding that male slaves take off all their clothes and females strip to the waist. Buyers looked for scars and signs of beatings, which could indicate a slave's defiant nature or a history of misbehavior. Some buyers also took advantage of the opportunity to molest or shame a girl or young woman who could not defend herself.

Watching a girl near her being manhandled, Emily burned with humiliation and anger. How could one person treat another with so little dignity? Of course, Emily knew that when she was chosen, she, too, would have to accept such treatment without complaint in order to avoid beatings—or worse.

Unfortunately, it wasn't long before an interested buyer came to the slave trader and asked for a young, attractive girl to hire as a housekeeper. The trader called for Emily.

Emily stepped forward, trembling. Fear and outrage left her cold and hollow. Surely no one would want her; she was just a girl. She could not be taken. She did not know what she would do without her sister. She tried to appear cheerful, but her chin quivered and tears slipped down her cheeks. The buyer looked her over and dismissed her. He told the slave trader that he refused to consider buying Emily because he had "no room for the snuffles in his house."

Once they were off the porch and out of view of the buyers, the trader slapped Emily across the face, hard. Her tears had lost him a $1,500 sale. He warned her that there would be worse if she didn't stop crying and look pleasant and willing in front of future customers.

Shades of Black

In addition to physical and emotional abuse, many female slaves were sexually abused by their owners and by other men they encountered in positions of power. Since they were considered property, enslaved women had no legal defense or recourse if they were raped or sexually molested. As a result, many black slaves gave birth to mixed-race children.

By law, any child of an enslaved mother was legally a slave, regardless of the legal status of the father. This practice resulted in several race classifications:

- *Mulatto* referred to a person with one black and one white parent; the word is derived from the Spanish word *mula*, meaning mule.
- *Quadroon* referred to a person with one-quarter black ancestry.
- *Octoroon* referred to a person with one-eighth black ancestry.

These terms had legal significance in the South, since many people who had fair skin were legally slaves. In many cases, light-skinned slaves were chosen for domestic work inside the home, while darker-skinned slaves worked in the fields.

Today, these race classifications are considered offensive, and a growing number of Americans classify themselves as "mixed race"—nine million people, almost 3 percent of the population, in the 2010 census.

All their lives, Emily and her siblings had been taught by their mother to conduct themselves with dignity and modesty. Now, they had to stand before strangers and allow them to violate their privacy and touch them as they pleased—and they had to smile all the while or face the whip. She had been spared for the moment, but Emily knew that it was a matter of time before she and her sister would be chosen.

WITNESS TO HORRORS

Behind the closed doors of the showroom, beyond the view of the
public, Emily witnessed the horrors and cruelty of the southern
slave system. Not long after she arrived at the slave pen, Emily

The Second Wife

I n New Orleans, attractive black women,
both free and enslaved, were sometimes
chosen as mistresses or second wives by
wealthy French, Spanish, and Creole men.
Through a social system known as *placage*,
these men would take a woman of color as a
secret common-law wife and separate their
time between their two homes and families:
one white, the other black; one public, the
other private.

The women in these arrangements
were not legally recognized as wives; they
were known as *placées*, from the French
word *placer*, meaning "to place with." Some
women became *placées* voluntarily, if they
were chosen by partners at so-called quadroon balls, formal dances where white
men met fair-skinned women of color.

Many of these mixed-race families
lived in neighborhoods not far from the
slave pen where the Edmonsons were held.

"Creole women of color taking
the air," an 1867 watercolor
painting by Edouard Marquis.
While these women would
have been free in 1867, the
placage system of "left-handed
marriages" was well-established
at the time the Edmonsons were
in New Orleans.

met a young woman who was also from Alexandria, Virginia. The girl was quite small, and very fine looking, with beautiful long, straight hair. Emily didn't know her age, but she thought she was Mary's age, 15, or perhaps even younger. Shortly after they met, the girl was sold.

Emily didn't expect to see her again, but a few days later the girl returned. Emily overheard the overseer say that she had been returned because she did not suit her purchaser. The seller had to refund the dissatisfied buyer's money, and he was enraged at the girl for not being more cooperative. Emily did not watch the girl getting flogged, but she saw the brutal consequences. The girl had been whipped so viciously that sections of her flesh had been shredded into bloody strips. Emily was not surprised that the girl was beaten, but she did not understand why the slave owner would express his anger by destroying his property, or what was considered his property in the eyes of the law.

Not long after the beating, Emily heard the overseer say that he would never flog another girl in that way again because, he said, it was too much for anyone to bear. Emily wondered if the guard experienced this change of heart because he observed his victim's ongoing suffering during weeks of painful recovery; it is one thing to snap a whip and another to witness the gore.

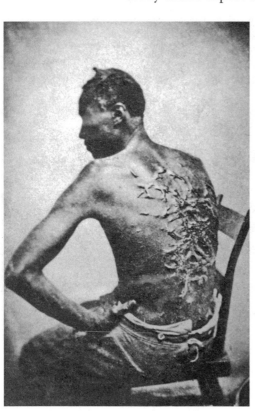

This iconic 1863 photograph shows the scars of a Mississippi slave who was beaten by his overseer.

The cruelty never seemed to end. Not long after the incident with the Alexandria girl, a young man was also returned to the slave trader. The man who bought him claimed that he was not a good worker; the enslaved man said that he was brokenhearted because he and the woman he loved had been sold to different owners and separated. The slave owner refunded the buyer's money and then pledged to flog the slave nightly for a week.

THE LASH.

Each stroke of the slave trader's bullwhip cut a bloody gash across the man's back. After about 200 lashes, the slave trader tired. He then demanded that each of the male slaves in the prison lay on five additional lashes with all his strength. Anyone who did not whip his fellow slave harshly enough was subjected to being flogged himself.

In the slave yard, beatings were not limited to adults. No one confined there—male or female, young or old— was allowed to sleep in the daytime. Sometimes young children would become drowsy and take a brief nap in the afternoon; if the overseer caught the children asleep, they were beaten. Emily and Mary would watch the little ones and let them doze off for brief periods of time, rousing them when they heard the keepers approach.

While most punishments were not designed to kill, in the New Orleans pen, the girls learned of two people—a

This 1863 lithograph by Henry Louis Stephens depicts a slave being whipped. Beatings often ranged from 10 to 40 lashes, sometimes more. A pregnant woman would be forced to lie facedown with her abdomen in a pit so that she could be whipped without injury to the baby.

woman and a young boy—who were whipped to death. Emily did not know how she was going to survive the ongoing abuse. In times of despair, other slaves found themselves almost envying those who had died: In death, they had at last found freedom; their suffering had ended.

~ TEN ~

An Unexpected Reunion

RICHARD EDMONSON ARRIVED in New Orleans a free man. He had to wait for weeks for his return voyage to Baltimore, so he decided to try to locate his older brother, Hamilton, the oldest of the 14 Edmonson children. Hamilton had run away from his owner's house in Washington, D.C., on July 1, 1833. The only information Richard had was that his brother had been captured and sold at auction in New Orleans, destined to work in the cotton fields. Sixteen years had passed; Richard had no reason to believe he would ever find out what happened to Hamilton.

Richard interviewed every willing black person he encountered. He went from shop to shop, asking for information about a slave meeting Hamilton's description coming from Washington 16 years before. After several days of searching, Richard wandered into a cooper shop at 121 Girard Street in New Orleans. Although they had grown up together, Richard did not recognize the store owner at first. After several questions, however, it became clear that Richard had found his oldest brother.

As they became reacquainted, Hamilton told Richard of his experiences as a southern slave. After spending years on a cotton plantation, Hamilton was sold again and given the last name of his new owner, Taylor. Hamilton Taylor became a cooper, a skilled tradesman who made barrels. While not a common practice, Hamilton's owner allowed him to keep a portion of his wages to encourage loyalty and to reduce the risk that he would run away. In time, Hamilton had saved enough money to buy his freedom for $1,000. As a free man, Hamilton started his own business making barrels near the shipping yard.

After 16 years away, Hamilton was eager to see the other members of his family. Mary had been a baby when Hamilton last saw her and Emily had not been born. Richard told Hamilton about his other siblings: Their five older sisters—Elizabeth, Eveline, Martha, Henrietta, and Eliza—were free, having purchased their freedom or married men who secured their freedom before the weddings. Their owner refused to sell any of the others because he depended on the steady income he received from hiring them out. The six who ran away on the *Pearl*—Emily, Mary, and their four brothers—had worked as domestic slaves before escaping. The two youngest, Josiah and Louisa, remained at home with their parents because they were still too young to be hired out. When he left the Culvers', Hamilton never expected to see his family again; now somehow Richard had found him. They had been given a second chance at brotherhood.

SURVIVING NEW ORLEANS

Emily did not know him and Mary did not remember him, but it did not take long for Hamilton to become a trusted member of the Edmonson family. The girls had heard stories about him, but they never expected to meet their runaway brother; finding Hamilton was their one experience of joy since they had arrived in New Orleans. Hamilton had not only survived, but thrived, even in the South.

Hamilton tried to do all he could to help his brothers and sisters. At the New Orleans slave pen, Emily and Mary slept on the floor in the female section with about 20 or 30 other women. Mosquitoes and other insects swarmed the room at night, and every morning the girls woke to find their feet itchy and swollen with bug bites. Hamilton and Richard approached the slave trader and asked him for permission to have Emily and Mary sleep at Hamilton's house, with the understanding that they would return to the showroom each morning. The trader wanted his slaves to look as healthy and free of disease as possible, so he agreed to the arrangement, knowing that the promise of a life-threatening beating would be enough to prevent the girls from trying to run away.

On the first night in Hamilton's home, Emily lay down on a mattress free of bugs and woke feeling more rested than she had in weeks. True to their word, she and Mary promptly returned to the slave pen to present themselves for sale.

Not long after, Emily's confidence was shaken when she saw the overseer take Samuel away in a carriage. They had no chance to speak or say good-bye. When they learned that he had been sold, they were not allowed to weep or appear sad; they needed to appear joyful and industrious on display. Emily did not know if she would ever see Samuel again, but the following day he returned to the slave pen and told the girls that he had been sold as a butler to Horace Cammack, a wealthy cotton merchant who had paid $1,000 for him. Hamilton may have helped him secure the position, but the details aren't known. Relieved that Samuel had avoided the harshness of field work, Emily found peace in knowing that he had found what he thought would be the best possible arrangement under the circumstances. The similar sale of Ephraim and John, the two other enslaved Edmonson brothers in New Orleans, followed.

While Emily waited to be sold, she noticed that many of the enslaved people in the showroom fell ill, complaining of fever, nausea, and headache. Some bled from their mouths or vomited a substance that looked like blackened tar. As the days wore on, a growing number of those around her turned a ghastly shade of yellow, a sign of liver failure and the final stages of the disease known as yellow fever.

Every day more people succumbed to illness. Surrounded by death, the Edmonsons did not know how long they would be spared. They were not used to the weather and conditions in the South, and purchasers often hesitated to pay full price for slaves who might come down with "yellow jack." Would they fall victim to disease before they had a chance to experience freedom?

Just as abruptly as they had been sent to New Orleans, Emily, Mary, and Richard were ordered to go back to Virginia before they became sick. On July 6, after three weeks in the South, they boarded the *Union* for the second time. Emily may have hesitated to return to the ship, but she longed for home more than she feared seasickness. The slave trader had told Emily and Mary that their family had raised a significant amount of money on their behalf. Richard was returning to life as a free man and the girls hoped that when they arrived, freedom papers would be waiting for them, too.

Beware! Yellow Fever

Yellow fever was a serious health problem in 1848. The year before, the disease had claimed almost 3,000 lives in New Orleans. When the disease began to spread among the slaves, no one had any idea how many would die. To minimize the risk of losing valuable property, traders often moved their slaves out of the area when disease broke out.

The mosquito known as *Stegomyia aegypti* is responsible for spreading yellow fever.

At the time, no one understood that yellow fever is a virus spread by the bite of an infected mosquito. Three to six days after being bitten, a person would experience headache, muscle aches, fever, flushing, loss of appetite, vomiting, and jaundice (yellow skin and eyes). After three or four days, these symptoms would disappear; some people would recover at this point, and others relapsed after about 24 hours. If the disease progressed, an infected person experienced organ failure, seizures, coma, and death. In 1848, there was no prevention or cure for yellow fever. Today there is a vaccination for the disease and there are modern treatments for the symptoms.

❧ ELEVEN ❧

$2,250: The Price of Freedom

AS SOON AS Emily boarded the *Union*, she realized that the return trip to Baltimore wasn't going to be much easier than the trip to New Orleans had been. The belowdecks cargo area that had been crowded with slaves during their journey south was now packed to the ceiling with bales of cotton, barrels of molasses, and loaves of sugar. Emily and Mary were left with a space about eight or ten square feet directly under the hatchway door. To keep from getting seasick, Emily decided to avoid the confined cargo space, instead spending as much time as possible on deck in the fresh air. To make them more comfortable during the trip, Richard had been able to acquire and bring along a mattress, blankets, and extra food and drink.

After 16 days at sea, they arrived in Baltimore. The slave trader took Emily and Mary back to the same pen where they had been held the month before. Emily anticipated good news of her release when she met Jacob Bigelow, a Washington lawyer, who arrived a few hours later. He told Emily and Mary that he came to make sure that Richard was not delayed or harassed on his trip home to his wife and children, but, he explained, they were to remain. Not enough money had been raised to pay for their release.

Devastated, Emily realized that this time she and Mary would have to manage without the support and protection of their brothers.

Over the next few weeks, Emily and Mary fell into a predictable routine. In the mornings they were forced to exercise by marching around the yard to the music of fiddles and banjos; in the afternoons they washed and ironed, slept some, and often wept.

A few weeks later, Emily had a chance to see her father, Paul Edmonson, and her older sister, Elizabeth Brent, when they traveled to Baltimore to try to negotiate for the girls' release. The slave trader told Paul that he had two weeks to raise the funds or the girls would be moved to another slave market.

That night Elizabeth stayed with Emily and Mary in the women's area and Paul slept in the room above his daughters. Emily could hear her father crying and groaning through the night. In the morning, Paul stood in the yard of the slave pen and watched the slaves marching around. The yard was narrow and the girls walked past him, so close that their skirts almost brushed up against him, but they had to keep walking and he had to let them go. Overwhelmed with grief, Paul could not stop from crying out, "Oh, my children, my children!" Emily knew that her father feared that he would not have enough time to raise the necessary funds to buy his children's freedom.

BACK TO BRUIN & HILL

Weeks passed and Paul Edmonson did not return. Instead, Joseph Bruin, the slave trader from Alexandria, came to reclaim Emily and Mary. He roused the girls from their cell at about eleven o'clock at night and told them to come with him because they were returning to Virginia.

This time, Emily did not dare to consider the possibility of freedom. Surely, if she and Mary were to be free, Bruin would tell them. He said nothing.

At about 2 a.m., they arrived at Bruin & Hill in Alexandria, Virginia, the first place they were taken after leaving the Washington City Jail. They were placed in the same room where they had been held after their initial capture. Weeks had passed and they were back where they started.

Emily and Mary spent the sweltering days of August in the Alexandria slave pen washing, ironing, and sewing. Sometimes they were allowed to work in Bruin's house, located less than a block from the slave pen. They spent a lot of time looking after Bruin's children, seven-year-old Mary and four-year-old Martha, who developed a special affection for their caregivers.

COMING TO TERMS

Several weeks later, Paul Edmonson visited Bruin in Alexandria, trying once more to negotiate for his daughters' freedom. He planned to go north to raise funds but he wanted Bruin to state in writing the exact terms that he would accept for their release.

In response, Bruin drafted the following document:

Alexandria, Va., Sept. 5, 1848

The bearer, Paul Edmondson, is the father of two girls, Mary Jane and Emily Catherine Edmondson. These girls have been purchased by us, and once sent to the south; and upon the positive assurance that the money for them would be raised if they were brought back, they were returned. Nothing, it appears, has as yet been done in this respect by those who promised, and we are on the very eve of sending them south the second time; and we are candid in saying that if they go again, we will not regard any promises made in relation to them. The father wishes to raise money to pay for them; and intends to appeal to the liberality of the humane and the good to aid him, and has requested us to state in writing the conditions upon which we will sell his daughters.

We expect to start our service to the South in a few days; if the sum of twelve hundred ($1,200) dollars be raised and paid to us in fifteen days, or we be assured of that sum then we will retain them for twenty-five days more, to give an opportunity for the raising of the other thousand and fifty ($1,050) dollars; otherwise we shall be compelled to send them along with our other servants.

Bruin & Hill.

Paul Edmonson took the paper and left.

THE COFFLE DEPARTS

Emily and Mary waited anxiously for a letter or message from their father, but day after day passed without word from him. The letter stated that their father had 15 days, until September 20, to raise the ransom. Emily watched as the deadline approached—and then passed. Had the price been set so high that he would be unable to raise the money? Since Bruin had not received any payment, Emily realized that he was free to sell them any time he wished.

Just as Bruin had promised, he began preparations to send about 35 slaves in a coffle to South Carolina. Emily and Mary would be part of that chain gang.

The girls were given bright calico fabric and ordered to sew the show dresses that they would wear when they arrived and were exhibited for sale. Emily did as she was told, although all the time she spent cutting and stitching the fabric she felt as if she were sewing her own funeral shroud. Would she and Mary have to endure the same horrors and humiliations they had experienced in New Orleans?

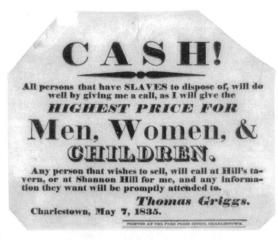

CASH!

All persons that have SLAVES to dispose of, will do well by giving me a call, as I will give the

HIGHEST PRICE FOR

Men, Women, & CHILDREN.

Any person that wishes to sell, will call at Hill's tavern, or at Shannon Hill for me, and any information they want will be promptly attended to.

Thomas Griggs.

Charlestown, May 7, 1835.

PRINTED AT THE FREE PRESS OFFICE, CHARLESTOWN.

Slave traders advertised in newspapers and broadsides for the purchase of slaves.

The night before the coffle was to leave, Emily and Mary went to Bruin's house to tell his family good-bye. His young daughters clung to Emily and Mary and begged them not to go. Mary explained that they did not want to leave, but they had to obey her father. Emily told Bruin's daughters that if they wanted them to stay, they should go and talk to their father. The children ran away to beg their father to allow Emily and Mary to remain in Virginia.

That night, Emily and Mary wept in the darkness of their cell. Bruin heard their cries and came up to see them. Mary begged for compassion, urging him to think of his own dear daughters. Bruin listened to Mary's words and hesitatingly agreed that if his business partner, Captain Henry Hill, approved, he would not force them to join the coffle leaving in the morning. That said, he warned the girls not to expect special treatment, since Hill had already said that he thought the girls should have been sold long ago.

Emily and Mary continued to weep and pray through the night. Morning dawned, but they had not been told that they could stay. Had Hill ignored their pleas? They gathered their few possessions and put on their bonnets and shawls. Had all their prayers gone unanswered?

Emily knew that in just a few moments, they would be forced to gather in the yard and line up—men, women, and children, two and two, the men handcuffed together, the right wrist of one to the left wrist of the other. A chain would be passed through the handcuffs, one after the other, linking the group together. The prisoners would form a line and travel on foot; the traders would travel on horseback on either side of the line, carrying whips to control both the horses and the people. At the time of their departure, they would be forced to set off singing—singing!—accompanied by fiddles and banjos, the steady crash of the chains creating the rhythm of the march.

A Slave-Coffle passing the Capitol.

From the 1881 book, *A Popular History of the United States*, by William Cullen Bryant. The men were typically handcuffed and chained together, while the women and children marched behind. The etching shows the U.S. Capitol as it appeared in 1815, without a dome.

Would they be able to survive the journey? Death was not unexpected when traveling on a chain gang.

Emily looked out the upstairs window of their quarters, watching the slaves gather in the yard below. When would she and Mary be called to join them?

The enslaved took their places in line, shackled together.

The fiddle and banjo began to play.

The gates to the pen opened and the coffle began to shuffle forward.

Sorrow Songs

Coffles were often led by fiddle and banjo players to keep the enslaved marching at a steady pace and to conceal their sorrow. Frederick Douglass reflected on the meaning of music and song among slaves in his 1845 book, *Narrative of the Life of Frederick Douglass, An American Slave*:

> I have often been utterly astonished, since I came to the north, to find persons who could speak of the singing among slaves as evidence of their contentment and happiness. It is impossible to conceive of a greater mistake. . . . The songs of the slave represent the sorrow of his heart; and he is relieved by them, only as an aching heart is relieved by its tears.

Frederick Douglass (1818–1895), a reformer and leader in the abolitionist movement, understood the extreme hardships of living within slavery. He was born Frederick Augustus Washington Bailey and changed his name to Douglass after escaping to the North.

Emily and Mary watched them leave, watched the last person in line move out of the yard and the gates close behind him. They had been spared. When they understood they would *not* be going to South Carolina, they hugged each other and wept with relief. They were not free, but they did not have to go south, not yet, not that day.

What Emily and Mary did not know was that the night before the coffle departed, Joseph Bruin met with one of the Edmonsons' supporters, probably William Chaplin, and worked out a last-minute agreement to keep the girls in Virginia. The man offered Bruin a $600 deposit, which he could keep if Paul Edmonson failed to come up with the balance of the money due by a new deadline.

Bruin, eager to pocket the $600 bonus, agreed to the arrangement. He no longer expected the Edmonsons to be able to raise the money. After all, they had been trying for months without success. Why would things be different this time?

TWELVE

Ransomed

P AUL EDMONSON ASKED everyone he knew for help raising the money he needed to buy his daughters' freedom, but he had only limited success. When he approached abolitionist sympathizers in Washington, they didn't have money to offer, but they did make arrangements for him to go to New York City to ask for assistance from the American and Foreign Anti-Slavery Society. After a 12-hour train ride, Paul arrived in Manhattan and followed the directions he had been given to the main office of the society. He explained his situation and shared testimonials about the girls' good character as well as a letter from Rev. Mathew Turner, the white minister at Asbury Methodist Church where the Edmonsons had worshiped, which stated that they were exemplary members of the congregation and worthy of support. A representative from the Anti-Slavery Society agreed to follow up by writing to Bruin to authenticate the facts of the case and to see if he would lower the ransom.

In the meantime, Paul was directed to the Rev. James W. C. Pennington, an escaped slave from Maryland who was also a founding member of the American Anti-Slavery Society and pastor of

The American Anti-Slavery Society

The American Anti-Slavery Society was founded in 1833 and dedicated to ending slavery in the United States. Within five years, it had about 1,500 state and local chapters and more than 200,000 members. Slavery was a divisive moral and economic issue, and pro-slavery mobs sometimes disrupted meetings and attacked speakers.

Even within the society, members did not agree on how to achieve their goals. The more radical members of the group denounced the U.S. Constitution as pro-slavery and favored allowing women to take leadership roles within the group. The more conservative faction supported working for change within the government, and it expected women to leave the work of the organization to the men. In 1839, a more conservative group known as the American and Foreign Anti-Slavery Society splintered off. At the same time, some members left and formed a third group, the Liberty Party, which aimed to end slavery through the political process. Following this organizational change, most work in the abolitionist movement was done through state and local branches or chapters.

Union with Freemen---No Union with Slaveholders.

ANTI-SLAVERY MEETINGS!

Anti-Slavery Meetings will be held in this place, to commence on
in the   at

To be Addressed by

Agents of the Western ANTI-SLAVERY SOCIETY.

Three millions of your fellow beings are in chains--the Church and Government sustains the horrible system of oppression.

Turn Out!

AND LEARN YOUR DUTY TO YOURSELVES, THE SLAVE AND GOD.

EMANCIPATION or DISSOLUTION, and a FREE NORTHERN REPUBLIC!

HOMESTEAD PRINT, SALEM, OHIO.

This woodcut image titled "Am I not a man and a brother?" was originally used as the seal of the Society for the Abolition of Slavery in England in the 1780s. It was widely used in the American abolitionist movement as well.

the Shiloh Presbyterian Church in New York City. Pennington preached about the Edmonson case in his church the following Sunday and his congregation raised $50 in donations, a significant amount of money considering that most members of the church were quite poor and many were saving their money to free their own family members. Paul didn't want to appear ungrateful—he did appreciate the efforts being made to help his family—but $50 wasn't nearly enough for him to reach his goal in

time. Pennington understood and sent Paul to visit the home of
the Rev. Henry Ward Beecher, a preacher and the editor of the
New York *Independent*, an abolitionist newspaper.

When Paul arrived at Beecher's house in Brooklyn, no one
was home, so he sat on the front steps to wait. Overcome with
stress and grief, he could no longer hold back the tears and he
began to weep. When Beecher arrived, Paul gathered his compo-
sure and explained his situation. Beecher invited him inside to his
library to tell his story.

Before that time, Beecher had not taken up the cause of slavery from the pulpit, but Mary and Emily's story horrified him.
The girls were so young and innocent that he felt compelled to
act. Beecher, who had led the Plymouth Church in Brooklyn for
about a year, reached out to other churches and congregations,
inviting them to attend a public rally to benefit the girls. This
ecumenical appeal was the first time New York clergy from different denominations had come together to assist slaves in need.

GATHERING AT THE TABERNACLE

On the night of October 23, 1848, 2,000 people from across New
York City jammed into the Broadway Tabernacle at Worth and
Catherine streets. Paul watched Beecher captivate the audience
with his zeal and theatrics. Early in his remarks, Beecher held up
shackles and chains and dramatically clashed them onto a table in
front of him.

Paul admired the way Beecher carefully chose his words.
Rather than wrestling with broad questions about the system of
slavery itself, Beecher focused on the plight of Emily and Mary
Edmonson, two devout and virginal Christian girls who faced a life
of prostitution in the South if he and his congregation failed to act.

Rev. Henry Ward Beecher: Finding His Voice

Henry Ward Beecher was born in Litchfield, Connecticut, in 1813. He was a shy and sensitive child with a severe speech impediment. "When Henry is sent to me with a message, I always have to make him say it three times," said one of his aunts.

Beecher took oratorical training at Mount Pleasant Classical Institute, a boarding school in Amherst, Massachusetts, before studying at Amherst College and later at Lane Theological Seminary outside Cincinnati, Ohio. In his own words:

Henry Ward Beecher was one of the best-known clergymen of the day. Several of his brothers and sisters became respected educators and abolitionists, including his sister Harriet Beecher Stowe.

> I had from childhood a thickness of speech arising from a large palate, so that when a boy I used to be laughed at for talking as if I had pudding in my mouth. When I went to Amherst, I was fortunate in passing into the hands of John Lovell, a teacher of elocution; and a better teacher for my purpose I cannot conceive. His system consisted in drill, or the thorough practice of inflexions by the voice, of gesture, posture, and articulation. Sometimes I was a whole hour practicing my voice on a word, like justice.
>
> I would have to take a posture, frequently a mark chalked on the floor. Then we would go through all the gestures; exercising each movement of the arm, and the throwing open the hand. . . . It was drill, drill, drill, until the motions almost became second nature. Now I never know what movement I shall make. My gestures are natural because this drill made them natural to me.

Beecher overcame his speech problems, and his antislavery preaching then made him one of the most prominent orators of his time.

While sympathetic to the Edmonsons as individuals, not everyone believed that ransom should be paid for slaves. Some people thought that negotiating with slaveholders recognized and legitimized the institution of slavery. Others believed that paying ransom would just supply money to those who would use it to buy other slaves. In addition, some didn't consider it fair to use limited resources to ransom the fortunate few rather than promote the emancipation of all enslaved people.

Despite these objections, most audience members found Beecher's plea hard to resist because it focused on the fate of two specific individuals. It wasn't abstract, it was personal. The audience at the Broadway Tabernacle wasn't trying to take on the institution of slavery; it was trying to help two innocent Christian girls, Emily and Mary Edmonson.

The Broadway Tabernacle was a center of antislavery activism from its founding in 1836. A pro-slavery mob burned it down while it was under construction, but it was rebuilt.

Beecher presented Paul to the audience and asked: "The father! Do goods and chattel have fathers? Do slaves have daughters?" He spoke of the girls' spirituality and faithfulness, begging the audience to protect the virtue of these Christian girls. When he noted that they were pious members of the Episcopal

PLYMOUTH CHURCH. REV. HENRY WARD BEECHER SELLING A SLAVE.

Methodist Church and that their faith would make them worth more on the slave market, the crowd responded with fury.

Paul watched as a fire was lit within Beecher. The chains before him became a symbol of the chains that bound Emily and Mary, as well as those that held the wrists of millions of other slaves, and in an outburst of passion Beecher seized them, slammed them to the floor, and ground them beneath his heel as though he were grinding the institution of slavery to dust beneath his feet. The audience cheered; their applause thundered throughout the hall.

"I thank you for that noise!" Beecher said. "It cheers me and makes me feel that I am among brethren." Beecher paced the stage—talking, preaching, waving his hands. A man in the audience later described him as "popping about like a box of fireworks

Rev. Henry Ward Beecher held mock auctions to raise funds to ransom enslaved persons, including Emily and Mary Edmonson.

Was It Wrong to Ransom Mary and Emily?

Many abolitionists were reluctant to pay to ransom slaves, even though they wanted to end slavery. They had several key concerns:

- Negotiating with slaveholders recognized and legitimized the institution of slavery. If abolitionists didn't believe one person had the right to own another, how could they engage in this kind of commerce?
- Paying ransom provided money to those who could use it to buy additional slaves. Wouldn't buying slaves drive up the prices and give slave traders the money they needed to stay in business?
- Using money to ransom individual slaves misused funds that could otherwise be used to promote the emancipation of all enslaved people. Should the resources of the abolitionists be used to free all slaves, not just the fortunate few?
- Engaging in the buying and selling of human beings was sinful and morally wrong. Was it ever appropriate to do what is wrong, even if the goal was to achieve a greater good?

accidentally ignited and going off in all shapes and directions—a rocket here with falling stars, a fiery wheel there."

Beecher then called for a donation, urging the audience to be generous.

When the money was counted, it amounted to a mere $600. Edmonson needed $2,250. Beecher expressed his displeasure and a voice came from the crowd: "Take up another!"

The collection boxes circulated again. This time members of the audience dug deeper into their pockets. Some women in the audience removed their rings and earrings and added their valuable jewelry to the collection. The money was counted, and again it fell several hundred dollars short.

One by one, additional pledges were made. Mr. S. B. Chittenden gave his name for another $50; his brother, Henry Chittenden, matched the pledge with $50 more. From time to time a voice in the audience yelled, "How much is wanting now?"

When all but $50 had been raised, Beecher said, "I never did hurrah in a public meeting, but when this account is closed up, I will join in three of the loudest cheers that ever rang through this old building."

"I'll take the balance," called a member of Beecher's Plymouth Church.

The room erupted in cheers and shouts. Men waved their hats and handkerchiefs offering three cheers for Beecher and the benefactors.

Paul broke down in tears.

After a moment of revelry, Beecher quieted the crowd and reminded them of the gratitude they each owed to God. Those in attendance sang the doxology, "Praise God from whom all blessings flow," not with thunder and applause, but with tenderness and thanksgiving.

The meeting closed with a joyful benediction, celebrating the fact that the Edmonson sisters would soon be free.

PAYMENT IN FULL

On an afternoon in early November, Emily was sewing near the open window of Bruin's home when she looked outside and said: "There, Mary, is that white man we have seen from the North." A moment later and they noticed a second man—their father!—walking with the man.

They sprang up and ran through the house and into the street, shouting as they went. The girls knew their father had been collecting money in the North. Emily rushed to him and asked if he had been successful. Paul's hands shook and his voice trembled as he told his daughters that he needed to speak with Bruin but would talk to them soon. Paul Edmonson and his companion entered Bruin's office and shut the door.

Emily and Mary returned to their room while their father conducted his business with Bruin. Did their father have the money for their ransom?

Did he have enough for both of them?

The longer they waited, the more they worried. They focused on their father's trembling hands and unsteady voice. Could he, in fact, be bringing them bad news? They had heard that their mother had been quite ill. Was she dead or in failing health? They strode back and forth as anxiety turned to excitement and back into anxiety again.

Inside the office, Bruin said that he was sincerely glad that Paul had arrived with the payment and that he would honor their agreement, but he was disappointed that Beecher had spoken so harshly about him at the meeting at the tabernacle. Bruin considered himself a good Christian and a more humane and sophisticated man than other slave traders. (Most slave traders were wealthy and influential citizens from well-to-do plantation families.) Bruin may have been well dressed and had impeccable manners, but he still made his fortune buying and selling human beings. Business was business.

Bruin counted the money, $2,250 cash, and signed the bill of sale. It read:

> Received from W. L. Chaplin twenty-two hundred and fifty dollars, being payment in full for the purchase of two negroes, named Mary and Emily Edmonson. The right and title of said negroes we warrant and defend against the claims of all persons whatsoever; and likewise warrant them sound and healthy in body and mind, and slaves for life.

Given under our hand and seal, this seventh day of
November, 1848. $2,250 BRUIN & Hill. (Seal.)

Bruin handed the paper to William Chaplin, who had helped
plan the escape on the *Pearl*. When Bruin let go, Mary and Emily
Edmonson were no longer his.

FOREVER FREE

Upstairs, Emily paced and prayed and tried to stay calm. She
tried to accept Mary's reassurance that God's will would be done,
whether she and Mary would be freed or if they would suffer
another setback.

Finally, a messenger came shouting to them, "You are free!
You are free!"

The girls jumped and clapped and laughed and shouted.

Paul held his daughters tenderly and tried to quiet them. He
certainly shared their exuberance, but he may have known that
even as free women their lives would not be free of hardship and
discrimination. He told them to prepare to go home and see their
mother. The girls gathered their belongings and said good-bye
to members of the Bruin family, this time with joy rather than
sadness.

A carriage took the girls and their father to their sister Elizabeth's house in Washington, where family and friends had gathered to celebrate their emancipation. Their brothers lifted the girls
in their arms and ran about with them, almost frantic with joy.
Their mother wept and gave thanks to God. They spent the night
rejoicing, grateful for the chance to be together.

In the morning, Mary and Emily went with Chaplin to
City Hall and watched him sign the deed of manumission. In

exchange for a payment of one dollar, the document assured that "the sisters Mary Jane and Emily Catherine Edmonson, daughters of Paul Edmonson," were "hereby, each of them, declared forever free from any and all restraint or control." After a lifetime of slavery and more than six months in various slave pens and auction houses, Mary and Emily belonged only to themselves. They were, at last, free.

⌒ THIRTEEN ⌒

The Trial of
Captain Daniel Drayton

WHILE EMILY AND Mary were ransomed about seven months after they first tried to escape, the captains of the *Pearl* remained in prison. Although there were two captains aboard the ship on the night of the escape, the central figure in the plot was 46-year-old Captain Daniel Drayton.

After the passengers and crew of the *Pearl* were captured, Drayton was questioned about the events of that night. Those who interrogated him wanted to know who had masterminded and financed the escape, but Drayton refused to tell them. He knew that to reveal the names of his contacts in New York and Philadelphia would not only put his associates at personal risk but could also compromise the broader abolitionist movement.

The names he kept secret were William L. Chaplin's, of the New York Anti-Slavery Society, and Dr. Charles Cleveland's, of the Philadelphia Anti-Slavery Society. These two men had raised the money and organized the escape plan, arranging for Drayton to be paid $100 to smuggle a group of enslaved people out of Washington, D.C. Drayton was given another $100 to hire a boat and captain.

Most of the seamen Drayton approached refused to help him with a scheme as risky as a slave escape. Captain Edward Sayres needed work and the $100 fee was significantly more than he could earn in another trip of similar duration. The men agreed that Drayton would control the cargo—the enslaved people—and Sayres would control the ship itself.

Drayton did not tell his captors anything, and he was sent back to his cell. When it came time to sleep, one of the keepers threw Drayton two thin blankets and left him to rest as well as he could on the stone floor. The room was virtually empty—no chair, table, stool, just a night bucket and a water can.

A WELCOME VISITOR

In the morning, Ohio Congressman Joshua Giddings and his friend Edwin Hamlin, editor of the Cleveland daily *True Democrat*, an antislavery newspaper, arrived at the jail to visit Drayton and Sayres. As they entered the building, they had to work their way through a cluster of slave owners and slave traders doing business in the lobby. When 53-year-old Giddings asked to visit the prisoners, the jailer hesitated. He knew who was standing before him; Giddings, who believed that slavery violated not just the Constitution but a higher natural law, was known as one of the most outspoken antislavery legislators of his day. He wasn't sure it would be safe to let a well-known abolitionist and a newspaper editor inside the jail to visit the accused.

Eventually the jailer allowed them in, relocking the front gate and passing the key back to another guard. He then escorted the men up the winding stone staircase to a second locked gate, which he opened to allow Giddings and Hamlin to pass through to the cells where Drayton and Sayres were held.

When the congressman met Drayton, he reassured the captain that his friends in the abolitionist movement would not abandon him. In that moment, Drayton had the power to derail several leading members of the Underground Railroad by linking them to criminal activity. Giddings reiterated that he and his abolitionist associates would take care of Drayton's family if he stayed quiet and did not provide the names of those who had planned the escape. In addition to financial support, Giddings offered Drayton representation by an attorney, David A. Hall, a lawyer from the District of Columbia who had experience defending several people who had been implicated in another Underground Railroad escape.

While Giddings spoke with Drayton, the noise of the rioters echoed in the staircase. Not long after, their voices grew louder and Giddings could hear dozens of feet pounding up the stairs. Downstairs, someone in the mob had gained possession of the key and unlocked the first gate, allowing the men to rush up the stairs and continue to threaten and yell at the congressman, who had become the target for their anger.

Although they were still separated by a second locked iron gate, someone in the crowd told Giddings to leave immediately or his life would be in danger. Giddings ignored the threats and completed his business with Drayton. He refused to show fear or any willingness to retreat.

The jailer eventually regained control of the crowd and convinced the men on the stairs to move back behind the main gate so that the visitors could leave. Giddings calmly faced the mob, meeting the eyes of those who had come to do him harm. The protesters had felt bold enough to assault the congressman with words, but no one touched him as he passed. Giddings and Hamlin walked down the stairs and out the front door unharmed.

Addressing Congress About the *Pearl* Escape

After visiting Captain Daniel Drayton in the Washington City Jail, Congressman Joshua Giddings went to the floor of the House of Representatives to speak about the escape on the *Pearl*. The following is an excerpt of his April 25, 1848, speech:

> It is said that some seventy-six men, women, and children, living in this District, possessing the same natural right to the enjoyment of life and liberty as gentlemen in this Hall . . . went on board a schooner lying at one of the wharves of this city, and set sail for a "land of liberty."
>
> When they reached the mouth of the river, adverse winds compelled them to anchor. Thus detained, we may imagine the anxiety that must have filled their minds. How that slave mother pressed her tender babe more closely to her breast, as she sent up to the God of the oppressed her silent supplication for deliverance from the men-stealers who were on their track. . . . Bloodhounds in human shape were in her pursuit, clothed with the authority of the laws enacted by Congress, and now kept in force by this body. They seized upon those wretched fugitives and brought them back to this city, and thrust them into yonder prison, erected by the treasure of this nation.
>
> There they remained until Friday, when nearly fifty of them, having been purchased by the infamous [slave trader] Hope H. Slatter, who headed the mob at the jail on Tuesday, were taken . . . to the railroad depot, and from thence to Baltimore, destined for sale in the far south, there to drag out a miserable existence upon the cotton and sugar plantations of that slave-consuming region.
>
> The scene at the depot is represented as one which would have disgraced the city of Algiers or Tunis: Wives bidding adieu to their husbands, mothers in an agony of despair, unable to bid farewell to

their daughters; little boys and girls weeping amid the general distress, scarcely
knowing the cause of their grief. Sighs
and groans and tears and unutterable
agony, characterized a scene at which
the heart sickens, and from which
humanity shrinks with horror.

Over such a scene that fiend in human
shape, Slatter, presided, assisted by some
three or four associates in depravity, each
armed with pistols, Bowie-knife, and club.
Yes, sir, by virtue of our laws he held these
mothers and children, these sisters and
brothers, subject to his power, and tore
them from the ties which bind mankind to
life, and carried them south, and doomed
them to cruel and lingering deaths.

**Congressman Joshua R. Giddings
(1795–1864) represented Ohio's
16th district. He was an outspoken
opponent of slavery.**

Sir, do you believe that those
members of this body, who stubbornly
refused to repeal those laws, are less
guilty in the sight of a just and holy God
than Slatter himself? We, sir, enable
him to pursue this accursed vocation. Can we be innocent
of those crimes? How long will members of this House
continue thus to outrage humanity?

INDICTED

Later that day, a jailer escorted Drayton downstairs to an office where two justices of the peace, Hampton C. Williams and John H. Goddard, were prepared to hold court. They had decided to conduct official business inside the jail because they considered it too dangerous to move the accused over to the courthouse.

Before the proceedings began, United States District Attorney Philip Barton Key told Drayton's attorney that he should leave the jail and go home immediately, because the people outside were furious and he risked his life by representing Drayton. Unruffled, Hall replied that things had come to a pretty pass if a man no longer had the privilege of safely speaking with his counsel.

The grand jury, under the instructions of the district attorney, handed up 74 indictments against each of the prisoners. During the proceedings, the justices of the peace charged Drayton, Sayres, and Chester English with stealing and transporting slaves and fixed bail at $1,000 for each runaway aboard the *Pearl*, or $76,000 for each of the accused.

The district attorney wanted to find the men guilty of a penitentiary offense in addition to levying a fine, so he employed an arcane 1737 Maryland statute that provided that any person who steals a slave shall "suffer death as a felon and be excluded the benefit of clergy." A modification of the law in 1831 changed the punishment from death to confinement in a penitentiary for not less than 20 years.

Neither Drayton nor Sayres could come up with the money needed to post bail, so they remained in the Washington City Jail to wait for their trials to begin. Drayton did his best to make prison life tolerable. Nothing could be done to improve the fact that his small stone cell had no direct sunlight and poor ventilation, but after about six weeks he was able to obtain an old mattress to place on the hard floor. A sympathetic cook sometimes gave him extra food on the side, but he found the basic prison food unappetizing. As a prisoner, Drayton received two meals a day: breakfast, consisting of one herring, corn bread, coffee, and a dish of molasses; and dinner, a second helping of corn bread, half a pound of salted beef, and a soup made of cornmeal. No fresh fruit or seasoned vegetables were served. In fact, the menu remained the same, day after day, month after month.

This portrait of Capt. Daniel Drayton was used to illustrate his 1853 book, *Personal Memoir of Daniel Drayton, for Four Years and Four Months a Prisoner (for Charity's Sake) in a Washington Jail.*

To make time pass faster, Drayton worked on self-improvement. When he first entered the jail, he could read reasonably well and he could sign his name, but he could not write in complete sentences. While he was incarcerated, he practiced writing and he read the newspaper whenever he could borrow a copy.

He also had time to think. Rather than weakening his resolve, Drayton's time in prison taught him to appreciate his freedom, and living without liberty strengthened his conviction that slavery was wrong.

THE TRIAL

Although the escape on the *Pearl* involved a single event, Drayton and Sayres were indicted on 110 separate charges: 36 larceny indictments for stealing from the 36 people who owned slaves on the *Pearl*, as well as the 74 grand jury indictments for transporting slaves. (The charges against English were dropped in exchange for his testimony against the captains.) If convicted on all counts, each of the men could have been sentenced to more than 800 years in prison.

The first trial against Drayton began on July 27, 1848. That day the temperature soared above 90 degrees and the high humidity made the air in the packed courtroom oppressive, even with the windows open for ventilation. The first case involved the escape of two enslaved men, Joe and Frank, who were the property of Andrew Hoover, the 47-year-old owner of a shoe factory and retail store. The district attorney argued that Drayton stole the men and intended to take them to the West Indies to sell them, although he did not explain why Drayton would have set off in an undersized boat that was not capable of sailing in the open ocean.

During the trial, Drayton's attorney attempted to call Joe and Frank as witnesses, but the judge ruled that the men did not have the right to testify in a District of Columbia court. Instead, the defense attorney called Hoover, who admitted under oath that no one had broken into his house; the property—the two enslaved men—had walked away on their own. If they left of their own volition, how could Drayton be found guilty of stealing them?

The case went to the jury at 3 p.m. When the court reconvened the following day at 10 a.m., the jury had not made a decision. Four members of the jury hesitated to convict Drayton, but the others eventually pressured the holdouts to change their minds. After 24 hours of deliberation, the verdict was in: Drayton was guilty.

Drayton wasn't surprised by the verdict, but he still wondered: How could he be found guilty of stealing something that cannot be owned? How can one man own another, any more than he can own the sea or the sky or the stars?

One case followed another during legal maneuverings that lasted almost one year. Ultimately, Sayres was cleared of all larceny charges and convicted of 74 counts of transporting slaves; he was fined $7,400, or $100 for each conviction. Drayton was convicted of two counts of larceny and 74 counts of transporting slaves. The judge fined him $10,360, or $140 for each transporting conviction, a greater fine than Sayres's because he was deemed more responsible for the crimes. Drayton was also sentenced to 20 years at hard labor for the larceny convictions. Both men were to remain in jail until the fines were paid, which, as far as Drayton was concerned, meant that they would be imprisoned for life.

In November 1848, Drayton appealed his larceny convictions before a three-judge panel of the District of Columbia Circuit Court. On February 19, 1849, judges William Cranch, James Morsell, and James Dunlop struck down the decision, ruling that for Drayton's larceny conviction to stand, he would have had to profit from the escape. With these charges overturned, the 20-year jail sentence was dropped, although he still had to remain in prison until he could pay the outstanding fines.

~ FOURTEEN ~

A Radical Education

A FEW WEEKS AFTER Emily and Mary Edmonson were freed, Rev. Henry Beecher invited the young women to visit New York City so that they could personally thank their benefactors. He also planned a second rally on their behalf, hoping to raise money for their education. Emily and Mary accepted Beecher's invitation, excited to have a chance to thank those who had been so generous to them. On the trip, they were escorted by abolitionist William Chaplin, who had helped coordinate their release and took them to the ministers who had sponsored the first rally and contributed toward their ransom.

On the night of December 7, the hall at the Broadway Tabernacle was again filled with many of the same people who had helped raise the ransom for the girls weeks before. When the program started, the Rev. Samuel H. Cox, from the First Presbyterian Church in Brooklyn, took the podium and told the audience that he had been impressed with the gratitude and good manners shown by Emily and Mary, noting that he could not have expected better manners from the daughters of Queen Victoria of England.

Beecher took the podium and congratulated the crowd for having been so generous in the past. He introduced Emily and Mary, and the girls felt eyes—thousands of eyes—focusing on them, staring, pitying, judging, wondering what their suffering must have been like. Beecher held Emily and Mary's bill of sale over his head, waving it in the air, saying it was wrong to sell people as if they were animals.

As he spoke, Beecher's words became more radical and inflammatory. "Slavery is a state of suppressed war," he said. "The slave is justified in regarding his master as a belligerent enemy and in seizing him from whatever reprisals are necessary to aid him in effecting a retreat."

This is the only known photograph featuring the Edmonson sisters alone. Mary is standing with her hand on Emily's shoulder.

Emily had never heard such strong words about slavery before—certainly never from a preacher, never from the pulpit. Were his words true? Did enslaved people have the power to resist authority and run away?

When the audience seemed enthusiastic and responsive, Beecher called for contributions to establish an education fund for Emily and Mary. He urged the crowd to help them prepare for a life of usefulness, noting that they wanted to become teachers so that they could educate other black Americans.

The plate was passed, but this time few contributed.

Now that they were free, Emily and Mary had begun to recognize new possibilities in their lives. They were both eager to learn to read and then to teach. Emily knew that she would not let this lack of financial support stop her; she would find a way to learn to read and write and complete her education. Beecher tried, but even he could not make an appeal for the sisters' education fund as exciting as the appeal to save them from the chains of slavery.

Beecher did not want to accept defeat. He called for a second meeting at the Broadway Tabernacle a week later, but that crowd proved no more supportive. Many abolitionists did not consider black people to be their social or intellectual equals, even though they did favor ending slavery.

BOARDING SCHOOL

Even after they were freed, Chaplin con-tinued to support Emily and Mary. He believed that they put a sympathetic face on the abuses of slavery, and that citizens in the North would object to slavery if they knew the kind of people who were held in bondage. He covered their educational expenses and made arrangements for the girls to move to upstate New York to live and study in the homes of several lead-ing abolitionists, including Gerrit Smith and William R. Smith. Little is known about their early educa-tion, except that the girls excelled in their studies. By the fall of 1849 they were ready to attend New York Central College, a school run by abolitionists in McGrawville, New York.

For a time, the girls also stayed in the Syracuse home of Jermain Loguen, a runaway slave from Ten-nessee. Though surviving records don't describe details of the time they spent with Loguen, he was known to be a bold and fearless conductor on the Underground Railroad, the network of secret routes and safe houses used by runaway slaves during their escape to northern free states or Canada. Conductors

Jermain Wesley Loguen (1813–1872) ran away from slavery at age 21. He eventually settled in Syracuse, New York, where he opened his house to slaves on the Underground Railroad. In 1859, he wrote his autobiography, *The Rev. J. W. Loguen, as a Slave and as a Freeman, a Narrative of Real Life.*

sheltered fugitives and guided them from station to station, typically at night. Loguen operated his station so openly that he sometimes advertised in the newspaper that he offered assistance to runaway slaves. During the time they spent with Loguen, Emily and Mary almost certainly helped shelter and support fugitive slaves on their way to freedom.

BECOMING ABOLITIONISTS

In Loguen's home, slavery wasn't only personal, it was political. He not only assisted individual runaways, he also dedicated himself to changing public policy. In addition to their academic work, Emily and Mary often attended antislavery rallies with Loguen and other abolitionists. They lived in a household that discussed current events and politics, so they became familiar with the proposed Fugitive Slave Act, as well as legislation pending in Congress in 1850 that involved the spread of slavery into the new territories and states in the west. The act would give slave owners and their agents almost unlimited power to travel north to track down and reclaim runaway slaves. The law would also subject those who assisted fugitive slaves to fines of up to $1,000 and six months of jail time.

While Emily and Mary were legally free in both the North and the South, they were distraught that their good friend Loguen and other runaway slaves would be in jeopardy if the Fugitive Slave Act passed. For decades, Loguen had lived in the North as a free man, raising his family and serving as a minister. Passage of the new Fugitive Slave Act would mean that he could be uprooted and enslaved, captured and returned to his owner in Tennessee. Anyone who helped protect him—including Mary and Emily—could be fined and imprisoned.

Holy Bible.
Thou shalt not deliver unto the master his servant which has escaped from his master unto thee. He shall dwell with thee. Even among you in that place which he shall choose in one of thy gates where it liketh him best. Thou shalt not oppress him.
Deut. XXIII.15,16

Effects of the Fugitive-Slave-Law.

Declaration of independence.
We hold that all men are created equal, that they are endowed by their Creator with certain unalienable rights, that among these are life, liberty and the pursuit of happiness.

This lithograph, titled "Effects of the Fugitive Slave Law," includes two texts at the bottom. The first quotation comes from Deuteronomy: "Thou shalt not deliver unto the master his servant which has escaped from his master unto thee. He shall dwell with thee. Even among you in that place which he shall choose in one of thy gates where it liketh him best. Thou shalt not oppress him." The second quote is from the Declaration of Independence: "We hold that all men are created equal, that they are endowed by their Creator with certain unalienable rights, that among these are life, liberty and the pursuit of happiness." Antislavery activists sold prints like this one to raise funds to promote their cause. The artist, Theodore Kaufmann (1814–1896), was a German immigrant and dedicated abolitionist.

In the summer of 1850, Loguen planned to attend a convention in Cazenovia, New York, to protest the proposed act, and he invited Emily and Mary to join him. The girls accepted and were delighted to find out that their old friend and supporter Chaplin was planning to attend the convention as well. They had learned so much since they saw him last; what would he think of them now?

The Fugitive Slave Act
and the Compromise of 1850

By the middle of the 19th century, the slavery issue demanded Congressional action. Most northern congressmen wanted Texas, New Mexico, and the land in the Southwest claimed in the Mexican-American War to be free of slavery, and, of course, most southern legislators wanted to spread slavery into these new territories. After extensive debates and discussions, Congress reached a compromise, known, appropriately, as the Compromise of 1850. It held that:

- California, where the Gold Rush was in full force, would be a free state;

- Texas would give up its claim to New Mexico and other territorial land in exchange for debt relief;

- The other former Mexican lands, including the Utah and New Mexico Territories, would be divided between free and slave;

- The buying and selling of slaves would be prohibited in Washington, D.C., although slave-owning states would remain legal and slave traders could continue to do business across the river in Virginia;

- The Fugitive Slave Act would be enacted. This act gave slaveholders almost unlimited power to track down and capture runaway slaves in the northern free states. It required federal marshals and other law enforcement officers to assist in the return of runaway slaves based only on the word of the claimant. It also made it illegal to assist fugitive slaves, with a penalty of up to a $1,000 fine and six months in prison. Suspected slaves had no right to jury trial or to testify or present evidence on their own behalf.

The Compromise consisted of five separate bills, all of which were passed in September 1850.

☞ FIFTEEN ☜

Chaplin's Surrender

A FEW WEEKS BEFORE the Cazenovia Convention, William Chaplin was in Washington, D.C., working with other abolitionists to defeat the Fugitive Slave Act. As part of a flamboyant plot designed to draw attention to the cause, Chaplin planned to arrive in Cazenovia with two runaway slaves hidden in his private two-horse carriage. To make the ploy even more worthy of news coverage, the slaves he planned to smuggle north belonged to Congressmen Robert Toombs and Alexander H. Stephens, both of Georgia.

On the appointed night, Chaplin drove his carriage down Seventh Street and out of Washington with the two fugitives, Allen and Garland, hidden in the back of his carriage. Although the specifics are unknown, someone alerted John Goddard of Washington's auxiliary guard to the plan. Goddard and six other men (four police officers and two civilian slave catchers) were waiting to ambush Chaplin and the runaways on their way out of town. As Chaplin crossed the Maryland state line, Goddard and his men leaped from the shadows and thrust a heavy wooden rail into one of the carriage wheels to stop it.

The carriage crashed to a halt. Rather than surrender peacefully, Chaplin and the runaways drew their pistols and shot at the officers,

William Chaplin (1796–1871) worked with the American Anti-Slavery Society and the Society for the State of New York.

who returned fire. During a five- or six-minute shootout, 27 bullets were fired, but astonishingly, no one was killed. One of the enslaved men was shot in the hand but still managed to run; the other survived the gun battle only because he had been carrying a large pocket watch that deflected a bullet that otherwise would have injured him.

After some hand-to-hand fighting, Chaplin was eventually taken into custody and arrested, and the fugitives were returned to their owners. Rather than making a heroic entrance at the convention, as he had planned, Chaplin joined the captains of the *Pearl* in the Washington City Jail.

THE CAZENOVIA CONVENTION

On August 21, 1850, Emily, Mary, and about 400 other people crowded into the Free Congregational Church in Cazenovia, New York, for the opening of the Cazenovia Fugitive Slave Law Convention. Hundreds of others gathered outside the building, unable to find a seat in the pews. Frederick Douglass, already famous for his 1845 autobiography, *Narrative of the Life of Frederick Douglass, An American Slave*, presided over the meeting and told the audience about Chaplin's arrest.

The first piece of business at the convention was to devise a plan to support Chaplin. The group broke into committees to plan ways to raise the considerable amount of money needed for his bail. In addition, those in attendance passed a resolution; it read:

> We call on every man in the Free States, who shall go to the polls at the approaching elections, go with this motto

burning in his heart and burst from his lips: "CHAPLIN'S RELEASE, OR CIVIL REVOLUTION."

That revolutionary spirit continued throughout the convention. In fact, the Cazenovia Fugitive Slave Law Convention adopted one of the most radical attacks on slavery that had ever come out of an antislavery meeting. A letter written and endorsed by the convention members encouraged Southern slaves not to hesitate to violate the law in order to escape slavery, because their personal right to freedom superseded the property rights of their owners. The letter concluded: "by all the rules of war, you have the fullest liberty to plunder, burn, and kill, as you may have occasion to do so to promote your escape."

Emily and Mary were eager to do whatever they could to help raise bail for their good friend Chaplin, who was held in the Blue Jug, the jail they knew all too well from the days they spent there after their capture. It was unusual for a woman—even more so for a woman of color—to address a large audience, but Mary felt compelled to step forward at the convention and say a few heartfelt words about the important role that Chaplin had played in her life. Some in attendance described her effort as touching and eloquent.

JUMPING BAIL

On September 18, 1850, the same day that President Fillmore signed the Fugitive Slave Act into law, Chaplin appeared in court before Judge William Cranch. Chaplin sighed with relief when the judge set his bail at $6,000—a lot of money, no doubt, but Chaplin knew that his supporters would be ready and able to meet that bail.

But Chaplin wasn't freed. After he posted bail, he was handed over to the Maryland authorities, who took him directly to another jail, in Rockville. The charges against him in Maryland were far more serious than they were in the District of Columbia. In addition to two counts of larceny for attempting to steal slaves and two counts of assisting runaways to escape, he was charged

During the Cazenovia Convention, the organizers commissioned a daguerreotype, an early type of photograph, to send to William Chaplin in prison. Frederick Douglass is seated on the left side of the table. Mary Edmonson is the tall woman standing behind him with a plaid shawl. Emily Edmonson, also in plaid, is standing to the right of the abolitionist Gerrit Smith, the central figure.

with three counts of assault and battery with intent to kill for firing at the officers in the shootout. This time, the judge set Chaplin's bail at an exorbitant $19,000.

Chaplin languished in prison as those in the abolitionist community worked on raising the money for his second bail. Chaplin was not cut out for prison life. In the weeks that followed, his bruises faded and his wounds healed, but Chaplin was haunted by his memory of the beatings. Jittery and afraid, he questioned himself and his role in the abolitionist movement.

Emily and Mary joined other abolitionists who spent much of September 1850 making appearances in small towns across upstate New York raising money for Chaplin. The girls spoke and sang and begged and pleaded everywhere they could, every day they could, even on Sundays, which they didn't consider to be sinful because they believed that working to earn Chaplin's freedom was doing the Lord's work.

Three and a half months later, the entire $19,000 had been collected for Chaplin's second bail. In January 1851, Chaplin was released from the Montgomery County, Maryland, jail.

When he was released, Chaplin fled, refusing to return for trial and forfeiting $25,000 in bail money—the $6,000 that had been paid to the District of Columbia and the $19,000 paid to Montgomery County, Maryland. While they understood his anxiety about returning for trial and running the risk of going back to jail, Chaplin's supporters expected him to make an effort to raise funds to reimburse his donors. To their surprise and regret, Chaplin made very little effort to repay his debts. He refused to put himself at risk any longer. Chaplin retired and abandoned his antislavery work. It is unlikely that Emily and Mary ever saw their friend again.

≈ SIXTEEN ≈

Pardoned

MONTH AFTER MONTH, Drayton and Sayres remained in prison, waiting for their associates in the abolition-ist movement to come up with a plan for their release. Drayton's patience ran out, however, when he learned that William Chaplin had been arrested and that money had been raised for his bail while Drayton and Sayres remained in the Blue Jug. How could his abolitionist associates have found so much money for Chaplin so quickly when he and Sayres had been sitting in jail for more than two and a half years?

Angry and annoyed, Drayton wrote to abolitionist William R. Smith and explained that Chaplin's supporters should not hold it against him if he revealed Chaplin's involvement in the *Pearl* escape. He wrote that the abolitionists "must not blame him if the chains weigh so heavily upon his limbs he should lose his power of endur-ance and seek that relief which his fellow citizens have not afforded him."

Not long after sending the letter, Drayton received word that his associates had renewed their efforts to get both of the captains pardoned and released from jail. With that understanding, Drayton agreed to maintain his silence, at least for a while.

The plan to free Drayton and Sayres required that the abolitionists convince a majority of the slaveholders to whom they owed fines to drop their claims for compensation. Drayton understood that his case was complicated by a Maryland law that required him to pay half his fines to the District of Columbia and half to the owners of the fugitive slaves. He also knew that his wife and his attorney, Daniel Radcliffe, had been going door-to-door making personal appeals and trying to persuade the slaveholders to waive their claim to the fine money. But months had passed and no visible progress had been made in his case, and at the end of the day, Drayton was still behind bars, still waiting.

While there were only 36 slave owners to visit, it took more than two months to execute the plan. Drayton learned that some of the slaveholders believed that Drayton and Sayres had served enough time for the crime and they signed the waiver with enthusiasm; others signed with some hesitation. Even years after the failed escape, a few still maintained that the captains should be hanged or, alternatively, tarred and feathered for their role in the escape.

A PRESIDENTIAL PARDON

Once a majority of slaveholders dismissed their claims against Drayton and Sayres, Senator Charles Sumner of Massachusetts wrote to President Millard Fillmore and asked him to pardon the captains. On August 12, 1852, President Fillmore signed a presidential pardon that released Drayton and Sayres from jail but left them financially responsible to the slave owners who did not waive their fines. While Drayton and Sayres were still required to pay thousands of dollars in fines, no one involved in the case expected that they would ever be able to do so.

As soon as the pardons had been executed, Senator Sumner arrived at the jail and demanded the immediate release of the captains. The U.S. marshal refused. He had received word from the Secretary of the Interior to hold the men until the next morning because the Virginia authorities wanted an opportunity to arrest and prosecute them for theft and the illegal transportation of two *Pearl* fugitives who had been owned by Virginians.

Stunned, Sumner hurried to the office of the *National Era* to consult with Lewis Clephane, the newspaper's 23-year-old business manager, who was in charge of removing the two men from the District of Columbia once they were released. Clephane shared Sumner's concern that like Chaplin, Drayton and Sayres would be released from the District of Columbia jail only to be immediately jailed in another jurisdiction.

When his Whig Party nominated Winfield Scott as their candidate in the coming election, President Millard Fillmore (1800–1874) knew his political career was over. With nothing at risk, he then pardoned captains Daniel Drayton and Edward Sayres. The pardon left the men financially responsible to those slaveholders who did not waive their fines.

Together, Sumner and Clephane returned to the jail to plead their case. Word of the presidential pardon had spread and local gossip included talk of a mob gathering at the jail. Sumner warned the marshal of the possibility of unrest if he waited any longer, so the officer grudgingly agreed to let the prisoners leave. As the door of the Blue Jug opened and Drayton and Sayres walked out of jail, the black prisoners inside cheered. After more than four years and four months of incarceration, Drayton and Sayres were free.

But that didn't necessarily mean that they were safe.

RACE TO FREEDOM

Clephane, a native Washingtonian, first ushered the captains to his home a few blocks away from the jail. Drayton and Sayres feasted on their first meal as free men while Clephane tried to line up a carriage and driver to take them to Baltimore later that night. Several days of heavy rain had damaged area bridges and washed out a number of roads, so many drivers refused to consider making the journey. Clephane eventually found a driver willing to make the treacherous trip, but for a substantially higher fee than normal.

By 10 p.m., Drayton, Sayres, and Clephane were on their way to the railroad station in Baltimore, where they hoped to board a train without being recognized. The unpaved roads were waterlogged and muddy. Near Bladensburg, Maryland, the river had overflowed its banks and the driver insisted they would have to turn back because the footing wasn't safe for the horses.

If they returned to Washington, they would be intercepted by the Virginia authorities and arrested. Unwilling to accept a change in plans, Clephane reached into his pocket and pulled out the large iron key that opened the door to the *National Era* offices. From the back seat, he reached forward and pressed the cold, hard metal into the back of the driver's head as if it were a gun and demanded that they keep going.

The driver urged his horse forward.

By the light of dawn, the carriage reached Baltimore. Drayton and Sayres were put on different trains: Sayres went directly to Philadelphia, while Drayton traveled to Harrisburg then east to Philadelphia. When he arrived in Philadelphia, Dr. Cleveland greeted Drayton and gave him $100 to help him get back on his feet, the same amount he gave Sayres.

Drayton took the cash, but no amount of money could make up for his compromised health. Drayton no longer resembled the able-bodied, 46-year-old man who first entered the Washington City Jail. He was withered and weak and unable to work; he walked stiffly and coughed often. He was unsure of his future, but grateful for his freedom.

SEVENTEEN

"The Last Two Drops of Blood in My Heart"

IN THE FALL of 1851, Emily and Mary Edmonson enrolled at New York Central College, in McGrawville, a small town in upstate New York. Emily was about 16 years old and Mary was about 18. They studied grammar, geography, and arithmetic, among other subjects, with the hope of someday founding a school for runaway slaves in Canada.

The girls made ends meet without Chaplin's financial support by working at school; the college paid female students three cents an hour for domestic work in the kitchen and dormitories and male students six cents an hour for agricultural work on the campus farm. They also received some support from abolitionist friends.

Their semester at school was interrupted by news that their younger siblings, Louisa and Josiah, were to be sold. As Emily and her siblings had feared at the time of their escape, their owner, Rebecca Culver, needed money. Her business agent had contacted Bruin to find out what the last two Edmonson children were worth. Valdenar, Culver's agent, then told Paul Edmonson that he would sell the children for $1,200 — either to the family or to Bruin.

At that time, Louisa, about 12 years old, still lived at home with her parents. Josiah, about 14 years old, had been hired out to live with and work for Valdenar, probably because his overseer considered the risk of Josiah's running away too great to send another one of the Edmonsons into the District of Columbia to be hired out.

Their father, now 65 years old, had gone north to try to raise the money, but he could collect only $100. Paul considered selling his 40-acre farm, but it was worth only $500. He owned farming equipment worth $35, and three horses, three cows, and five pigs, together worth $120. Just as was the case when he tried to raise money for Mary and Emily, if he sold everything he had, he would be left without the means to support himself and he would still fall far short of what he needed to buy their freedom.

Emily and Mary knew that it would be up to them to find a way to ransom their brother and sister. They feared that if they weren't able to raise the money, their siblings would have to endure the beatings and harsh conditions in the slave pens, as well as the threat of being sold south. They reached out to their abolitionist friends for help. This time, their mother, Milly, wanted to make an appeal to those who might be able to help the family. It is not known whether Milly had permission from her owner to travel out of the area. She would not have been considered a fugitive because her owner had faith that she would return; it was not conceivable that she would leave her family behind.

Their friends made arrangements for the girls and their mother to go to New York for a meeting with Harriet Beecher Stowe, author of the best-selling novel *Uncle Tom's Cabin*. At the time, Stowe was in Brooklyn visiting her younger brother, the same Rev. Beecher who had been instrumental in raising Emily and Mary's ransom. Stowe had learned about the Edmonsons from her brother, and she modeled several characters in her novel after Emily and Mary.

Harriet Beecher Stowe's Heartbreak

Harriet Beecher Stowe understood Milly Edmonson's sorrow. The year before she wrote *Uncle Tom's Cabin*, Stowe lost her son, Charley, to cholera. On December 16, 1852, Stowe wrote to friend and fellow abolitionist Eliza Cabot Follen:

> I have been the mother of seven children, the most beautiful and most loved of whom lies buried near my Cincinnati residence. It was at his dying bed and at his grave that I learned what a poor slave mother may feel when her child is torn away from her. In those depths of sorrow, which seemed to be immeasurable, it was my only prayer to God that such anguish might not be suffered in vain.

Stowe's grief inspired and motivated her to write her best-selling novel *Uncle Tom's Cabin*.

In addition to *Uncle Tom's Cabin*, Harriet Beecher Stowe (1811–1896) wrote more than 20 books, including several under the pen name Christopher Crowfield.

MEETING HARRIET BEECHER STOWE

Emily and Mary met their mother at Beecher's home in Brooklyn. The girls had not seen their mother in the four years since they moved north to attend college. They hugged and stared at one another; Emily noted that her mother was older, grayer, and more stooped than when she last saw her, but her spirit remained the same.

After all the necessary introductions, Milly settled in to tell Stowe about the pressure of raising children in the shadow of

UNCLE TOM'S CABIN;

OR,

LIFE AMONG THE LOWLY.

BY

HARRIET BEECHER STOWE.

VOL. I.

ONE HUNDRED AND FIFTH THOUSAND.

BOSTON:
JOHN P. JEWETT & COMPANY
CLEVELAND, OHIO:
JEWETT, PROCTOR & WORTHINGTON.
1852.

The Importance of *Uncle Tom's Cabin*

After Congress passed the Fugitive Slave Act, editor Gamaliel Bailey asked Harriet Beecher Stowe to write a serialized novel to be published in the abolitionist newspaper *National Era* in 1851. Stowe agreed and wrote *Uncle Tom's Cabin* in protest of the law and in sympathy with grieving slave mothers.

The novel appeared as a series of 40 weekly installments, or about one chapter each week. The first part of the series, titled "Uncle Tom's Cabin, or the Man That Was a Thing," appeared on June 2, 1851, filling most of the first page of the paper. (When it was released in book form, the title was changed to *Uncle Tom's Cabin; or, Life Among the Lowly*.) Stowe was paid $300 for 43 chapters, but she made her fortune in the later sale of the book that collected all the installments in a single volume.

Uncle Tom's Cabin became one of the most important books of the 19th century. It galvanized public sentiment against slavery, helping to ignite the Civil War. It became the best-selling novel of the 19th century and the second best-selling book behind only the Holy Bible in the number of copies sold that century. It remains influential today, with 150 editions in print worldwide.

Aspects of *Uncle Tom's Cabin* have been widely debated since its publication. Literary critics have condemned the work as sentimental and melodramatic. While many readers saw the character of Uncle Tom as strong, principled, and courageous, ultimately dying to protect other runaway slaves, others criticized him for using submissive behavior to get along with white society rather than standing up to his owner. In the decades after the book's release, the Uncle Tom character appeared in a number of other works that portrayed him as weak and subservient. The term "Uncle Tom" eventually became a negative label for a black person willing to use servility to win the approval of white people. *Uncle Tom's Cabin* nonetheless is credited with igniting a reform movement and mobilizing support for the abolitionist movement throughout the country.

In response to southern critics who asked Stowe to prove that the events in her novel were based in truth, in 1853 Stowe published a second book, *A Key to Uncle Tom's Cabin.* The book included "the original facts and documents upon which the story is founded, together with corroborative statements verifying the truth of the work." The book included a detailed account of the Edmonsons' story, based on the meeting she had in Brooklyn with Milly, Emily, and Mary.

slavery. She explained how she had taught her children to value liberty and to work for their freedom. She recounted the story of her daughter Henrietta, who had a chance to buy her freedom when she was sick and facing death. Henrietta's doctor told her not to bother buying her freedom because she would not live long. She told him: "If I had only two hours to live, I would pay down that money to die free." True to her word, Henrietta spent her savings and died a young—but free—woman. Milly couldn't have been more proud.

Stowe's 1853 book *A Key to Uncle Tom's Cabin* provides an account of Milly's comments. When Milly told Stowe about the horror she felt when six of her children were sold to a slave dealer after they attempted to escape on the *Pearl*, Emily and Mary chimed in with a bitter description of all slaveholders.

"Hush, children!" said Milly. "You must forgive your enemies."

"But they're so wicked," one of the girls responded.

"Ah, children, you must hate the *sin* but love the *sinner*."

"Mother," said one of the girls, probably Emily. "If I was taken again and made a slave of, I'd kill myself."

Milly stared at Mary and Emily in disbelief: How could her children have such unchristian things to say? Had slavery—and freedom—changed her daughters? "I trust not, child—that would be wicked."

"But Mother, I *should*. I know I never could bear it."

"Bear it, my child? It's they that bears the sorrow here is they that has the glories there," Milly said, referring to the promise of Heaven.

The discussion turned back to the family's common concern about ransoming Louisa and Josiah.

Emily could see that her mother's story touched Stowe profoundly. In their meeting, Milly explained to Stowe that her two

Mary and Emily, Emmeline and Cassy

The story of Mary and Emily Edmonson's attempted escape on the *Pearl* helped inspire Harriet Beecher Stowe when she was writing *Uncle Tom's Cabin*. In fact, Stowe based her characters Emmeline and Cassy in part on the stories of Mary and Emily Edmonson.

In *Uncle Tom's Cabin*, chapter 45, "Concluding Remarks," Stowe wrote:

The public and shameless sale of beautiful mulatto and quadroon girls has acquired notoriety from the incidents following the capture of the *Pearl*. . . . There were two girls named Edmundson [*sic*] in the same company. When about to be sent to the market, the older sister went to the shambles, to plead with the wretch who owned them, for the love of God, to spare his victims.

He bantered with her, telling what fine dresses and fine furniture they would have [if they became sex slaves for wealthy men in New Orleans].

"Yes," she said, "that may do very well in this life, but what will become of [us] in the next?"

They too were sent to New Orleans, but were afterwards redeemed, at an enormous ransom, and brought back. Is it not plain, from this, that the histories of Emmeline and Cassy may have many counterparts?

youngest children, Louisa and Josiah—"the last two drops of blood in [my] heart"—were to be sold away from her. She begged Stowe for her support in raising the money needed for their ransom.

Stowe pledged to help free Josiah and Louisa, promising Milly that she would help raise the money needed to free them and if it fell short, she would make up the difference. Milly thanked God—and Stowe—now that she was one step closer to having her family free.

True to her word, Stowe quickly raised the $1,200 needed to free Louisa and Josiah, but Valdenar, the agent for his sister-in-law, their owner, refused to honor their agreement. First, he increased his asking price by $300. When Stowe agreed to pay the higher price, he refused to sell them again, this time arguing that Josiah was still needed to work the fields. Stowe, unwilling to disappoint Milly, grudgingly agreed to accept the delay and continued the negotiations until the two youngest Edmonson children were safely at home with their mother.

Meeting Milly Edmonson

Harriet Beecher Stowe was impressed with Milly Edmonson from the first time they met. In *A Key to Uncle Tom's Cabin*, Stowe wrote:

> Milly Edmonson is an aged woman, now upwards of seventy. She has received the slave's inheritance of entire ignorance. She cannot read a letter of a book, nor write her own name; but the writer must say that she was never so impressed with any presentation of the Christian religion as that which was made to her in the language and appearance of this woman during the few interviews that she had with her. . . .

This is the only known photograph of Amelia ("Milly") Edmonson.

> Milly is above the middle height, of a large, full figure. She dresses with the greatest attention to neatness. A plain Methodist cap shades her face and the plain white Methodist handkerchief is folded across the bosom. A well-preserved stuff gown and clean white apron with a white pocket-handkerchief pinned to her side, completes the inventory of the costume in which the writer usually saw her. She is a mulatto and must once have been a very handsome one. Her eyes and smile are still uncommonly beautiful but there are deep-wrought lines of patient sorrow and weary endurance on her face, which tell that this lovely and noble-hearted woman has been all her life a slave.

During their interview, Milly's story and her demeanor touched Stowe deeply. In Milly, Stowe had found a woman as humble and Christ-like as Uncle Tom, the protagonist in *Uncle Tom's Cabin*. She was impressed with Milly's character and her common sense. Stowe wrote to her husband, Calvin Stowe, that until she met Milly she had not met a "living example in which Christianity had reached its fullest development under the crushing wrongs of slavery." She continued: "I never knew before what I could feel till, with her sorrowful, patient eyes upon me, she told me her history and begged my aid."

⸙ EIGHTEEN ⸙

Emily, Alone

ARRIET BEECHER STOWE's friendship with the Edmonsons continued after Louisa and Josiah were freed. In the fall of 1852, Stowe made arrangements for Emily and Mary to attend Oberlin College in Ohio, one of the few schools in the country that accepted students without discrimination based on race or sex. In addition to the core subjects of mathematics, English, geography, and music, Stowe insisted that the girls learn basic housekeeping and sewing, which she argued would prove useful when they became teachers.

From the time they arrived on campus, Emily became concerned about Mary's health. Mary complained of "spinal difficulty," so at Stowe's recommendation, Emily applied hot and cold wet bandages to Mary's aching back as part of a water cure that was popular at the time. Mary remained thin and weak, plagued by a chronic cough, fever, and night sweats. The girls lived in the home of Henry Cowles, a minister and member of the Oberlin board of trustees, who provided Mary with healthy meals and plenty of rest. Nothing helped.

After several months, the sisters decided they wanted to go home to be with their family in Washington. Both of them longed to see their parents, and Emily worried that Mary's health was not improving and she might not survive to see her family again if they waited too long. Stowe discouraged them, arguing that travel to Washington in Mary's weakened state could make her worse. She may also have been worried that if their visit home was made public, the girls might be threatened by people who objected to their involvement in Stowe's latest book, *A Key to Uncle Tom's Cabin*, which documented the abuses of slavery. A full chapter of the controversial book discussed the Edmonsons. In any case, they did not make the trip.

By March of 1853, Mary's health had worsened further. Her symptoms were classic, but the news was still devastating when the doctor made a diagnosis: tuberculosis. By the end of April, the doctors warned that she would not live much longer. Emily hated to see her sister suffer, but she did not feel ready to let go. Emily had depended on Mary her entire life in slavery and in freedom as older sister, best friend, and spiritual guide. Emily's love for her sister defined who she was, and it shaped who she thought she would be in the future. Mary had been by her side through every experience in her life. What would she do without her?

Paul Edmonson came to Oberlin to be with his dying daughter; Milly couldn't make the trip. When he arrived on campus, Paul joined the 24-hour vigil at Mary's bedside. Helpless and heartbroken, Emily and her father dabbed sweat from Mary's forehead and wiped bloody spit from the corners of her mouth. They told her they loved her and listened to her struggle for each raspy breath in reply. They knew it wouldn't be long—no one could hang on to life like that for more than a few hours. Emily believed that someday she would see her sister again in Heaven, but still, it was impossibly hard to let go.

With her father and sister at her side, 20-year-old Mary Jane Edmonson died of tuberculosis on May 18, 1853. She was buried in Oberlin's Westwood Cemetery.

FROM STUDENT TO TEACHER

After the funeral, 18-year-old Emily wanted to return to Washington with her father rather than remain in Oberlin without Mary. Five years after attempting to escape on the *Pearl*, Emily was going home to the District of Columbia, but this time as a free and literate woman ready to build a life of her own.

Still, Emily felt incomplete without Mary. In the weeks after her return, she struggled to redefine herself as a young woman alone, rather than half of the duo known as the Edmonson sisters, Emily and Mary. On June 3, 1853, she wrote about her sister in a letter to Mr. and Mrs. Cowles, whose family she had lived with while at Oberlin:

> Though I am in Washington with all my dear friends, my heart still lingers around Oberlin, for I have left there beneath the green turf, one that I loved as I did myself, but we are far separated now, for she is in Glory and I am now in a land of chains and slavery. . . .

It took time to move beyond the sadness, but Emily wanted to follow through on the plans she and Mary had made to become teachers. Once again, Stowe provided Emily with the connections she needed to follow her dreams. Stowe recommended Emily to Myrtilla (Myrtle) Miner, the zealous headmistress at the Normal School for Colored Girls in Washington, D.C., a school dedicated to teaching black girls to become teachers themselves.

From their first meeting, Emily was struck by Miner's commitment. For a time Emily wondered whether she should instead return to Syracuse to stay with Jermain Loguen and his family, where she could work with the abolitionists. Stowe convinced her to become Miner's assistant, replacing a young Quaker woman who had spent a year at the school. Emily was to begin teaching primary school, with the understanding that she would move on to more advanced classes over time. A teacher! Emily would return to school, but this time as a teacher rather than a student. What would Mary think if she could see her now?

As they got to know each other, Emily listened to Miner tell stories about the founding of the school and its difficult beginnings. When Miner announced that she wanted to open a school for black girls in the nation's capital, many abolitionists and would-be supporters questioned her plan, telling her that they considered it futile and foolish. Even Frederick Douglass, an avowed proponent of education, discouraged her, considering the school an impractical and ludicrous idea because the community would never tolerate a school for black girls. Only Rev. Beecher of New York, the same man who had helped to raise Emily's ransom, thought that founding a school was an excellent idea; he promised to send money to buy furniture.

Myrtilla Miner (1815–1864) founded the Normal School for Colored Girls in order to train black students to become teachers.

Miner told Emily that she begged money from friends for the school. "Give me anything you have," she said. "Paper, books, weights, measures. I will make each one an object lesson for my girls." Ultimately, Miner returned to the District of Columbia with $100 and a teaching assistant. On December 3, 1851, the school opened with six students in a small apartment rented for $7 per month. Six months later, there were 41 students, and the classroom was equipped with carpet, desks, textbooks, and a small, select library donated by publishers and friends.

More than half of the students regularly paid the $1.50 monthly tuition.

Emily could see that Miner and her school had come a long way in a short time. The school recently had raised $4,300 to buy land and expand the facilities, and one of Emily's first tasks was to help Miner settle into the new campus, an abandoned three-acre farm in the District, which included a two-story main house and three small cabins, surrounded by shade trees, fruit trees, raspberry bushes, rhubarb plants, strawberry patches, and asparagus plants.

When Emily and Miner moved to the new location, there were no fences around the property or locks on the doors. In a letter to a friend, Miner wrote: "Emily and I live here alone, unprotected, except by God." Some in the community objected to the education of black girls. At times, troublemakers gathered near the school to insult the girls as they walked home after school. According to her 1851 memoir, Miner responded by yelling out the window: "Mob my school! You dare not! If you tear it down over my head, I shall get another house. There is no law to prevent my teaching these people and I shall teach them, even unto death!"

Vandals regularly stoned the house, trying to frighten Miner and Emily into leaving. Once, their house was set on fire; someone walking past woke them and helped extinguish the flames. At one point, the threats against the school had become severe enough that Miner had to seek help. She rushed into town and met with a night watchman. About 15 minutes later, four very burly men armed with clubs appeared on the school grounds and the troublemakers disappeared.

In order to defend herself and her school, Miner bought a revolver, and she and Emily learned how to shoot. When the troublemakers tried to harass them at the window of the schoolhouse with the weapon in plain view, she said she would shoot

The Normal School became Miner Teachers College in 1929 and the program is now part of the University of the District of Columbia. The college building, built in 1914, houses the School of Education at Howard University.

the first man who came to the door. "I have been seen practicing shooting with a pistol," Miner wrote in a letter to a friend, noting that, since that time "we have been left in most profound peace."

To further improve security, Miner invited Emily's parents to move into one of the cottages on the grounds, where Paul could cultivate a garden and Milly could work as a seamstress. When the Edmonsons moved onto the campus, bringing the family dog, their presence made Emily and the others at school feel safer, especially at night.

The school became an established and accepted part of the community. In the years that followed, Emily realized her dream of being a teacher—and because of her efforts, the next generation of Edmonson children did not have to struggle as much as she had to receive an education. Emily Brent, Emily Edmonson's niece, attended the Miner school and was a member of one of the first classes to graduate. After finishing her studies, Emily Brent moved to Wilmington, Delaware, where she began her career as a teacher, the second generation of Edmonsons to become educators.

Who Was Myrtilla Miner?

Myrtilla Miner, founder of the Normal School for Colored Girls, in Washington, D.C., had an interest in education her entire life. When Miner was a young girl, her father explained that he considered education beyond the basics to be superfluous, so he encouraged his daughter to drop out of school after a few years. She respected her father, but Miner couldn't bring herself to quit; she was curious and eager to learn.

Miner picked hops to earn money to buy books. She began to teach at age 15, and then wrote to the principal of the Young Ladies Domestic Seminary in Clinton, New York, asking for admission with the understanding that she would pay her tuition and room and board from her future earnings as a teacher. The principal accepted her terms.

Unfortunately, Miner's physical strength was not as great as her intellectual strength. As a first-year student, she suffered from severe spinal problems requiring back surgery. Her injuries kept her confined to bed, but she kept up with her studies, eventually attending class while lying on the floor at the back of the room.

After graduation, she accepted a teaching position in the Rochester, New York, public schools. She then moved to Providence, Rhode Island, followed by Whitesville, Mississippi, where she taught a plantation owner's daughter to read and write. In the South, she encountered slavery for the first time. The realities of holding men and women in bondage horrified her.

Miner thought that enslaved people should be educated. She asked the plantation owner—her employer—if she could teach the slaves on his plantation. He explained that it was a crime to teach a slave, suggesting she go north to teach the slaves if it was so important to her. That's just what she did.

One of the best descriptions of Miner on record comes from a letter Frederick Douglass wrote on May 4, 1883, to a trustee of the Miner school when asked to reflect about the life and mission of the school's founder. He wrote:

> It is now more than thirty years (but such have been the changes wrought that it seems a century) since Miss Miner called upon me at my printing-office at work, busily mailing my paper, the "North Star." . . . A slender, wiry, pale (not over-healthy), but singularly animated figure was before me, and startled me with the announcement that she was then on her way to the city of Washington to establish a school for the education of colored girls. I stopped mailing my paper at once, and gave attention to what was said. I was amazed, and looked to see if the lady was in earnest and meant what she said.
>
> I saw at a glance that the fire of a real enthusiasm lighted her eyes, and the true martyr spirit flamed in her soul. My feelings were those of mingled joy and sadness. Here, I thought, is another enterprise, wild, dangerous, desperate, and impracticable, destined only to bring failure and suffering. . . . To me, the proposition was reckless, almost to the point of madness. In my fancy, I saw this fragile little woman harassed by the law, insulted in the street, a victim of slaveholding malice, and, possibly, beaten down by the mob. . . .
>
> My argument made no impression upon the heroic spirit before me. Her resolution was taken, and was not to be shaken or changed. . . . I never pass by the Miner Normal School for Colored Girls in this city without a feeling of self-reproach that I could have [tried] to quench the zeal, shake the faith, and quail the courage of the noble woman by whom it was founded, and whose name it bears.

❦ NINETEEN ❧

Homecoming

ON APRIL 5, 1860, three generations of the Edmonson family gathered in the District of Columbia to celebrate the wedding of 25-year-old Emily. Her husband-to-be, 45-year-old Larkin Johnson, was a freed slave, widower, and father of four children: 17-year-old Benjamin, 16-year-old Mary, 13-year-old Martha, and 9-year-old Charles.

The celebration marked not only Emily's new status as wife, but also her new role of mother in a ready-made family. After the wedding, she planned to move to her new family's ten-acre farm in Montgomery County, Maryland, just a few miles away from where she grew up.

Larkin Johnson had lived in Montgomery County all of his life, so it is very likely that he had known the Edmonson family for years before marrying Emily. He had been freed in 1846 when his owner died. Little is known about Johnson's early life and his first marriage, except that his first wife, Lucy, died sometime in the 1850s.

In preparation for the wedding, Emily may have reflected on her past, as well as her future. She may have thought about her mother's frequent warning:

Now, girls, don't you never come to the sorrows that I have. Don't you never marry till you get your liberty. Don't you marry to be mothers to children that ain't your own.

On this day, both mother and daughter could think about how far they had come: Of Milly and Paul's children, Emily and her 13 brothers and sisters, all were known to have lived free, except one. Only John, the missing brother, may have remained enslaved at the time of the wedding. After the escape attempt on the *Pearl*, John was taken to New Orleans and sold from the showroom. There is no definitive evidence that he obtained his freedom, and there is no report that he ever saw his family in Washington again.

Emily and her family had overcome extraordinary odds. They had devoted their lives to the pursuit of freedom—both for themselves and for other family members—and their efforts paid off. Emily would never know her slave mother's sorrow: She would not have her babies sold away from her or be forced to raise ransom to buy them back. Emily was free, her husband was free, and every one of her children would be born free. Although they would face the challenges of racism and discrimination that dominated post–Civil War America, Emily and her family would spend every day of their lives in liberty, just as Milly Edmonson had dreamed.

Elizabeth Edmonson: Free to Marry

Some time in the 1840s, Elizabeth, the oldest of the Edmonson daughters, fell in love and wanted to marry John Brent. He was a "free dealer," meaning that his owner gave him permission to perform extra work for wages. His owner took the pay John earned as an employee for the War Department, but John kept the wages he earned working on weekends and evenings as a butler for wealthy Washingtonians. John saved his money and at the age of 25, he paid his owner $600 and bought his freedom.

Once he was free, John continued to work and save his wages, and a few years later he had saved $800 and purchased his father's freedom. He fell in love with Elizabeth—Lizzie—but, following her mother's advice, she refused to marry him until she was free. Brent sawed wood at night to make extra income and after two years, he had enough money to buy Lizzie's freedom and make her his wife.

Samuel's Story

The story of Samuel Edmonson's second escape from slavery was recorded by his nephew John Paynter and published in The Journal of Negro History *in 1916. The following is a summary of Paynter's account.*

Not long after Samuel Edmonson arrived in New Orleans, he was purchased to serve as a butler in the home of Horace Cammack, a prosperous cotton merchant. When he arrived at Cammack's home, Samuel immediately became infatuated with an 18-year-old slave named Delia Taylor, who served as a maid to Mrs. Cammack. They courted and eventually married; before long Delia gave birth to a son they named David.

Samuel and his family thrived until Cammack's son, Tom, returned from college. Tom disliked Samuel from the first time they met, and he did everything possible to make Samuel's life miserable. Eventually, the two clashed; Samuel wrote a letter explaining the situation and then he fled. It was not his intention to run away, but he did not feel safe with Tom. When he learned about the situation, Cammack ordered Samuel to return to the house and he sent his son out to live in the country. Samuel returned to the estate and to his family and willingly resumed his duties.

The following year, Cammack was killed in a violent storm while yachting with friends off the coast of Norway. Tom inherited Samuel and almost immediately decided to get rid of him. Rather than be sold to another family or risk becoming a field slave, Samuel decided to run away.

Samuel bought a set of forged free papers. Initially, he planned to escape up the Mississippi River, but he worried that that approach would be too dangerous. He went down to the riverfront to study the activity at the wharf and consider other options for escape. Lost in thought, he startled when a stevedore yelled at him to move out of the way. The sudden disruption broke his focus and gave him an idea: He could escape by impersonating a merchant from the West Indies in search of a missing bale of goods. Once he was in the islands, he would be protected by English law and free from slavery.

Samuel found a ship captain planning to leave that night for Jamaica. It wasn't a passenger ship, but the captain offered Samuel an extra bunk in the cabin, explaining that if he didn't mind roughing it, the seaman would be glad to have his company.

With only a few hours before his departure, Samuel hurried home to say good-bye to his wife and baby. Delia urged him to escape at once; Tom had already sent law enforcement officers out to look for him. Tearfully, Samuel left his wife and young son behind, aware that risking escape was the only way the family could possibly be reunited in the future. He slipped through the shadows and boarded the waiting ship.

Later that evening the customs officer boarded the ship to inspect the transit papers and found Samuel resting in the upper bunk of the ship's cabin. Had the officer been alerted to his escape? Was he looking for a runaway slave?

The captain spread the ship's papers out on a table in the cabin for inspection.

"Heigho, I see you have a passenger this trip," said the customs officer. "Samuel Edmonson, Jamaica, West Indies, thirty years old. General Merchant."

"Yes," said the captain. "Mr. Edmonson asked for passage at the last moment and as he was alone and we had a bunk not in service, I thought I'd take him along. He has a valuable bale of goods astray, probably at Jamaica, and is anxious to return and look it up."

"Well, I hope he may find it. Where is he? Let's have a look at him."

"Mr. Edmonson, will you come this way for a moment?" called the captain.

Samuel had been listening intently to the conversation. Now that he had to present himself, he murmured, "God help me," and jumped nimbly to the deck.

"This is my passenger," said the captain. To Samuel he said, "The customs officer simply wished to see you, Mr. Edmonson."

Samuel bowed and forced himself to stand at ease, resting one hand upon the table. He didn't look away or hold back when the customs officer looked him over, staring into his face, then reaching for his hands to assess their condition. Samuel let the inspector look at his hands, turning them over to examine his palms for signs of a lifetime of manual labor. Samuel's clean-cut appearance, callus-free hands, and trimmed fingernails weren't typical even of household slaves.

The customs officer shook Samuel's hand and said: "I hope you may recover your goods."

Samuel Edmonson thanked the officer and climbed back into his bunk. He had passed as a free man.

➤ ◄

Samuel sailed on to Jamaica and then traveled without arousing suspicion on a schooner carrying a cargo hold full of wool to Liverpool, England. He took a job with an English merchant and saved his money. Although the details of their emancipation and reunion are unknown, three years after Samuel fled, his wife and young son were freed by Mrs. Cammack and joined him in England. The family then moved to Australia and supported themselves by raising sheep just outside Melbourne. Delia gave birth to three more children, but only two survived.

The details of their return were not documented, but sometime before 1868, the family returned to Washington, D.C. Samuel Edmonson died in 1907 at age 80.

Emancipation in the Nation's Capital

Enslaved people in Washington, D.C., were freed almost nine months before those in other parts of the country. On April 16, 1862—a date annually recognized in the District as Emancipation Day—President Abraham Lincoln signed a law that immediately freed all slaves living in the nation's capital. In addition, the bill allowed for slave owners to be compensated for their loss of property. Over a period of months, the Secretary of the Treasury paid nearly one million dollars to 966 slave owners to cover the liberation of 3,100 enslaved people.

Freedom was extended to millions of additional slaves in the South when President Lincoln signed the executive order known as the Emancipation Proclamation, on January 1, 1863. This act freed the three million slaves living in the ten Southern states that seceded during the Civil War. It also allowed freedmen, as the emancipated slaves were called, to enlist in the Union army.

But the Emancipation Proclamation did not ensure freedom for all. It did not apply to another one million enslaved people living in the five border states on the Union side, nor did it apply to Tennessee or certain areas of Louisiana and Virginia where Union forces were in control. It was not until the Thirteenth Amendment to the Constitution was adopted on December 16, 1865, that slavery was made illegal throughout the entire United States.

On April 16, 1862, President Abraham Lincoln signed the Compensated
Emancipation Act, which freed an estimated 3,000 slaves living in the
District of Columbia.

Death of a Martyr

Captain Daniel Drayton did not live long enough to see slavery outlawed. After his release from the Washington City Jail, he tried to raise money to live on by writing his memoirs. *Personal Memoir of Daniel Drayton*, written with help from Richard Hildreth, was published in 1854, two years after Drayton's pardon. It cost 38 cents for a hardcover copy and 25 cents for a paperback. The book sold only modestly.

Although the details of his life after prison are not well documented, it is known that Drayton never recovered his physical or emotional health. In the five years after his release from jail, Drayton moved restlessly from Philadelphia to Cape May, New Jersey; to Boston; to Staten Island; and finally to New Bedford, Massachusetts, a city with a large black community and a long history with the Underground Railroad.

On June 24, 1857, Drayton spent an evening with an old friend, a former slave who had attempted escape on the *Pearl* almost ten years before. Drayton, at that time a widower who had fallen out of touch with the rest of his family, told the man that he had come back to New Bedford to die in a place where he would get a proper funeral. Drayton's old friend didn't take him seriously.

A week later, Drayton checked into the Mansion House Hotel. He skipped dinner and told the front desk clerk that he did not wish to be disturbed. That evening he barricaded the door of his room and swallowed one and a half ounces of laudanum, a liquid form of morphine. Drayton then rolled up his pants legs, placed his feet in a pan of water, and sliced open the arteries in his ankles. When Drayton did not come out of his room the next day, the landlord broke down the door and found him dead.

Drayton had been correct: New Bedford did give him a celebrated farewell. Led by the mayor and the board of aldermen, the town honored the captain of the *Pearl* at a well-attended funeral at City Hall. More than half the mourners in attendance were from the New Bedford black community.

Drayton was buried at a cemetery in New Bedford, where a monument was erected to mark the grave of "Captain Drayton, Commander of the Schooner Pearl." His obituary in the local paper was titled "Death of a Martyr."

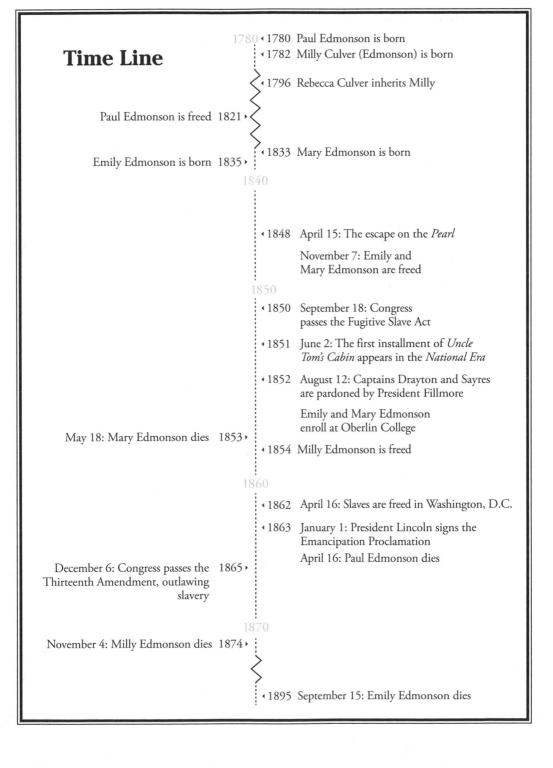

Time Line

1780 ‹ 1780 Paul Edmonson is born

‹ 1782 Milly Culver (Edmonson) is born

‹ 1796 Rebecca Culver inherits Milly

Paul Edmonson is freed 1821 ›

‹ 1833 Mary Edmonson is born

Emily Edmonson is born 1835 ›

1840

‹ 1848 April 15: The escape on the *Pearl*

November 7: Emily and
Mary Edmonson are freed

1850

‹ 1850 September 18: Congress
passes the Fugitive Slave Act

‹ 1851 June 2: The first installment of *Uncle
Tom's Cabin* appears in the *National Era*

‹ 1852 August 12: Captains Drayton and Sayres
are pardoned by President Fillmore

Emily and Mary Edmonson
enroll at Oberlin College

May 18: Mary Edmonson dies 1853 ›

‹ 1854 Milly Edmonson is freed

1860

‹ 1862 April 16: Slaves are freed in Washington, D.C.

‹ 1863 January 1: President Lincoln signs the
Emancipation Proclamation

April 16: Paul Edmonson dies

December 6: Congress passes the 1865 ›
Thirteenth Amendment, outlawing
slavery

1870

November 4: Milly Edmonson dies 1874 ›

‹ 1895 September 15: Emily Edmonson dies

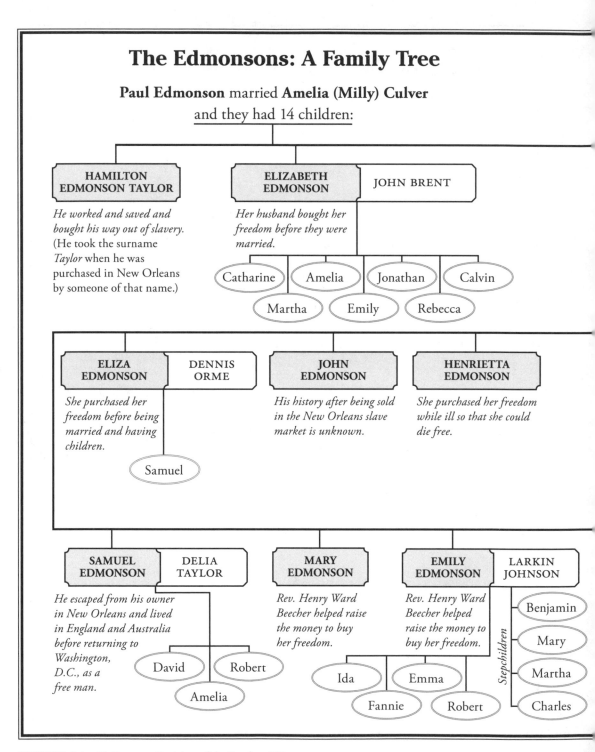

The Edmonsons: A Family Tree

Paul Edmonson married **Amelia (Milly) Culver**
and they had 14 children:

HAMILTON EDMONSON TAYLOR

He worked and saved and bought his way out of slavery. (He took the surname Taylor when he was purchased in New Orleans by someone of that name.)

ELIZABETH EDMONSON   **JOHN BRENT**

Her husband bought her freedom before they were married.

Catharine   Amelia   Jonathan   Calvin
Martha   Emily   Rebecca

ELIZA EDMONSON   **DENNIS ORME**

She purchased her freedom before being married and having children.

Samuel

JOHN EDMONSON

His history after being sold in the New Orleans slave market is unknown.

HENRIETTA EDMONSON

She purchased her freedom while ill so that she could die free.

SAMUEL EDMONSON   **DELIA TAYLOR**

He escaped from his owner in New Orleans and lived in England and Australia before returning to Washington, D.C., as a free man.

David   Robert
Amelia

MARY EDMONSON

Rev. Henry Ward Beecher helped raise the money to buy her freedom.

EMILY EDMONSON   **LARKIN JOHNSON**

Rev. Henry Ward Beecher helped raise the money to buy her freedom.

Ida   Emma
Fannie   Robert

Stepchildren
Benjamin
Mary
Martha
Charles

SOURCE: John H. Paynter, *Fugitives of the Pearl*, p. 204

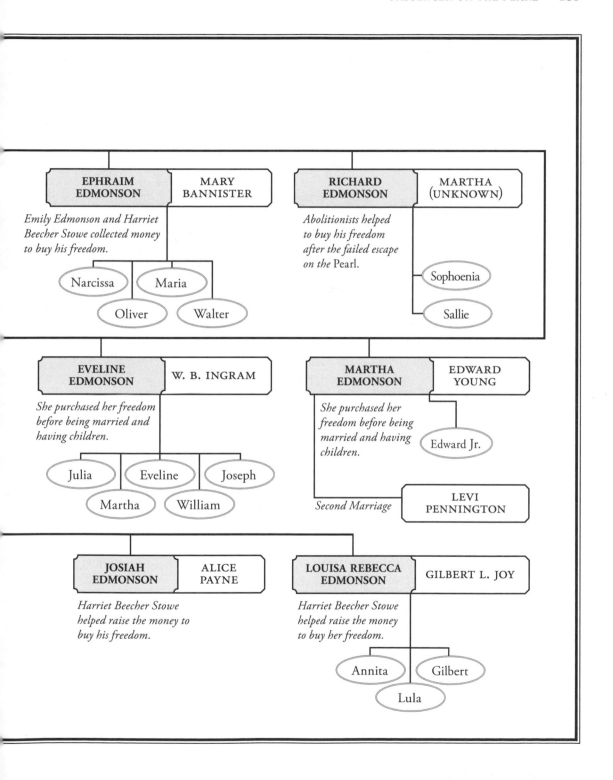

EPHRAIM EDMONSON — MARY BANNISTER

Emily Edmonson and Harriet Beecher Stowe collected money to buy his freedom.

Narcissa Maria Oliver Walter

RICHARD EDMONSON — MARTHA (UNKNOWN)

Abolitionists helped to buy his freedom after the failed escape on the Pearl.

Sophoenia Sallie

EVELINE EDMONSON — W. B. INGRAM

She purchased her freedom before being married and having children.

Julia Eveline Joseph Martha William

MARTHA EDMONSON — EDWARD YOUNG

She purchased her freedom before being married and having children.

Edward Jr.

Second Marriage — LEVI PENNINGTON

JOSIAH EDMONSON — ALICE PAYNE

Harriet Beecher Stowe helped raise the money to buy his freedom.

LOUISA REBECCA EDMONSON — GILBERT L. JOY

Harriet Beecher Stowe helped raise the money to buy her freedom.

Annita Gilbert Lula

Sources and Notes

The following notes provide sources for quoted material. In some cases, the punctuation and spelling have been updated within quotations to reflect current usage, although the word choice remains unchanged.

Epigraph

"No man can tell the intense agony . . ." Frederick Douglass, *My Bondage and My Freedom*, ch. 19, "The Run-Away Plot." New York and Auburn: Miller, Orton & Mulligan, 1855, p. 284.

Chapter 1: A Mother's Sorrow

"I loved Paul very much . . ." Harriet Beecher Stowe, *A Key to Uncle Tom's Cabin: Presenting the Original Facts and Documents Upon Which the Story Is Founded Together with Corroborative Statements Verifying the Truth of the Work.* Boston: John P. Jewett & Co., 1853; replica: Elibron Classics; elibron.com, Adamant Media Corporation, p. 156.

"Well, Paul and me, we was married," Stowe, p. 156.

"I had mostly sewing . . ." Stowe, p. 156.

"I never seen a white man . . ." Stowe, p. 156.

"Now, girls, don't you never come . . ." Stowe, p. 157.

Chapter 2: Escape: April 15, 1848

"What will Mother think?" Stowe, p. 158.

"At that time, I had regarded . . ." Daniel Drayton, *Personal Memoir of Daniel Drayton, for Four Years and Four Months a Prisoner (for Charity's Sake) in Washington Jail.* Boston: B. Marsh, 1853 (e-book release December 8, 2003, Project Gutenberg; gutenberg.net; e-book #10401-8), p. 8.

"I no longer considered myself . . ." Drayton, p. 6.

Chapter 3: Against the Tide

"Be good children . . ." John H. Paynter, "The Fugitives of the Pearl," *The Journal of Negro History* 1, no. 3, July 1916. Reproduced by the Association for the Study of African American Life and History, Inc., Howard University, HU ArchivesNet, WorldCom (2000), huarchivesnet.howard.edu/0008huarnet /paynter1.htm> [May 22, 2010]; p. 2.

Chapter 5: Capture

"Do yourselves no harm . . ." Stowe, p. 159.

Chapter 6: Back to Washington

"Aren't you ashamed . . ." Paynter, "Fugitives," p. 6.

"Damn the law!" Drayton, p. 15.

"Lynch them!" Drayton, p. 15.

"This community is satisfied . . ." Drayton, p. 19.

"Let me say to you . . ." Drayton, p. 19.

"We advise you to be out of the way!" Drayton, p. 21.

"I cannot surrender my rights!" Drayton, p. 21.

"Down with the *Era*!" Drayton, p. 21.

"fearful acts of lawless and irresponsible violence." Keith Melder, *City of Magnificent Intentions: A History of Washington, District of Columbia.* Washington, D.C.: Intac, Inc., 2001, p. 126.

Chapter 7: Sold

"Have I not the same . . ." Stanley Harrold, *Subversives: Antislavery Community in Washington, D.C., 1828–1865.* Baton Rouge: Louisiana State University Press, 2003, p. 132.

"God bless you, sirs . . ." Harrold, p. 132.

"despised and avoided," Paynter, "Fugitives," end notes.

Chapter 8: Baltimore

"Last evening, as I was passing . . ." Drayton, p. 24.

Chapter 9: New Orleans

"Stop crying or I'll give you . . ." Stowe, p. 161.

"no room for the snuffles . . ." John H. Paynter, *The Fugitives of the Pearl.* Washington, D.C.: The Associated Publishers, 1930, p. 7.

Chapter 11: $2,250: The Price of Freedom

"Oh, my children . . ." Stowe, p. 163.

"Alexandria, Va., Sept. 5, 1848 . . ." Stowe, p. 163.

"I have often been utterly astonished . . ." Frederick Douglass, *Narrative of the Life of Frederick Douglass, An American Slave.* Boston: Anti-Slavery Office, 1845, ch. 2, p. 3.

Chapter 12: Ransomed

"When Henry is sent to me . . ." Lyman Abbott and S. B. Halliday, *Henry Ward Beecher: A Sketch of His Career with analyses of his power as a preacher lecturer, orator and journalist, and incidents and reminiscences of his life.* American Publishing Co., 1887; quinnipiac.edu/other/abl/etext/beecher/beechercomplete .html, p. 134.

"I had from childhood a thickness of speech . . ." Abbott, p. 135.

"The father! Do goods and chattel . . ." Abbott, p. 147.

"I thank you for that noise!" Abbott, p. 147.

"popping about like a box . . ." Abbott, p. 147.

"Take up another!" Abbott, p. 147.

"There, Mary, is that white man . . ." Stowe, p. 165.

"Received from W. L. Chaplin . . ." *Washington National Era*, November 30, 1848.

"You are free!" Stowe, p. 166.

"the sisters Mary Jane and Emily Catherine . . ." *National Anti-Slavery Standard*, November 30, 1848.

Chapter 13: The Trial of Captain Daniel Drayton

"It is said that some . . ." *Congressional Globe*, 30th Congress, 1st Session (December 1847–August 1849), p. 520.

"suffer death as a felon . . ." Drayton, p. 28.

Chapter 14: A Radical Education

"Slavery is a state of suppressed war . . ." *New York Independent*, December 21, 1848.

Chapter 15: Chaplin's Surrender

"We call on every man . . ." Hugh Humphreys, "Agitate! Agitate! Agitate! The Great Fugitive Slave Law Convention and Its Rare Daguerreotype" (monograph). *Madison County History Society Heritage*, no. 19. Oneida, N.Y.: Madison County Historical Society, 1994.

"by all the rules of war . . ." Humphreys.

Chapter 16: Pardoned

"must not blame him . . ." Mary Kay Ricks, *Escape on the Pearl: The Heroic Bid for Freedom on the Underground Railroad.* New York: HarperCollins, 2007, p. 228.

Chapter 17: "The Last Two Drops of Blood in My Heart"

"I have been the mother of seven children . . ." Henry Louis Gates Jr.,
The Annotated Uncle Tom's Cabin by Harriet Beecher Stowe. New York:
W. W. Norton & Co., 2007, p. xxxv.

"If I had only two hours . . ." Stowe, p. 157.

"Hush, children!" Stowe, p. 167.

"The public and shameless sale . . ." Gates, p. 464.

"the last two drops of blood . . ." Stowe, p. 166; Paynter, *Fugitives*, p. 15.

"Milly Edmonson is an aged woman . . ." Stowe, p. 56.

"living example in which Christianity . . ." Ricks, p. 236.

Chapter 18: Emily, Alone

"Though I am in Washington . . ." Emily Edmonson to Mr. and Mrs.
Cowles, June 3, 1853. Henry Cowles Papers, Box #3, Series: Correspondence,
Personal; Folders: Aug.–Dec. 1852 and Jan.–July 1853; Record Group 30/27,
Oberlin College Archives.

"Give me anything you have . . ." Ellen O'Connor, *Myrtilla Miner:
A Memoir.* Boston and New York: Houghton, Mifflin & Co., 1851, p. 26.

"Emily and I live here alone . . ." O'Connor, p. 51.

"Mob my school! You dare not!" O'Connor, p. 56.

"I have been seen practicing . . ." O'Connor, p. 51.

"It is now more than thirty years . . ." O'Connor, pp. 21–25.

Chapter 19: Homecoming

"Don't you never marry . . ." Stowe, p. 157.

"Heigho, I see you have a passenger . . ." Paynter, *Fugitives*, p. 9.

"I hope you may recover . . ." Paynter, *Fugitives*, p. 9.

"Captain Drayton, Commander of the Schooner . . ." *New Bedford
Evening Standard* (Massachusetts), July 2, 1857.

Bibliography

Abbott, Lyman, and S. B. Halliday. *Henry Ward Beecher: A Sketch of His Career with analyses of his power as a preacher lecturer, orator and journalist, and incidents and reminiscences of his life.* American Publishing Co., 1887 (www.quinnipiac.edu/other/abl/etext/beecher/beechercomplete.html).

Drayton, Daniel. *Personal Memoir of Daniel Drayton, for Four Years and Four Months a Prisoner (for Charity's Sake) in Washington Jail.* Boston: B. Marsh, 1853 (e-book release December 8, 2003, Project Gutenberg; www.gutenberg.net; e-book #10401-8).

Foner, Philip S., and Josephine F. Pacheco. *Three Who Dared: Prudence Crandall, Margaret Douglass, Myrtilla Miner, Champions of Antebellum Black Education.* Westpoint, Conn.: Greenwood Press, 1984.

Gates, Henry Louis Jr. *The Annotated Uncle Tom's Cabin by Harriet Beecher Stowe.* New York: W. W. Norton & Co., 2007.

Hanchett, Catherine M. "What Sort of People & Families . . . The Edmondson Sisters." *Afro-Americans in New York Life and History* 6, no. 2 (1982), pp. 21–37.

Harrold, Stanley. *Subversives: Antislavery Community in Washington, D.C., 1828–1865.* Baton Rouge: Louisiana State University Press, 2003.

———. "The Pearl Affair: The Washington Riot of 1848." *Records of the Columbia Historical Society, Washington, D.C.* 50 (1980), pp. 140–60.

Humphreys, Hugh. "Agitate! Agitate! Agitate! The Great Fugitive Slave Law Convention and Its Rare Daguerreotype" (monograph). *Madison County History Society Heritage,* no. 19. Oneida, N.Y.: Madison County Historical Society, 1994.

Loguen, Jermain Wesley. *The Rev. J. W. Loguen, as a slave and as a freeman: a narrative of real life.* Syracuse, N.Y.: J. G. K. Truair & Co., 1859; Sabin Americana, Print Editions, pp. 1500–1926.

Melder, Keith. *City of Magnificent Intentions: A History of Washington, District of Columbia.* Washington, D.C.: Intac, Inc., 2001.

O'Connor, Ellen. *Myrtilla Miner: A Memoir.* Boston and New York: Houghton, Mifflin & Co., 1851.

Pacheco, Josephine F. *The Pearl: A Failed Slave Escape on the Potomac*. Chapel Hill: University of North Carolina Press, 2005.

Paynter, John H. *The Fugitives of the Pearl*. Washington, D.C.: The Associated Publishers, 1930.

———. "The Fugitives of the Pearl." *The Journal of Negro History* 1, no. 3 (July 1916). Reproduced by the Association for the Study of African American Life and History, Inc., Howard University, HU ArchivesNet, WorldCom (2000), <huarchivesnet.howard.edu/0008huarnet/paynter1.htm> [May 22, 2010]

Ricks, Mary Kay. *Escape on the Pearl: The Heroic Bid for Freedom on the Underground Railroad*. New York: HarperCollins, 2007.

Stowe, Harriet Beecher. *A Key to Uncle Tom's Cabin: Presenting the Original Facts and Documents Upon Which the Story Is Founded Together with Corroborative Statements Verifying the Truth of the Work*. Boston: John P. Jewett & Co., 1853; replica: Elibron Classics; elibron.com, Adamant Media Corporation.

Stowe, Harriet Beecher. *Uncle Tom's Cabin; or, Life Among the Lowly*. Boston: John P. Jewett & Co., 1852.

For More Information

About Harriet Beecher Stowe

Fritz, Jean. *Harriet Beecher Stowe and the Beecher Preachers.* New York: Puffin, 1998.

Hedrick, Joan. *Harriet Beecher Stowe: A Life.* New York: Oxford University Press, 1995.

Koester, Nancy. *Harriet Beecher Stowe: A Spiritual Life.* Grand Rapids, MI: Wm. B. Eerdmans Publishing Co., 2014.

Morretta, Alison. *Harriet Beecher Stowe and the Abolitionist Movement.* New York: Cavendish Square, 2014.

About Abolition and Slavery

Aronson, Marc. *Sugar Changed the World: A Story of Magic, Spice, Slavery, Freedom, and Science.* New York: Clarion, 2010.

Davis, David Brion. *Inhuman Bondage: The Rise and Fall of Slavery in the New World.* New York: Oxford University Press, 2008.

Horton, James Oliver. *Slavery and the Making of America.* New York: Oxford University Press, 2006.

Lowance, Mason, editor. *Against Slavery: An Abolitionist Reader.* New York: Penguin Classics, 2000.

Marrin, Albert. *A Volcano Beneath the Snow: John Brown's War Against Slavery.* New York: Knopf Books for Young Readers, 2014.

McNeese, Tim. *The Abolitionist Movement: Ending Slavery.* Reform Movements in American History. New York: Chelsea House, 2007.

Sanders, Nancy. *Frederick Douglass for Kids: His Life and Times.* Chicago: Chicago Review Preview, 2012.

Stewart, James Brewer. *Holy Warriors: The Abolitionists and American Slavery.* New York: Hill and Wang, 1997.

Thomas, William David. *William Lloyd Garrison: A Radical Voice Against Slavery.* Voices for Freedom. New York: Crabtree Publishing, 2009.

Slave Narratives and Oral Histories

Burton, Annie L. *Women's Slave Narratives*. New York: Dover, 2006.

Gates, Henry Louis, Jr. *The Classic Slave Narratives*. New York: Signet Classics, 2012.

Mellon, James. *Bullwhip Days: The Slaves Remember: An Oral History*. New York: Grove Press, 2002. First published 1988.

Perdue, Charles Jr. *Weevils in the Wheat: Interviews with Virginia Ex-Slaves*. Charlottesville, VA: University of Virginia Press, 1991.

Yetman, Norman. *Voices from Slavery: 100 Authentic Slave Narratives*. Mineola, NY: Dover, 1999.

———. *When I Was a Slave: Memoirs from the Slave Narrative Collection*. Mineola, NY: Dover, 2002.

In addition, many 19th and early 20th century slave narratives are in the public domain and are available to download free or for a nominal fee. Most are available in print editions as well.

Burton, Annie L. *Memories of Childhood's Slavery Days*, 1909.

Douglass, Frederick. *Narrative of the Life of Frederick Douglass*, 1845.

Du Bois, W.E.B. *The Souls of Black Folk*, 1903.

Hughes, Louis. *Thirty Years a Slave from Bondage to Freedom: The Institution of Slavery as Seen on the Plantation and in the Home of the Planter*, 1897.

Jacobs, Harriet. *Incidents in the Life of a Slave Girl Written by Herself*, 1861.

Northup, Solomon. *Twelve Years a Slave*, 1853.

Truth, Sojourner. *Narrative of Sojourner Truth*, 1850.

United States Work Projects Administration. *Slave Narratives: A Folk History of Slavery in the United States from Interviews with Former Slaves*, 1936–1938.

Washington, Booker T. *Up From Slavery: An Autobiography*, 1901.

Museums and Organizations of Interest

Alexandria Black History Museum
902 Wythe Street
Alexandria, VA 22314
(703) 746-4356
www.alexandriava.gov/BlackHistory

**Frederick Douglass National
Historic Site (National Park Service)**
1411 W Street, SE
Washington, DC 20020
(202) 426-5961
www.nps.gov/frdo

The Harriet Beecher Stowe Center
77 Forest Street
Hartford, CT 06105
(860) 522-9258
www.harrietbeecherstowecenter.org

**National Abolition Hall of Fame
and Museum**
5255 Pleasant Valley Road
Petersboro, NY 13035
(315) 366-8101
www.nationalabolitionhalloffameand
    museum.org

**National Underground Railroad
Freedom Center**
50 East Freedom Way
Cincinnati, OH 45202
(513) 333-7500
www.freedomcenter.org

The Pearl Coalition
(202) 650-5606
www.pearlcoalition.org

**Smithsonian National Museum
of African American History and
Culture**
1400 Constitution Avenue, NW
Washington, D.C. 20004
(202) 633-1000
www.nmaahc.si.edu

Acknowledgments

I offer special thanks to those who helped with this book, specifically:

Dr. Edna Green Medford, Professor of History at Howard University, for reviewing the manuscript;

the writing community at the Vermont College of Fine Arts, especially The Bat Poets and my VCFA critique group, for inspiring me as a writer;

Sarah Davies of the Greenhouse Literary Agency for representing my work;

Emily Parliman, Anne Winslow, Laura Williams, Steve Godwin, Brunson Hoole, Kelly Bowen, and the rest of the team at Algonquin;

Judit Bodnar for watching my p's and q's;

and, of course, Elise Howard, my editor. To paraphrase Wilbur in *Charlotte's Web*, it is not often that someone comes along who is a true friend and a good editor. Elise is both.

Index

Page numbers in italics refer to photos or illustrations and their captions.

WHEN
CHICAGO
RULED
BASEBALL

Also by Bernard A. Weisberger

America Afire

WHEN CHICAGO RULED BASEBALL

The Cubs–White Sox World Series of 1906

Bernard A. Weisberger

WILLIAM MORROW
An Imprint of HarperCollins*Publishers*

HarperCollins books may be purchased for educational, business, or sales promotional use. For information, please write: Special Markets Department, HarperCollins Publishers, 10 East 53rd Street, New York, NY 10022.

FIRST EDITION

Designed by Renato Stanisic

Printed on acid-free paper

Library of Congress Cataloging-in-Publication Data

Weisberger, Bernard A., 1922–
    When Chicago ruled baseball: the Cubs–White Sox World Series of 1906/Bernard A. Weisberger.
        p. cm.
    ISBN-13: 978-0-06-059227-1 (alk. paper)
    ISBN-10: 0-06-059227-3

    1. World Series (Baseball) (1906) 2. Chicago Cubs (Baseball team)—History—20th century. 3. Chicago White Sox (Baseball team)—History—20th century. I. Title.

GV878.4.W45 2006
796.357'64'0977311—dc22

                                                                                    2005056136

---

06 07 08 09 10 JTC/QWF 10 9 8 7 6 5 4 3 2 1

To Michael Remer
Kinsman, Friend, and Fellow Fan

Contents

Acknowledgments

Most of the research for this book was done in the library of the Chicago Historical Society, whose helpful staff I am glad to thank, with a special note of gratitude to curator Peter Alter, for pointers to sources. The other major location of documentation was the A. Bartlett Giammati Research Center in the National Baseball Hall of Fame in Cooperstown, New York, and there I was given particular aid and comfort by Tim Wiles.

I am also greatly indebted to Blair Namnoum, my research assistant. Thanks to Robert Johnston for giving the manuscript an early reading, and to Vera Chatz for solving a research problem by her impressive memory for song lyrics. And thanks to editor Michael Shohl for his input.

As usual, none of the above are responsible for any errors I may have made.

1

Opening Day

Chicago, Tuesday, October 9, 1906. From the standpoint of baseball weather, the outlook was rotten. Frigid blasts that gave Chicago its unflattering "Windy City" nickname whipped through the streets. A pale sun fought a losing battle with clouds that now and then spat snow flurries. If quality play was expected, the day almost shouted for a postponement.

But nothing short of a blizzard, or an earthquake like the one that had destroyed San Francisco that spring, or a renewal of the Great Fire that had left Chicago a pile of smoking ashes just thirty-five years earlier to the day was going to postpone the big event. Chicago, rebuilt and renowned, was going to strut. It was opening day of the World Series, and both contending teams, champions of the thirty-year-old National League and its five-year-old American League rival, were from Chicago. And so, in the plummy prose of *Chicago Tribune* sportswriter Hugh Fullerton a few days earlier, "Since last night a combination pennant pole marking the site of Chicago has served as the earth's axis, and around it something less than 2,000,000 maddened baseball fans are dancing a carmagnole of victory."[1]

The earth on the whole was unaware of the relocation of its axis. *World* Series? Probably 99 percent of the earth's peoples at that time had never seen, heard of, or cared about the game of baseball. But in Chicagoan eyes, baseball was the national pastime of the United States of America, and by definition a contest for its professional championship had to be earth altering. So Chicago was collectively excited, even if not every one of its slightly fewer than 2 million inhabitants could tell a carmagnole (a dance popular during the French Revolution) from a catcher's mitt.

The anticipation had been building for the six days since it became certain that both of Chicago's teams were pennant winners. The town's major daily newspapers (in those preconsolidation days of 1906, there were some nine in English and an equal number in German, Yiddish, Czech, Norwegian, and one or two other languages) gave baseball front-page coverage, beginning on Thursday and with the volume increasing over the weekend.[2] The *Tribune* devoted most of its Sunday sporting section to a long review of the championship seasons of both White Sox and Cubs. It shared space with coverage of Saturday's Big Ten college football matchups—baseball's only serious rival for attention back then. But college football appealed mostly to college graduates, an influential but still miniature slice of the population. Americans without higher education, however, had taken the diamond game to heart by the millions. They wanted a steady and generous diet of baseball scores, standings, and gossip in the daily papers that plugged them into the world (at 2 cents a copy), and publishers fed it to them willingly and profitably.

Front-page editorial cartoons, usually political, were temporarily shelved in favor of baseball gags: baseballs with smiley faces, deliriously happy fans and families, the latter including pets and babies. Two in particular carried implicit social messages. One, a story in four panels appearing in the *Tribune,* introduced a pair of characters already familiar from the comic strips: the boss and the office boy. The boss corners the reluctant youngster, who is planning to sneak away, and demands that the boy "do something" for him that afternoon, which happily turns out to be to "go to the ball game with me and explain the finer points." The lesson was that first, there were "fine points" to the game that made it a craft worth studying and not an idle pastime, and second, that mutual delight in Chicago's baseball prowess bound together generations and classes—benign old employer and lowly kid jobholder. In that simple form the text was clear even to the barely literate reader.

Compared to that theme of harmony, one of the *Daily News*'s pregame cartoons radiates realism. The image of Mrs. O'Leary's angry cow starting the Great Fire of 1871, as legend had it, by kicking a lighted lantern into a pile of straw is succeeded by the "Mild and Gentle Animal of Today" wearing a contented grin as uniformed Cubs and Sox players cheerfully milk her into a bucket stamped with a large, eye-catching dollar sign. Whatever else professional baseball bestowed on society at large, it was a business whose chief end and aim was to generate cash.

That contradiction between baseball's public face as the simon-pure recreational expression of the American spirit and the reality of big-league, big-city baseball as a market enterprise (and a monopoly at that) anchored in a growing commercial entertainment industry and culture—that discord between image and reality—is clear in any hard-eyed look at that 1906 crosstown series in a Chicago banging and barging its metropolitan way into a new century. It's a sports story that helps to explain how we American urbanites have come to be who we are and how we see ourselves.

But songs of social significance aren't the only music of baseball history. The Series itself was wonderfully exciting, an electric week of surprises, thrills, exploits and errors, hopes roused and hopes dashed. For those who were there, time was suspended, the world outside the playing field faded into the background, and individual problems were forgotten in the single, roaring life of

3

the crowd riding the same emotional roller coaster with every swing and every pitch. That is what any popular spectator sport still does for its fans. In America, baseball did it first.

It was a different world then. But a lover of baseball in 2006 isn't all that estranged fron the grandstand throngs caught in those grainy black-and-white news photos of a century ago. We know more than we want to now about the private sins of the players, about multimillion-dollar payrolls and agents and unions and TV revenue shares—sometimes it's hard to tell the sports pages from the business news. We follow *our* game through a welter of background noise from other athletic goings-on that now have equal or better claims to be *the* national pastime.

But we stay tuned and, when we have the chance, spend an extravagant afternoon or evening at the new stadiums built especially to cater to the luxury-box crowd, because we find the game between the foul lines beautiful. It wasn't any less so then. So in the pages that follow, the contests themselves are always the place to which the story returns after digressions and excursions into history. The narrator hopes that his readers will be a little wiser and sadder, perhaps, but still eager for the on-field action to start—just like those crowds heading for Game One, one hundred years ago, via four converging streetcar lines and two elevateds. Two hours before the entry gates opened at noon they were already shivering and stamping in line before the ticket windows. Who were they, and what was the Chicago of their day like? And what form would the first-ever intracity World Series take?

The opener would be at the Cubs' park, as determined by a coin toss at a meeting the day before. In attendance were both teams, their owners, and the three-man National Commission that then ruled organized baseball. It consisted of the presidents of both leagues and a third member chosen by them. The games would alternate between the two contestants' parks until one of them had won four. No final decision was made that day as to who would be home team for the deciding game if the Series reached a 3–3 tie. There was a possibility of moving it to a neutral site, and bids were actually made by at least two other cities, but relieved Chicago fans saw that idea shot down early. Other points that were settled raised ticket prices to double the regular season rates—Series seats would cost 50 cents for the bleachers, $1 or $1.50 for the grandstand and "pavilion" and $2 for boxes. These hikes were imposed over the objection of White Sox owner Charles Comiskey, who argued that they were hard on his regular patrons with small incomes. His complaints do not seem groundless considering that thanks to inflation, a 1906 dollar's purchasing power in 2006 would range somewhere between $14 and $20. That was the "real" price of a $1 grandstand seat back then. And since blue-collar Chicagoans of 1906 worked an average ten-hour day to earn just $2 or $3, a 100 percent hike in admission fees was no light matter.[3]

There would also be a pool of four umpires, two from each league, one pair to work each game, one in reserve.

It was all more or less virgin territory because this was only the third World Series to be played since a late-1902 peace treaty between the American and National Leagues had ended a war for dominance. The first, in 1903, had matched Boston and Pittsburgh in a best-of-nine set, won by Boston in a thrilling comeback. There had been none in 1904, when the New York Giants, National League winners, still held out against dignifying the AL champions—Boston once more—with major-league status. But the Giants came into the fold at last in 1905, and beat Philadelphia in a brilliantly pitched set, 4–1, every victory a shutout.

The best-of-seven formula decreed for 1905 would also govern the 1906 Series, but no precedent was entirely solid yet, and that seven-game format would change briefly back to best-of-nine before solidifying. Even the teams' names were not yet firmed up. A modern reader of sports pages in the very early 1900s would easily be confused by references to the Pilgrims (today's Red Sox,) Highlanders (Yankees), Spiders (Indians), and Spuds (Cubs), the last named in recognition of owner Charles Murphy's Irish roots. A Chicagoan of today might be more startled to find that the Cubs' home field then was not in its current ninety-year-old location in Wrigley Field on the city's North Side, but on its West Side. It was in fact called simply West Side Park. Thereby hangs a tale of urban geography and baseball economics.

Physically, Chicago is divided into northern and southern sections by the Chicago River, a somewhat pretentious name for a very short stretch of water. The river is formed by the junction of two other streams (unpoetically named the North and South Branches), and ran eastward for a mile into Lake Michigan at the time of the city's settlement. Its banks were wilderness then and later became part of the heart of downtown Chicago. The river's current was reversed around 1900 by an engineering feat, when the Sanitary Canal was created to divert sewage from Lake Michigan's waters and ultimately into the drainage basin of the Mississippi River. In the Chicago of 1906 the West Side was roughly whatever lay west of the South Branch. There was not much of a North Side at the time; its residential boom would come later.

West Side Park filled most of a block bounded by Polk, Taylor, Wood, and present-day Wolcott (then named Lincoln) streets now occupied by part of the Medical Center of the University of Illinois at Chicago. It was well west of Lake Michigan and south of the Chicago River; but apparently the South Side, which was White Sox territory, did not begin until present-day 35th Street, some three miles farther south, so far as organized baseball was concerned.

West Side Park's location was not random. The lots on which big-league stadiums stood were often picked as a result of cozy relationships among team owners, real estate speculators, and local politicians.[4] But they also needed to be in neighborhoods where land was cheap and plenty of public transportation was available, which explains why West Side Park was in what city planners labeled the Central Manufacturing District. And if there had been no manufacturing district, it is unlikely that there would have been a major-league baseball team (let alone two) in Chicago. The sixteen teams of the National and American Leagues that topped the pyramid of organized baseball were concentrated in the well-populated commercial, financial, and industrial centers of the Northeast or the smoky workshop cities of the Midwest. Four cities—St. Louis, Chicago, Boston, and Philadelphia—had two teams each; New York had three, counting Brooklyn, which had been an independent city until absorbed into Greater New York in 1898. Four others were in Pittsburgh, Cleveland, Cincinnati, and Detroit. Only factory-free and smallish Washington, D.C., was an exception, for reasons of state.

Of those ten major-league towns, Chicago's manufacturing credentials were the most impeccable. Carl Sandburg had yet to call the city hog butcher to the world, but both the Cubs' and Sox' parks were only minutes away by streetcar from the Union Stockyards and associated packinghouses, where, as of 1901, some 25,000 workers were daily slaughtering and processing 13,000 porkers per day and about 60 cattle per hour.[5] When the wind was right, the sounds and especially the smells of those penned creatures waiting their turn to die pervaded the vicinity. Miles of piping spewed their offal into the South Branch of the river, creating the water-pollution problem that the Sanitary Canal was built to correct.

Chicago's southern outskirts were already noted for turning out steel and railroad cars, especially the celebrated Pullman sleepers, in workshops where an 1894 walkout had triggered a devastating nationwide sympathy strike of railworkers' unions. And in block after block of the West Side, ready-made garments poured out of sweatshops and lofts like the one in which Dreiser's "Sister Carrie" Meeber briefly and unhappily punched eyelets for shoelaces. Chicago workers also produced books, glassware, and furniture, and were found by the thousands in foundries and breweries, machine shops and printing plants, sawmills and distilleries. The city had the third highest number of manufacturing employees in the nation.[6]

At the Lake Michigan and Chicago River docks more vessels tied up annually than in New York, Philadelphia, Baltimore, Mobile, and San Francisco combined.[7] They were freighters unloading timber and the iron and copper ores of the Great Lakes region. In the nearby freight yards, boxcars clashed and banged, incoming ones loaded with the wheat, corn, and cattle of the Great Plains, empties ready to carry finished products from warehouses and storage bins to every part of America. Chicago, "Nature's Metropolis," as historian William Cronon calls it, sat in the middle of all of this bounty and the transportation network that moved it, and thousands more Chicagoans were part of the small army of employees, white collar and blue, required to keep the wheels turning. The city was part of a great industrial surge.

So was modern baseball. It fed off the mass production of wood, leather, and textiles that went into bats and gloves and uniforms. It reached its followers through newspapers that, thanks to high-powered presses, could run off hundreds of thousands of copies in a few hours. It depended on railroads that allowed big-market cities to schedule each other regularly—none of the ten big-league towns was more than an overnight jump from any other. It existed by the grace of electric streetcars and elevated or underground trains that could move thousands to and from the parks quickly, and of technology that supplied them there with necessities like plumbing and amenities like thousands of bottled drinks and bags and boxes of peanuts and Cracker Jack. Big-league baseball needed all that as much as it needed the urban throngs who provided enough customers to make it a paying proposition. Not for nothing does its now-traditional anthem (not yet written in 1906, however) demand: "Take me out to the crowd."

No one could doubt that a major crowd was forming outside West Side Park hours before the 2:30 start of the game, thirty minutes earlier than usual in order to allow more daylight if the game should go into extra innings. The waiting thousands stamping and shivering looked like a late-season football audience despite the calendar that showed Indian summer. Men wore overcoats and gloves, women furs and muffs, and here and there someone flashed a pocket flask brought to provide internal warmth. Reserved seats were sold out, and the lines to buy tickets at the grandstand and bleacher entrances stretched for a block and a half in two directions, jamming the streets so thoroughly that it was impossible for horse-drawn traffic to pass, and teamsters needed help from the crowd to turn their animals' heads around in order to retreat. There is no record of automobiles trying to make it through. They were still a rarity, operating at less than 10 miles per hour. The 77,000 horses remaining in the city still played a sizable part in moving goods and people around town. But most of the milling throng had gotten there on solidly packed public transportation. Two branches of the Metropolitan Elevated had nearby stations, and no fewer than six streetcar lines had stops, in the words of the *Tribune*, "fairly close to the park." Fares were in pennies.[8]

Considering the discomforts of the weather there were few outbreaks of quarreling or episodes that required crowd control, though some 500 of Chicago's 2,600 police were on hand, probably including a detachment of the small mounted patrol that had been activated only a month earlier.[9] Arrests were made, but not for rowdyism. The miscreants were scalpers who were hovering near the entrances and hawking seats at up to $20 apiece. Eight of them were caught and booked. How many escaped detection is unrecorded.

The fans were too happy to be troublesome. As the *Daily News's* late-afternoon "Sporting Extra" put it:

FANS ARE IN FULL BLAST. THRONG STREETS, CROWD STANDS, CHEER CHICAGO AND HER DAY AND MIGHTY BASEBALL TEAMS IMPARTIALLY. *ROOTING IS INTENSE AND NOISE*

*RULES EVERY NOOK IN BIG WEST SIDE PARK.
FLASHES OF SNOW FAIL TO MAR GOOD
HUMOR SEEN ON FACES.* Bleachers Are a Howling,
Joyous Mob.[10]

They were all in a holiday mood, and for some it was literally a holiday. The city council, in a Monday-night session filled with laughter and cheering (COUNCIL CHAMBER IN SESSION RESEMBLES COLLEGE CAMPUS ran the headline), had passed a resolution freighted with no fewer than seven "Whereases" and a carload of platitudes that gave municipal workers the day off. The Board of Trade closed as well, and some of the city's banks planned to release parts of their workforce on a rotating schedule throughout the Series. The *Daily News,* which saw CHICAGO SEIZED BY A BASEBALL FRNZY, was of the opinion that "until the world's championship in baseball is decided commerce is threatened with paralysis."

The term "hype" was not yet invented, but no current sports promotion could exceed the efforts of the local press to make the Series a historic event only slightly rivaled by the American Revolution and the Second Coming combined. The *Record-Herald's* headline ran: WORLD'S CHAMPIONSHIP SERIES WILL OPEN BEFORE ARMY OF WILD ROOTERS. HUNDREDS OF ENTHUSIASTS FROM OTHER CITIES ARE HERE FOR THE STRUGGLE. And there were inevitable references to the coincidence of Chicago's darkest moment having fallen precisely three and a half decades earlier. The *Tribune* proclaimed on the morning of the opener that " 'Chicago Day' will be celebrated this afternoon by the most historic event that has occurred on Oct. 9 since the year 1871. Today is the day set for the beginning of the greatest struggle in baseball's history, the series for the world's championship between two of the grandest ball clubs ever in knickerbockers, both belonging to Chicago. . . . The city was swept by a destructive fire. . . . Today a fire is raging through the city that . . . will burst into its full fury at 2:30 o'clock this afternoon. . . . But it will be a harmless fire of loyalty to one team or the other."

The *Inter-Ocean*'s editorial page used the occasion to repeat a cherished Chicago theme, the city's miraculous comeback: "In education, in art, in custom . . . we have made colossal progress within the last three and a half decades . . . for a community . . . which received in middle life a shock that seemed calculated to stupefy and stunt it."

As a result of all that media churning and bubbling the original crowd expectations were in the range of 25,000, which would have exceeded the capacity of both ballparks. Both team presidents, the White Sox' Charles Comiskey and Charles Murphy of the Cubs, had immediately set contractors to work adding extra seats, and Murphy confidently told the world that he would be ready to handle up to 26,000, of which only 2,000 would have to be standees.

As it happened, the seating limits of West Side Park were not tested in that initial game, probably because of the brutal weather conditions. The announced paid attendance came to 12,693. That was still more than the entire population of thousands of America's rural hamlets, and sufficient to generate enough noise to be heard by the indigent patients and hardworking doctors of Cook County Hospital, which was located in the block immediately north of the stadium. Since reporters later described the park as nearly full, Murphy's promise of more than 25,000 seats was undoubtedly exaggerated in hopes of swelling the gate receipts, but he was lucky not to have drawn such a crowd.

Many potential spectators frightened off by the chilly day chose to "view" the games in indoor comfort provided courtesy of the *Tribune*. As a circulation-boosting public service, the paper had leased the great downtown Auditorium Theater and the First Regiment Armory on South Michigan Avenue, with a combined seating capacity of 9,000, and arranged for a huge bulletin board to be displayed containing a reproduction of the diamond. Telegraphers would receive instantaneous information from the park and move counters with the players' names around the bases as indicated. Likewise, the number of balls, strikes, and outs would be posted, so that the audience would know who was at bat, how many men on base, and, as the *Tribune* put it, "everything that a real fan wants to know about a ball game." Seating would be free, and first-come first-served.[11] So at least a quarter of a century before baseball broadcasts became available, and almost half a century prior to regular telecasts from the stadiums, the concept of being able to "watch" the games in seated indoor comfort was implemented.

Organized baseball's public relations flourished on this merger of its game with civic festival. That marriage deflected attention from the sport's actual history as a business and how its existing 1906 structure had emerged only after a long period of teams raiding one another's turf and rosters; of bankruptcies, broken contracts, and lawsuits; of ugly confrontations among owners and between owners and their employee-players—a kind of capitalist guerrilla warfare on the road to economic stability through concentration of ownership. There had also been cheating scandals, drunkenness, and on-the-field violence against umpires and players. It was better to paint the owners as the guardians of a pure and purely American game, played by virtuous heroes, while ignoring such inconvenient dissonances as the fact that few of those hundreds of thousands of industrial workers who contributed to Chicago's glory would or could be on hand to see the games, all played in the afternoon. The average industrial workweek was six ten-hour days.

Nor could hundreds of thousands of Chicago workers understand the "national pastime," either as played or as reported by the press. In 1906, the entire country was at the midpoint of an enormous transatlantic migration that brought some 13 million Europeans to the United States between 1890 and 1920. Chicago was one of the great magnet cities of this ingathering that built the infrastructure of industrial America. Chicago's population in 1890 was slightly over 1 million, and approximately double that by 1910. A large share of that expansion came from overseas arrivals; by one estimate, almost three-quarters of all Chicagoans in 1900 were either born abroad or were children of foreign-born parents. The sources of immigration were new too. The early waves of Irish, German, and Scandinavian newcomers were now outnumbered by a so-called new immigration from southern and eastern Europe. The year 1910 would find, for example, 210,000 Poles, 100,000 Russian and Polish Jews, and 110,000 Bohemians (to list only the most numerous nationalities) crowding the row houses and tenements within a short distance of the Cubs' and Sox' ballparks.[12] Barriers of language and culture alone kept first-generation immigrants from following the game. It was their children who would become fans by the millions, and to that extent baseball was the "Americanizing" influence it was claimed to be, fitting neatly into a period that gave the nation the Pledge of Allegiance(1892), "America the Beautiful" (1893), Flag Day (1914), and assorted patriotic exercises in the public schools. But baseball's big tent was not all-encompassing. The several thousand African Americans in the city in 1906 were neither encouraged nor likely to attend the Series, because by mutual agreement among owners dating back to the 1880s, black players had been banned from sharing the diamonds with whites. The national pastime was nowhere more national at that moment in history than in its unapologetic racism. African Americans were in fact attracted to the game, but they played and watched it in segregated leagues.

Baseball was not unique in accentuating its positive image, a habit shared by humanity at large but raised to a special art form labeled "boosterism" in America. Chicago, too, put its best face forward. Visitors to the Series who stayed in the hotels of the city's business and civic center, fifteen minutes from West Side Park, were urged to admire the sights of the city that had rebounded so magnificently from disaster: the bold new high-rise architecture of office buildings designed by Sullivan and Adler, or Burnham and Root, or William Le Baron Jenney; the Symphony Hall and Art Institute virtually opposite each other on wide and handsome Michigan Avenue; Marshall Field's elegant department store, and some of the fine new homes along the near-north lakefront being built for the millionaire entrepreneurs who owned the factories and mills and packinghouses; or the new University of Chicago campus that had risen near the grounds of the great World's Columbian Exposition of 1893. They were *not* encouraged to look around, en route to the games, at nearby blocks of slums where crowded and unsanitary conditions bred typhoid and tuberculosis (3,679 deaths from the latter in 1905), and where the nearest thing to a tourist attraction was Jane Addams's celebrated settlement, Hull House, ten blocks from the Cubs' park, which struggled to help the immigrant poor to cope through its adult-education classes, free clinics, home nursing, and other services.

The celebrants of Chicago's glory also skated past other evidence of unlovely life among the lowly, like the still-existing miles of unpaved streets; the unprotected railroad grade crossings at street level that killed hundreds each year (one of them on the very day before the opening game); the Municipal Lodging Houses opened in 1902 for the overflow of unemployed and homeless men previously allowed to sleep in police stations; the thousand-odd Loop buildings that had only a single stairway, often locked, that could be used as a fire exit; the coal smoke; the gambling dens and whorehouses of the vice district on the West Side that made a disdainful editor of the *Tribune* in 1907 describe the area as a place where "murderers, robbers and thieves of the worst kind are born and reared to maturity."[13] Chicago was no alabaster city undimmed by human tears.

Who, then, made up the stadium crowd during the week? A large share came from a swelling white-collar cohort like the thousands of clerical workers in government and private offices, which, unlike factories, were willing to release workers in time for a first pitch at 2:30 or 3:00 P.M. That left patrons of the game in those happier days plenty of time to get home for dinner, since contests rarely took more than two hours.[14]

Other spectators could have included students, owners of retail businesses, independent craftsmen with their own shops, traveling salesmen, lawyers, doctors and dentists, nighttime employees—people, in short, who still exercised some control over their hours of work. Women, preferably accompanied, were included because the leagues were already bidding for their patronage (which conferred a respectability that they wanted to cultivate) with Ladies' Day promotions and other enticements like elective separate seating and well-appointed restrooms. The box seats harbored sports-minded members of the elite, but the bulk of the paying audience came from that part of the population defined by the elastic and politically confusing term "middle class." And in 1906 they showed it by wearing their Sunday best to the park.[15]

But awareness of the left-outs among those in the stands that delirious autumn week shouldn't erase the fact that there was genuine citywide excitement. The contagion of enthusiasm spread by the headlines did make the judge and the janitor, the tycoon and his tailor, the school chums whose fathers came from Rome, New York, and Rome, Italy, feel like fellow members of one community for at least a few days. Still, it was an artificial, rather than a face-to-face, community like those in the dwindling number of 1906 America's small and middling-sized towns or in distinctive urban neighborhoods. None of the players on either team was native to Chicago, and large numbers of the onlookers in a constantly moving population had probably not been born and raised there.

That pretense that cities are actually represented in professional sports leagues goes on still, and is part of a larger reality about the social organization of huge metropolitan areas. Neither necessarily good nor bad in itself, it's simply part of the way we Americans live now. It's the way Americans were just getting used to living a century ago.

At noon the gates were finally opened, and a wave of people poured in past street vendors proffering pennants, seat cushions, megaphones, horns, team pictures, and other souvenirs. As they seated themselves they looked out on a setting still recognizable. The stands and bleachers were festively draped in red-white-and-blue bunting for the great occasion. The diamond itself was laid out according to dimensions that had finally stabilized (like almost all the rules) in the form that they still keep: 90 feet between bases set in circular patches of bare earth, the marked base paths themselves, an unsodded alley covering the 60½ feet between pitcher's mound and home plate (not there in most modern parks), and the batter's boxes. All the rest of the infield and outfield was covered in the green of a natural-grass park. The left- and right-field dimensions were familiar too—340 feet down the left-field foul line, 316 down the right, but an impossibly deep 560 to the center-field fence covered with ads.

That depth was sharply reduced, however, by a 1906 practice that allowed overflow crowds to stand along the foul lines and in the outfield, separated from the players by a rope or wire cable located at the home team's discretion. That called for ground rules about balls that fell among the standees. Those agreed on for Game One of this World Series were that a ball that landed amid spectators on fair ground, either on the bounce or the fly, was unretrievable and would count as a double. There would be no pop-fly home runs into that shrunken center field.[16] A fielder's overthrow into the mob allowed a one-base advance. Spectators were supposed to return balls that fell among them, and if they did not, players or umpires went out to retrieve them. Recovery efforts weren't always successful, but the expectation was that an entire game should be played with one ball, no matter how scuffed, battered, and stained with dirt or the substances that still-legal spitball pitchers chewing tobacco, licorice, or slippery elm daubed on it before delivery.

Behind home plate benches and tables were set up for some three hundred reporters, photographers, and telegraphers poised to relay the action to the waiting nation. The sportswriters were especially important in a time when radio and television were nonexistent, serving as the eyes and ears of the millions of Americans who were followers of big-league ball but were not among the lucky thousands who filled the grandstands of small parks on any given game afternoon. How the absent multitudes of fans experienced the contests depended on a handul of men (and in 1906 men only) who could convey what they saw on the field realistically and excitingly in concise, understandable stories hammered out under heavy time pressure, stories that turned box scores into live drama.

But there was no specially located press section in or on the wooden stands, which had been expanded by the addition of extra front rows and field boxes, further reducing the room available to catch foul flies. There were no dugouts, either. The players, with bats, gloves, and other gear scattered at their feet, sat on field-level benches in what were more or less open sheds that on this day were flag draped for the occasion,

By a little before 1:00 P.M., with an hour and a half still to wait, the noise was enough to make life hard for the telegraphers tapping away at their keys. Rooters were waving pennants and team totems, including a two-foot-long bear-cub doll that someone was dangling over the upper grandstand railing and jiggling into occasional dances by means of a string. A party of Sox rooters from city hall, led by Chicago's official restaurant inspector, had brought a six-foot-long string of cowbells to jangle. Boasts and insults, good-natured and otherwise, were exchanged at high volume, amplified by tooting horns. PARTISAN FEELINGS RUN HIGH IN VAST THRONG OF EXULTANT FANS WHOSE HEATED ARGUMENTS COUNTERACT ICY BLASTS, ran one next-day headline. Amid all that din, bets were openly being laid, with those taking the Cubs obliged to offer odds of 2 to 1 or even 3 to 1 because, for all the excitement, the Series looked as if it would be a runaway for the Nationals, a David-and-Goliath rematch, this time without divine assistance on David's side.

★   ★   ★

The 1906 Chicago Cubs were one of the greatest teams of the twentieth century. That season they won 116 games, a record never surpassed, and not even equaled until 2001 by the Seattle Mariners, who did it in a 162-game season instead of the 154-game format in use when each league had only eight teams playing seven rivals twenty-two times apiece. The Cubs had lost only 36 games in the entire year. (Two meaningless ties were not made up.) In their own park they were 56–21, and on the road they reeled off 60 victories against a mere 15 losses. In the early part of the season the experts had predicted a tough battle between the Cubs and the New York Giants, the preceding year's world champions. But after an opening series in which the New York team took three games out of four, it was all Cubs. They wound up winning 14 of the next 18 games against John McGraw's team, including a monumental 19–0 shellacking at New York's Polo Grounds in June. It gave them an additional nickname in Chicago sport pages: "Giant-Killers." Never looking back after grabbing first place on May 28, they vaulted from strength to strength, with a 26–3 record in August, and victories in 50 of their final 57 games.[17] They led the league in batting with a team average of .262 and clouted 20 home runs, a high total then, but second in 1906 to the Brooklyn Dodgers' 25. In fielding they were the first modern team to post fewer than 200 errors (194 to be exact). Their double-play combination of shortstop Joe Tinker, second baseman Johnny Evers, and first baseman (and manager) Frank Chance was deadly, though not celebrated in Giant rooter Franklin P Adams's poem beginning "These are the saddest of possible words, Tinker to Evers to Chance" until 1910. (Actually, the trio made only 17 double plays in 1906, eight started by Tinker, but it was a goodly total and harder to reach when a deader ball got out to the infielders more slowly.)

In addition to almost flawless fielding and slugging power they had speed, a gigantic asset in a low-scoring era when a stolen base that helped build a run could decide a game. The Cubs had pilfered 283, with Chance alone taking 57.

The pitching was beyond expressions like "eye-popping." The combined staff's earned run average was 1.76. Its ace, Mordecai Brown, had posted a 26–6 record during the season and his ERA was 1.04. Behind him came left-hander Jack Pfiester, with 20 wins against eight losses. Ed Reulbach, 19–4, allowed opponents only 1.65 earned runs in every nine innings. Carl Lundgren was fourth in wins with 17, against six losses, but in contrast to the other mound misers seemed virtually generous in allowing runs: his ERA was 2.21. Jack Taylor, obtained from the St. Louis National League team in a midseason trade, was a Cub from only July 1 onward, but he won 12 games for the Chicagoans while losing three and had an ERA of 1.84 as a Cub. Orval Overall had an identical won-and-lost record, with a 1.88 ERA. Twenty-eight times, or every five and a half games on average, the Cubs had won by a shutout—and Brown alone had 10 of those.

In contrast, the White Sox had undergone a brutal season-long struggle. The midpoint of July 1 found them in the second division, and they'd barely been above the .500 mark two weeks earlier. But the pack leaders, New York, Philadelphia, and Cleveland, were tightly bunched, so when the Sox broke through with a record-setting 19-game win streak in August, they headed into the final month as front-runners. At that point a new wave of illnesses and injuries to key players swept their dugout while the New York Highlanders (later the Yankees) embarked on their own 15-game string of wins. On September 21, with only two weeks left, the visiting New Yorkers took three out of four and recaptured the league lead from the Sox, who were playing with a shifting series of emergency lineups patched together by thirty-two-year-old player-manager Fielder Jones—his real name. A final three-team scramble among New York, Cleveland, and Chicago ended in the late afternoon of October 3, when the White Sox' 91st victory clinched the title. They would add two more in the final standings to finish with a 93–58 mark.

The sense of a mismatch was increased by the numbers of a postseason exhibition series that the two Chicago teams had played in 1905. The Cubs easily captured that one 4–1. Moreover, the Sox were relatively weak at the plate—a .230 team average put them lowest in their league, and led Hugh Fullerton to dub them the "hitless wonders." But for all that, knowledgeable baseball men were not counting the American Leaguers out. They respected Jones's steady leadership and his support from owner Comiskey. They were also aware that the White Sox had four topflight "twirlers" whose records were not far inferior to those of the Cubs staff. Their big winner, right-hander Frank Owen, was 22–12, left-hander Nick Altrock had 20 wins and 13 losses, and the other starting southpaw, Guy Harris "Doc" White, had notched 18 victories and been beaten six times. Completing the quartet was Ed Walsh, a spitballer whose numbers were 17–13. Neither did position-by-position comparisons hugely favor the Cubs. Their dominance of the National League had been awe inspiring, but whereas they had run away with the pennant by midsummer, the White Sox had fought their way through a tougher season against several challengers.

The pre-Series predictions of the real experts, the rival managers, were therefore hedged. Five National League pilots picked the Cubs, but Philadelphia's Hugh Duffy announced his doubt "that the Cubs would have a runaway race." Their American League opposite numbers naturally differed, though only one would risk a flat-out prediction of a White Sox win. James McAleer of St. Louis declared that "the White Sox will spring a surprise" and that "making the Cubs 2–1 favorites is decidedly out of line." Connie Mack of the Philadelphia Athletics ruefully responded that "from the way the White Sox rubbed it into the Athletics this season it wouldn't behoove me to predict anything but an American League victory." Others were even more circumspect. Clark Griffith, at that time the pilot of the New York American Leaguers, declared: "You never can tell in baseball." Cleveland's Napoleon Lajoie more or less echoed that view with "It looks like a toss-up to me."[18]

Evolving World Series tradition seemed to require that at least some league officials plus the owners and the two managers be polled for their easily foreseeable opinions. At least as they were quoted—and it's impossible to be sure how much embroidery reporters might have added—they showed a two-tier hierarchy of stuffiness. The league presidents and the owners sounded like the politicians and businessmen that they were. The player-managers were more terse and colloquial. President H. C. Pulliam of the National League described the upcoming battle as if he were giving an after-dinner or election speech, careful to say nothing that would offend:

> The Chicago National League team will have a worthy antagonist in the Chicago American League team, led by Manager Jones. I do not look upon this series as being one sided, but I do know that in this series those fortunate enough to witness the games will see the highest type of skill, as displayed upon the baseball diamond.
>
> My faith in the Chicago National League team is such that I believe victory will perch upon the banner of Manager Chance's team. Baseball is an uncertain game, however, and the fortunes of war may go to President Comiskey's team.
>
> The city of Chicago is fortunate, indeed, to have the destinies of its two great clubs directed by such creditable representatives. They stand for all that is good, honest and sportsmanlike in baseball.[19]

Murphy reduced the pomposity level: "I have the greatest confidence in Manager Chance and the rest of the boys, and the Sox will have to go some to take the opener." And Comiskey spoke in the language of his own days on the playing field: "The boys will be there with the goods and take the opening contest by a fair score." The field managers were even crisper. "Picking winners in baseball," said Jones, "is a dangerous proposition. The dope goes wrong oftener than it turns out right . . . [but] I can't see where the Cubs have anything on us." Chance, who was apparently uninterested in furnishing good (or any) copy to the inquiring writers, was dismissive. His words were: "I don't care to play the post-season games through the press. . . . We beat the White Sox last fall in a gallop and, as the team is much stronger now . . . I don't see why we shouldn't repeat." Then the tongue-in-cheek clincher: "I can tell more after the post-season series is over."

That was the point, of course. Records accumulated over six months weren't safe predictors of what could take place in a week. Tim Murnane, an experienced Boston sports reporter, picked the Cubs in his pre-Series analysis but added a timeless bit of wisdom. "Baseball dope is often misleading especially in a short series."

The first on-field test of all predictions was ninety minutes away when, amid roars from the stands, the first Cub players began to arrive for pregame warm-ups, walking across the field to their brick clubhouse behind center field. Many were recognizable from firsthand familiarity, for a number of players on both teams (at least four Cubs and four White Sox according to city directories) lived in neighborhoods no more than a streetcar ride away from their ballparks. First came center fielder Art Hofman, whose skinny six-foot-tall frame was easily noticeable at a time when the average height of American men was several inches less than it would be two or three generations later; then came his two partners in the outfield, Jim Sheckard and Frank Schulte. They were followed by Tinker and Evers, the latter's small size and sharp features well known to be joined to a fiery competitive temperament. Each provoked a new round of cheers from Cub fans as he was recognized. Mordecai Brown, who would be the starting pitcher and could be spotted immediately by his malformed right hand, was followed by manager–first baseman Chance, another six-footer, who weighed 190 pounds and proudly carried the nickname of "Husk." These were followed by the rest of the players, who disappeared to change and reemerged in brand-new white uniforms (without numbers, a later addition) over which they had thrown overcoats to beat the chill as they waited their turns. Jack Taylor strolled to the mound to pitch batting practice. As each Cub stepped up for his practice swings, a man with a megaphone bellowed his name, followed by the words "champion of the world," provoking new outbursts of noise from the West Siders' loyalists.

At 1:30, the White Sox rooters got a chance to cheer when their heroes, already uniformed, made their entrance. Both parks had dressing rooms for the home team only, so by agreement the visiting squad of the day would dress at the Victoria Hotel downtown and be drawn through the streets to the playing field in a tallyho, a large open wagon with benches. In baseball's early years, now already fading into recall, both teams had arrived that way, often accompanied by a band and sometimes singing fight songs as if they were college cheerleaders. Out-of-town clubs had to ignore taunts, catcalls, and an occasional overripe vegetable hurled by local partisans. The worst that the White Sox and Cubs would have to endure on travel days, however, would be verbal harassment.

On this day there was music in West Side Park too. After the White Sox filed in to take their practice and the two managers "cordially" greeted each other amid continuous cheers, a man with a cornet stepped up to the plate and played "There'll Be a Hot Time in the Old Town Tonight," leading the audience to join in with words that Chicagoans were using to make tragedy into mock-heroic parody:

> *One fine night all the people were in bed*
> *Mrs. O'Leary took a lantern to the shed*
> *The cow kicked it over, winked an eye and said*
> *"There'll be a hot time in the old town tonight."*

At the conclusion of the chorus the soloist added a number entitled "How Would You Like to Be the Umpire," and then got a "hearty hand" when he wound up his performance with "Chicago," not the jazzy "toddlin' town" version well known since 1920, but a more solemn city anthem that ran in part:

> *Behold, she stands beside her inland sea*
> *With outstretched hands to welcome you and me.*
> *For every art, for brotherhood she stands,*
> *Love in her heart, and bounty in her hands*
> *Chicago, Chicago, Chicago is my home*
> *My heart is in Chicago wherever I may roam.*[20]

While the players now stripped down to sweaters and continued to whip the ball around the infield, celebrity spectators were arriving: the massive President Ban Johnson of the American League; Pulliam of the National; Gary Hermann, the third National Commissioner; an array of team owners and managers from both leagues; and then local political notables seeking visibility with an election just a few weeks away. They included "Bath House" John Coughlin, alderman of the First Ward, notorious for its toleration of bets, babes, and booze, who showed up wearing a blue shirt, white collar, and red tie, the shirt closed by three large diamond studs, which Bath House John exposed to admiring gazes by keeping his gray outer coat unbuttoned. Not mentioned prominently in newspaper accounts was Mayor Edward F. Dunne, who was vainly trying to close down the palaces of sin that contributed to Coughlin's popularity, and would as a result be dumped by the Democratic machine after a single term. On this day, Bath House was freely flaunting the wages of sin while, by coincidence, the National Purity League was holding a convention in the area of the Loop, the central core of downtown, outlined by four crisscrossing elevated lines.
Another, and very special, civic elebrity was Adrian C. "Cap" Anson, who had spent nineteen years as the manager of the Chicago National League team in the 1880s and 1890s, and guided it to several championships. Cries for a speech rose above the hub-

bub, but were declined by the popular veteran. Another celebrity guest was present by proxy, so to speak, for shortly before the game actually began, a White Sox fan with "an excellent baritone voice" and a megaphone led the Sox part of the crowd in mocking words set to the tune of a popular song, "So Long, Mary," a hit from George M. Cohan's musical *Forty-five Minutes from Broadway*. The version that emerged from the megaphone ran:

> *So long, Murphy*
> *How we hate to see you lose*
> *So long, Murphy*
> *We know you will have the blues*
> *We'll all feel sorry for you, Murphy*
> *While we cheer*
> *So long, Murphy*
> *Maybe you will win next year.*

Cohan himself, a baseball fan, was in Chicago but playing a matinee of another of his shows, *George Washington, Jr.*, and unable to attend. At a later game, his stage manager would present gifts to both managers. But gifts were also on tap for this opening day. In a brief lull in the noise, representatives of the Hamilton Club, a gentlemen's sporting association, presented silver loving cups to the captains of both Chicago teams, followed by a chorus of "Auld Lang Syne." All of this spectacle undoubtedly intrigued foreign visitors, one of them all the way from Siam, who had come to witness the "American game" for themselves.

Finally, 2:30 came. A gong clanged, its brassy echoes drowned in the rising tumult of expectation that still precedes the call to "Play ball." Umpires "Silk" O'Loughlin and J. Johnstone assumed their positions behind second and home plate. Mordecai Brown took the mound; the Sox leadoff hitter, right fielder Eddie Hahn, stepped into the box; and at last, the foreplay, the heart flutters, the heavy beathing, were over, and the Great Event, the game itself, began.

★   ★   ★

As Brown wound up for his first pitch, Cubs fans exulted, know-ing already that they were watching a future historic star. In his three seasons with the Chicago National League club, to which he came during his second year as a major-league player, he had already won 59 games while losing 28, and at thirty years of age, his best seasons were still ahead of him. His mere presence on a major-league baseball field at all was a wonder in itself. His right hand had been maimed in a childhood accident on his father's Indiana farm, when he stuck it into a feed cutter and lost the first joint of his index finger. A later fall had broken the third and fourth fingers on the same hand, which never healed correctly and made the use of his pinkie almost impossible. Yet "Three Finger" Brown was devastating because when he gripped the ball properly with his stiffened hand, the small knob on the stump of the forefinger put a spin on it that resulted in a nasty curve that broke sharply downward in either direction as it crossed the plate. (Ty Cobb called it the hardest pitch he ever faced.) Brown showed his mas-tery as he faced the first three White Sox hitters. He struck out Hahn, got Jones to lift an easy fly to center, and racked up another strikeout against second baseman Frank Isbell, whose .279 season average made him the best hitter on the White Sox.

It was the turn of the Sox' fans to cheer next, as left-hander Nick Altrock took the hill. "The bleachers howl with delight when 'Nick' goes in to pitch," reported one writer. "He hasn't the best curves in the world nor the most speed, but he has more nerve."[21] The combination of nerve and curve had been kind to the easygoing and popular twenty-eight-year-old. He had won 23 games in 1905 and 20 in 1906, and he faced the Cubs' lead-off hitter, center fielder Art Hofman, with unshaken confidence, especially as he had earned Comiskey's team its lone victory in the five-game exhibition series with the Cubs the preceding fall. The crowd leaned forward as the classic trio at the plate took their stances—Hofman in the box, the catcher and umpire both

masked, the catcher in a higher crouch than later became customary, the ump peering over his shoulder. Altrock, possibly inspired
by the presence of his easily visible and magnificently whiskered
father in the stands, and comforted by a large cud of tobacco in
his own cheek, went to work in earnest and got the first three
batters on easy ground balls, then walked back to the dugout past
the small army of news photographers clustered behind home
plate to record the first run, whenever it occurred.

But it would not occur in the first third of the game, as each
pitcher bore down and worked his way through the order. In the
second and third, Brown induced three of the six batters he faced
to ground out, and added three strikeouts to his total. But Altrock
was not to be outdone. Part of his crowd appeal was the lively
sense of humor that made him willing to rib the game itself, and
when not pitching or coaching on the baselines, he was noted for
clownlike mockery. (After retiring as a player, he would in fact put
on pregame comedy acts with another ex-player, Al Schacht, the
"Clown Prince of Baseball.") But there was no lack of serious-
ness about him this particular afternoon. "No frills in the work
of Nick," wrote the *Inter-Ocean*'s man at the game. "It was earnest, deadly earnest and never did a man work harder for victory.
His whole heart and soul was in every ball he hurled across the
plate." After retiring the first three Cubs to face him, Altrock in
the second inning got Chance, a .319 hitter during the season, to
hit a bouncing ball that White Sox first baseman Jiggs Donahue
handled unassisted. Next, he confronted the Cubs' leading hitter,
Harry Steinfeldt (.327). One of a number of players of German
descent in the big leagues, "Steinie" was popular with Cub fans,
and his lifetime totals were excellent. At third base he was part of
the Cubs' superb infield defense, but because he did not figure
in the famous Tinker-to-Evers-to-Chance poem, he is not preserved in history like his three infield partners. Altrock got him
to dribble a roller toward first again, so slowly that this time Altrock himself picked it up and tagged the Cub third baseman out.
Then he faced the relatively light-hitting Joe Tinker, who flied

out to Hahn in right. In the bottom of the third, the 5-foot-10-inch Altrock first leaped to cut off Evers's high bouncer over the mound and threw him out at first, then got catcher Johnny Kling to line to shortstop Lee Tannehill, and finally fanned Brown. The opener was on the way to becoming a pitching duel of aces, with only two of the first 18 batters getting the ball out of the infield. Alhough by one account "man after man faced the determined Nick, only to be mowed down with relentless regularity," the work of "Miner" Brown (another nickname, earned by early jobs in the coal shafts of southern Indiana) was "hardly a bit behind."

At the end of each inning the crowd stood, modifying the usual custom of stretching only at the end of the fifth (not the seventh) inning. One reporter noted that, given the weather, the object of the repeated stretch was probably to move around in order to prevent the water from freezing in the viewers' joints.[22]

After Brown set down the White Sox in the top of the fourth on two more grounders and a shallow fly, the Cubs finally broke through with the game's first hit, a two-out infield single by Frank Schulte. Schulte had speed, and when he hit a slow bounder over Altrock's head, he was able to sprint to first in time to beat Isbell's hurried pickup and throw. Promptly, he took off for second and added a postseason stolen base to the 25 he had already accumulated. That brought an anticipatory roar from Cub fans. But Altrock thwarted Chance's hope of bringing the run home by getting the Cub manager to rap sharply to first for the final out.

Not until the top half of the fifth was the great work of two hard-throwing pitchers sullied by a run scored, and that one on an error. Third baseman George Rohe, one of only three right-handers in the White Sox lineup that day, was the hitter. Listed as a utility infielder, he was there as a late replacement for George Davis, the regular shortstop, who was laid low with a severe cold. Lee Tannehill, who ordinarily handled third for Jones, was moved into the shortstop position, and Rohe took his spot. Offensively it was no downgrade. With a .258 season average in 74 games, Rohe was one of the more potent White Sox, and he proved it now by sending a bullet down the third-base line past a diving Steinfeldt, out to where left fielder Sheckard could manage only to deflect it into foul territory. There it rolled under some on-field seats or some lumber left over by a construction crew—newspaper accounts did not agree—and became a triple.

With Rohe standing on third and nobody out, Brown bore down. He fanned Donahue, then fired a pitch that the next batter, left fielder Pat Dougherty, found just enough of to send rolling slowly toward the mound. Rohe took off at full steam while Brown, a fine fielder, charged, pounced on the ball, and whipped a throw to his catcher that had the runner beaten. But Kling, perhaps beset with opening-game jitters, dropped the ball as Rohe slid in with a White Sox run. While White Sox rooters filled the air with exultant shouts, Brown, too, caught the contagion and threw a wild pitch (not officially charged as such) that got somewhere behind Kling, who retrieved it quickly but not before Dougherty had dashed to second. Brown now got the light-hitting (.214) Sox catcher Billy Sullivan to ground out to Tinker, moving Dougherty to third. With two out, Tannehill connected solidly with a Brown offering, but Tinker's "sizzling" stop arrested further damage.

Working with this slim advantage, Altrock retired the Cubs' power hitter, Steinfeldt, for the second time on a groundout. Tinker lifted a pop foul behind the plate, and Billy Sullivan raced back, scattering photographers and telegraphers in his path, and made "a beauty of a catch," after which little John Evers, who somehow at 125 pounds could carry a .255 batting average into the Series, struck out.

Brown walked Altrock to begin the sixth, and Hahn sacrificed his side's pitcher to second. Fielder Jones now poked a single over second that dropped into shallow center as Altrock tore around third en route to home. Hofman, likewise at full gallop inward, scooped up the Texas Leaguer and fired a perfect strike to Kling to get the out at the plate. While fans of both sides were still gasping with excitement, Brown, facing Isbell, threw another pitch that Kling could not handle, this time officially recorded as a wild pitch. Jones had gone to second on the play that nipped Altrock at the plate, and now moved to third. Sox fans were shrieking for "Izzy" to come through, and he obligingly did so, poking a soft single that brought Jones trotting easily in to score another run.

Chance now approached the mound to see if he could steady Brown, his march accompanied by Sox rooters' triumphant chant of "ONE! TWO!"—their team's score. But whatever Chance told Brown was effective, because he got Rohe to bounce one back to him for an easy flip to first and the third out.

The Sox now had two runs on three hits, the Cubs no runs on their one. But their turn came, as it does so often when a pitcher walks the first man in an inning to face him. Altrock gave Kling a ticket to first, and then Brown, after missing two attempts at bunting, swung at the next pitch and sent a bouncer over Altrock's head and up the middle. Isbell and Tannehill, converging on a collision course, hesitated for a second and let the ball roll between them into short center. Hofman's sacrifice moved the runners into scoring position with one out, electrifying the crowd. The White Sox battery faltered briefly in the middle of the uproar, and Altrock uncorked a pitch to lefty Jim Sheckard that was "scarcely an inch off the ground" and rolled through Sullivan's hands, allowing Kling to sprint home to cut the lead in half, while Brown moved to third with the tying run and only one out.

But the star turns of this afternoon belonged to the defense. Sheckard sent a soft looper toward left field. Tannehill broke speed records going out to catch it with his back to the plate, then whirled and in midpirouette threw in to Sullivan briskly enough to keep Brown frozen at third. Schulte, next up, rapped a sharp grounder to Rohe, who held it a fraction too long while Schulte flew down the line, then heaved it wide of first. Jiggs Donahue, all six feet and one inch of him, lunged for the throw at a full stretch, did a midair barrel roll, and thumped down on his back, with one foot just touching first a microsecond before Schulte's and one hand flourishing the ball in the air to show a completed catch.

Out number three, and in two plays as quick as a championship tennis volley at the net, the hitless wonders had shown why they needed few runs to win.

It had been a magnificent game thus far—close, wondrously pitched, and with defensive gems offsetting errors on each side. A letdown seemed to threaten as the tiring Brown bobbled an easy grounder that brought Donahue (who was greeted with cheers for his game-saving catch) safely to first, and next threw a wild pitch that advanced him to second with no one out. But Donahue was trapped in a rundown when Dougherty bounced to Brown, whose lightning throw to Tinker caught him leading too far. Cub fans exhaled, but relief was short. Dougherty had taken first on the fielder's choice while Donahue was being chased down and tagged out. Then he stole second. But intimations of Brown's demise were premature; he got Sullivan on a fly and Tannehill on a ground ball, and walked back to the bench still only one run behind.

Altrock, however, was getting stronger in the late innings. He set the Cubs down one-two-three in their half of the seventh, and then, batting leadoff in the Sox eighth, rubbed it in by hitting a single himself. Hahn forced him at second. Hahn himself then tried to steal, but Brown had smelled it coming and called for a pitchout. Hahn was out on Kling's throw to Evers, but in the collision at second, the runner spiked the skinny lightweight in the foot, so that Evers limped to the plate to begin the Cubs' offense in the bottom of the eighth and was easily thrown out by Isbell. Kling came through with the Cubs' third hit, a "pretty" single to center, and Brown dutifully moved him along with a sacrifice. But Hofman could only lift one of Altrock's curves to short center for the closing out. Brown, taking his last turn on the hill, got three quick outs, a ground ball, a fly, and, as a curtain-lowering flourish to the day's performance, a strikeout.

The bottom of the ninth brought those crowning moments in a tight and important game when the result can ride on any pitch and the suspense is relentless, tormenting, and wonderful. Twelve thousand–odd men and women in their high collars and long skirts were lashed by emotions still familiar to their great-great-grandchildren who follow the game—the rooters for the leading team screaming and pleading for the pitcher to wrap up the win, and those of the trailing club screeching, beseeching each batter to keep it alive. Pinch hitter Pat Moran, a right-hander, flied to center. Frank Schulte was out, short to first. Two down, and manager Chance, the fate of his team in the hands that gripped his bat, poked a single to center and passed the baton to Steinfeldt, the .327-hitting leader of the team, the one batter of all that any Cub loyalist would want to see. Over 12,000 people were on their feet, holding their breath. The count was not reported, but Steinfeldt swung at an Altrock offering that seemed his style. There was a crack, the ball sailed in a high arch toward center—high, but not deep. Fielder Jones gazed skyward, did a little jig, and stretched up his hands, and, as one word-intoxicated sportswriter put it, "the sphere dropped safely and snugly into its happy home in Mr. Jones's basketlike hands."

Ecstatic Sox fans poured onto the field, carried Altrock away on their shoulders, pummeled and hugged his teammates, tore at their uniforms. It was only one game, but a supposed walkover for the confident Cubs had turned into a loss for them. The mold of a season had been cracked; they were mortal and vulnerable after all. That was what the White Sox had needed to nerve them for further warfare against Goliath. American League president Ban Johnson crowed: "It's an awful crime to say 'I told you so' but I am compelled to use that hackneyed expression. I have no fear of the final result of the series so long as the American League champions play that kind of ball." Jones said much the same: "If all our pitchers show the form that Altrock displayed, the series ought to be over in three days more."

But Chance, who wasted few words, kept morale up with a simple declarative sentence: "We got away badly, but we will be heard from later." And owner Murphy pronounced, "One swallow does not make a summer."

Sportswriter Charles Dryden of the *Tribune* summed it up. "That they [the Sox] should slam the favorites by a score equal to the odds against them is what the bards would call poetic justice as she is meted out." Even more succinct was a cartoon on the same page showing a jubilant Sox player using a bat to stir a tub of "Mashed Potatoes."

It had been thrilling from start to finish. Still, it was just one game. Baseball remained unpredictable. Had any of the writers reached for a Shakespearean simile they could have found it in a line from the clown Feste's song in *Twelfth Night:* "What's to come is yet unsure."

2

The Cubs and the
Foundations of Baseball

Though Cubs fans among the homebound crowds exiting West Side Park into the chilly late-afternoon darkness were disappointed, they were hardly suffering crushed hopes. Their team remained one of the greatest ever to play baseball, and the odds still said that their favorites, who had won better than three out of every four games they played (3.22 to be exact), were unlikely to lose three of the six now remaining.

Where had that assemblage of great players come from? How was a championship professional team created? What breed of Chicago capitalists came together to create such a model of excellence? The answer properly begins with Albert Goodwill Spalding, whose name still adorns tennis rackets, basketballs, golf clubs, and a cornucopia of other sporting equipment marketed to hopeful amateurs hoping to imitate the stars who, for hefty fees, endorse them.

There are various contenders for the title of patriarch of American baseball as a popular sport. But it's hard to doubt that Spalding was the genius of baseball as an American business enterprise and as (at least until recent years) *the* "national pastime." That his own baseball roots were in Chicago made it all the sweeter for the city's two teams to be at the pinnacle of baseball's universe in 1906. For that shining moment the essences of dynamic metropolitan growth, big-time, big-dollar sports entertainment, and progressive America seemed to converge right there in the contenders' ballparks.

Spalding was born in 1850 in Byron, in rural Illinois. Calling the Prairie State quintessentially American in the nineteenth century simply records a fact, not a slogan. Among those born, educated, or making their careers there were Abraham Lincoln and Ulysses S. Grant, Jane Addams and William Jennings Bryan, Cyrus McCormick and George Pullman, revivalist Dwight L. Moody and poet Vachel Lindsay—in other words, some of the nation's most celebrated politicians, philanthropists, religious leaders, writers, soldiers, and captains of industry. All were part of the host of movers and shakers who put their stamp on America's surge into industrialism from 1865 to 1915. Spalding is of that number.

He was not born in a log cabin—his father was a successful businessman who died when the boy was eight. The widow sent Spalding to boarding school, which he hated, at nearby Rockford in the northern part of the state.

Spalding was a child of his time, eager to break out of the small-town upbringing that he and other successful children of Main Street acknowledged and sometimes celebrated, usually after their escape from it. He was steeped to the eyebrows in American go-getterism, patriotism, and evangelism—not religious, but the secular kind that strove to convert the world to correct, namely American, opinions. He was a firecracker waiting to be lit, and when he reached his middle teens, "Base Ball" was there in Rockford with the match in the form of a local team, the Forest Citys. Pitching ball became for him what steamboat piloting (likewise a specially American occupation) was to young Mark Twain, the first step on the path to celebrity.

Spalding was a small boy when the New York Knickerbockers, a club of gentleman amateurs, were the toast of the game. He was eleven years old when the Civil War broke out, during which soldiers on both sides sometimes played baseball in camp during lulls between battles. And at sixteen, when the war had been over for a year, he was invited to begin playing with the Forest Citys, who had discovered the husky kid with a strong arm and a knack for putting a good pitch out of a hitter's reach. By then Rockford's team was one of hundreds springing up in small communities during a brief, democratic, preprofessional period when players played and spectators watched for free.

But professionalism, drive by the boosters' will to win, was already setting in. Local teams, supposedly amateur, were already finding ringers and covertly compensating them. Two years after Spalding joined the Forest Citys, another "amateur" club, the Chicago Excelsiors, offered Spalding a $40-a-week job in a wholesale grocery store, with a clear understanding that his chief commercial duty would be to pitch. Strangely, considering the appeal of both Chicago and business in his later years, he did not take to the big city at first; he came back to Rockford and in the two years of 1869 and 1870 pitched 58 games for the Forest Citys and won 45 of them. Those meganumbers were recorded at a time when the pitcher had some advantages in baseball's constant search for rules that provide the nearly-ideal balance between offense and defense that is so central to the beauty of the game. Spalding stood only 45 feet away from home plate, giving the batsman less time to judge what was coming his way. He could throw up to nine pitches that missed the strike zone before the batter got a walk. And a foul ball caught on the bounce was an out. On the other hand, the hitter could request a high or low delivery, the pitcher did not work off a mound, and his hand had to be no higher than his hip at the time of release. While this reduced the ability to throw hard and with spin on the ball (despite the occasional modern-day presence of a few submariners), an underhand delivery put less strain on the arm, making it possible to pitch numbers of games and consecutive innings that would now be inconceivable.

Spalding's record caught the attention of Harry Wright, who in 1869 had been organizer and player-manager of the Cincinnati Red Stockings, the first 100 percent openly professional team. Wright moved to Boston in 1871 at the invitation of some local businessmen who hired him to give the "Hub of the Universe" a team whose virtues as a promotional tool they already saw. Wright put one together handsomely by luring stars, including Spalding, from wherever he could find them. It was a canny strategy. In four paid seasons for Boston, Spalding won 185 games against 43 losses, completed 205 of 234 starts, and had 15 shutouts and 11 saves. In 1875 alone he had an incredible 54–5 won-lost record (a .915 percentage) in 62 starts, with seven shutouts, and nine saves, helping Boston to dominate a recently formed league, the National Association of Professional Base Ball Players.

Then Chicago called again, and this time Spalding was listening. The bid came from a member of the Chicago Board of Trade, a merchant named William A. Hulbert, known as "a progressive wide-awake business man in the community, who had early evinced an interest in the game, all the more unusual for he had never been a player himself." He was already part owner of a team in the NAPBBP known as the Chicago White Stockings, the progenitors of the Cubs (a possible confusion to current readers, which will be unraveled in later pages). Hulbert was convinced that the eastern owners were rigging operations to Chicago's disadvantage, so he helped found a new chain of pro clubs, ambitiously called the National League of Professional Base Ball Clubs, to which he transferred the White Stockings. His first act as a National League owner (he would in time become its president) was to guarantee the White Stockings' competitiveness by waving a checkbook and hiring four key players, including Spalding, from Boston, plus Adrian Anson, a star from the Philadelphia entry in the National Association. The bait for Spalding was a guaranteed salary as player-manager of $1,500, plus a quarter of the gate receipts and, according to Spalding later, an appeal to his regional pride. Hulbert said to him that he had no place being in Boston as a western boy. "If you'll come to Chicago, I'll accept the Presidency of this club, and we'll give those fellows a fight for their lives."[1]

It was a great match. Spalding and Hulbert fully shared those Gilded Age values most prominently visible in a rebuilding, post-fire Chicago. The mood of America, especially in 1876, the nation's hundredth birthday, was furiously upbeat. The struggles of Reconstruction were ending, in good part thanks to white America's abandonment of support for Negro rights, a policy shortly to be reflected on the lily-white fields of baseball. In northern opinion makers' eyes, at least, the Union had survived, a noble cause had been sustained, and a backward slavery system that was not merely unjust but that shackled progress had been overthrown. The railroads were opening the Far West to quick settlement, the cities were booming, and the immigrant ships were bringing in hardworking future Americans every day. Mass production and inventions like electric power were unfailing blessings, and every problem had some reasonable solution soon to be discovered. The Roaring Eighties were a time of unquestioning joy (unless you were poor or black, in which case your opinion was not requested). "Everyone" knew that America was on the fast track to a great future. The self-made millionaire steelmaker Andrew Carnegie put it succinctly in a book he called *Triumphant Democracy*. Other nations, he wrote, plodded along the path of progress, but "the republic thunders by with the rush of an express."[2] Baseball epitomized what Walt Whitman called America's "fling and go" spirit, and began to flourish in this atmosphere.

Spalding was an immediate glowing success. He made 60 appearances, won 47 of them—that is, all but five of the White Stockings' total of 52 victories out of 66 games played—and led the club to the first National League championship. But in 1877 he pitched in only four games and turned the manager's role over to Anson; he played his last professional game in 1878. His eye was on bigger things. He had already started the sporting-goods business that would grow into a nationwide enterprise and make him a multimillionaire. In 1882, when Hulbert died, Spalding moved up to part ownership of the White Stockings. In 1887 he became president of the National League, and though he resigned in 1890, he kept a dominant influence in its councils. Likewise, he was the de facto ruler of the White Stockings even though he also resigned from that job around the same time.

National League baseball in Chicago *was* A. G. Spalding, who was determined to run it on "sound business principles," which meant regularizing schedules; preventing wildcat competition for markets and players; attracting audiences by making the game respectable, affordable, and patriotic; skillfully merchandising it; and making sure that the labor force, the players, stayed under owner control. For Spalding as entrepreneur, the rules on the field were the same as those in shops or offices. His advice to Spalding & Brothers employees in the company magazine in 1915, the last year of his life, was to be a team player and follow the manager's instructions. Successful employees learned "to hit the ball rather than knock the organization" and to be part of a "machine, which in order to produce . . . must have all its parts working in perfect harmony." There was a clear warning, too. Just as a "slouchy, incompetent, and unfaithful ball player" would soon find himself unemployed, so would anyone on the Spalding payroll who was "indifferent . . . dishonest . . . or disloyal."[3]

But then as now it was success that sold tickets, and in the 1880s Cap Anson, who succeeded Spalding as manager and played first base, provided plenty of that for the White Stockings. He was big and aggressive (he could enforce his rules for the players with 220 pounds of muscle on a six-foot-one frame), and his strategic thinking was farsighted back in the dead-ball days, when the game supposedly was focused on the one-run-at-a-time recipe for victory that relied on the bunt, the steal, or the hit-and-run play to advance runners. But Anson was aware that the first priority of a hitter was to become a base runner. So his self-described winning formula was "Round up the strongest men who can knock a baseball the farthest the most often, put yourself on first base and win."[4] In other ways, too, Anson was ahead of his time. He worked hard to stay in condition, turned teetotaler in his late twenties, and was a dietary faddist who abstained from fried food, starches, and rich desserts at a time when success in life was measured by the number of twelve-course banquets (with appropriate wines) that a public figure was invited to attend. He drove his players hard and demanded that they also pay conscientious attention to conditioning. Anson was one of the earliest managers to ask the front office to finance spring training—in Hot Springs, Arkansas, in 1886—to "boil out the fat."

But one area in which he was much in tune with his own era was in its virulent and open racism, though he himself was not a southerner but hailed from Iowa. Anson became a leader in the movement to force the handful of early (and much abused) black major leaguers off the field. In 1887, when Anson refused to let his team confront an opponent with a "colored" player in the lineup, National League owners backed him by agreeing that they would no longer offer contracts to blacks. Other baseball associations followed suit, and within a few years the big-league, big-time game was lily white. The ban, while never written down, remained effective for sixty years.[5]

Anson's personal statistics were Hall of Fame–worthy even allowing for the difficulty of comparing statistics between eras. In his twenty-two years with the Chicago team he batted less than .300 only three times, and those seasons all came after he was thirty-eight years old, the last being in 1897, when he was forty-five and hit "only" .285. His lifetime total of 3,418 hits still had him ranked seventh, as of midsummer 2005, among the thousands who had played the game by then.[6]

His record as manager was just as sparkling in the early going. In his first eight seasons the White Stockings captured five league championships, the first two in 1880 and 1881, the fourth and fifth in 1885 and 1886. In those last two seasons, an agreement was made between the National League and the rival American Association to have their respective winners play each other for the "championship of the world." Both times the American Association title was the St. Louis team then known as the Brown Stockings or Browns, unrelated to a later American League entry of the same name.

Officially nobody won the first of those best-of-seven matches. Each team was credited with three victories, and one game was a tie, called because of darkness. The series was considered in part a promotional exhibition, with the final three meetings "on the road" for both clubs, one in Pittsburgh and two in Cincinnati. In reality one of Chicago's wins was by forfeit when the St. Louis team left the field in protest against the umpiring; the White Stockings lost three of the five games actually played to a decision. In 1886, in a more straightforward home-and-home series, the White Stockings lost again, 4–2, despite the presence of Billy Sunday, the future evangelist (like Anson from Marshalltown, Iowa), who already was starting to believe that God gave him the speed to run down long drives and make impossible catches.

In a portent of future events, the player-manager at first base for St. Louis in both years was Charlie Comiskey, who would become owner of the Cubs' American League rival in 1900 and hold the reins until his death in 1931.

But after 1886 Spalding, now the principal owner, sold off a whole galaxy of stars of the Anson regime, and more were lost in 1890 when players in revolt against the owners' tight control of their salaries formed a league of their own, to which a number of top performers defected. It folded after a year, and there followed a shake-up in the National League structure and many player reassignments.

By then the White Stockings were in a long slide that lasted through the nineties. Plugging gaps with young players gave them a new nickname, the Colts. After a ninth-place finish in 1897 (in what had become a single twelve-team big league), the graying Anson, now called "Pop," left the team in the wake of a quarrel with team president Jim Hart, who was basically a shadow substitute for Spalding. Shorn of its "Pop," the forlorn team on the field became known as the Orphans.

But the White Stockings organization as a whole was not fatherless while A. G. Spalding lived. His combined experience as athlete and entrepreneur gave him a good command of the duties of the front office—the detailed work of financing, player and property acquisition, contracting with stadium concessionaires, outfitting and equipping the team, scheduling travel and reserving accommodations—that could no longer be handled in off-hours by those responsible for happenings on the playing field itself. Baseball was becoming big business; it demanded rationality, marketing, and large chunks of capital. Some of Spalding's player sell-offs in the 1880s may have been to shift cash from building winners into wooing customers, both with amenities that would make an afternoon at the park a pleasurable experience and by promoting the idea that the game itself was a genteel, uplifting, healthy, and patriotic undertaking that deserved support. Two cases in point are his ballparks for the White Stockings and the team's world tour of 1889.

The club's home for its first years of National League existence was a tiny park at 23rd and State Streets, on the South Side. It was enclosed by fences to exclude nonpaying viewers, and seated only about 1,500 in its wooden grandstand. By 1882, when Spalding became an owner, daily attendance was reaching 3,000 without any help from still-illegal Sunday games. The overflow stood in whatever nonplaying space was available. Spalding got the White Stockings to put $10,000 into a larger baseball "palace," which opened in 1884 at Michigan Avenue and Randolph Street, adjacent to the growing business heart of town. The covered grandstand could hold 2,000 customers (who could rent cushions), and there was a bleacher section with room for 6,000. Up to 2,000 standees were welcome. The most up-to-date feature was a set of eighteen luxury boxes atop part of the grandstand with armchairs and curtains to keep unmannerly winds and dust out of the hair and clothing of "parties of ladies and gentlemen." Spalding's own box held a telephone (only recently invented) so that he never needed to be out of contact with his booming business, then annually turning out half a million bats per year and baseballs in lots of 144,000.[7] There was also a bandstand in a pagoda above the main entrance. It took a staff of forty-one ticket sellers, gatekeepers, "cushion renters," "refreshment boys," and musicians to keep the operation going on games days. But that was a mere interim stop. With credit based on growing cash flow—over $30,000 annually as early as 1881—the White Stockings built yet another new stadium at Congress and Throop Streets, slightly to the south and west. This first version of West Side Park could seat 10,000 and had facilities for track, cycling, and lawn tennis in the off-season, plus a covered entryway for gentlemen driving their carriages to the park, and "a neatly furnished toilet room with a private entrance for ladies." There would be one more move before settling, in 1894, into the park where the 1906 World Series was played.

Spalding's biggest publicity stunt was worthy of Phineas T. Barnum, the patriarch of American hype. Between 1888 and 1889 he took the White Stockings on a worldwide tour, playing exhibitions against an "all-American" team of other pro players. The peripatetic nines performed for crowds in Hawaii, New Zealand, Australia, Egypt, and Europe. Spalding always saw to it that the arrival of the teams playing the "American game" was a major news event, preceded and accompanied by banquets and receptions, and with the audience well seeded with celebrities. In Hawaii, there was a luau with the royal family (Hawaii was still an independent kingdom). In Britain, no less a spectator was recruited than the Prince of Wales himself, the future King Edward VII, who confessed that he enjoyed the spectacle but preferred cricket. Spalding was also a master at newsworthy scene-settings. In Egypt one game was played in front of the Pyramid of Cheops. He even tried to land the Colosseum in Rome for one game, but the Italian government refused. Some games took place on improvised fields like meadows, race tracks, and cricket grounds. In one case a playing area had to be dug out of two inches of English snow. But when the tour was over, not only was baseball slightly familiar to newspaper readers abroad, it was a household word at American breakfast tables. At a banquet in New York given to honor the travelers on their arrival home, Mark Twain noted that "baseball is the very symbol, the outward and visible expression of the drive and push and rush and struggle of the raging, tearing, booming nineteenth century."[8]

All of this hoopla did not prevent the decline of the team in the 1890s and during the first two years of the new century, which were an unsettled period for all of baseball. The American League was created in 1900, and a number of National League players defected to it in the course of a business war that lasted until a peace treaty at the end of 1902 brought the rival leagues together under a single roof with eight teams apiece and launched a long period of stability, especially happy from the point of view of the owners, who kept continued ironclad control over the players' salaries and movements.

The end of the tumult and shouting allowed team president Jim Hart, now liberated by Spalding's total withdrawal into his personal business affairs, to begin thinking seriously about how to rescue the old winning tradition. In the process of renewal that would begin after 1901's sixth-place finish, so many young and new faces appeared that sportswriters began to substitute the term "cubs" for "Colts," which would seem to have fit as well. But "cub" was a generic and customary term for a young boy or an apprentice, going back as far as Mark Twain's learning the shape of the Mississippi as pilot Horace Bixby's cub. In 1907, Cubs became the official team name. For purposes of clarity and continuity, and strict historical accuracy be damned, that name will henceforth be the only one used in this story. Meanwhile, Chicago's new American League entry simply collared the "White Stocking" label, which was neither trademarked nor copyrighted, shortened it to "White Sox," and made the name its own.

Hart followed the pattern of Hulbert more than a quarter century earlier in raiding Boston, and brought to Chicago Frank Selee, who had led Boston's National League team (later the Braves) to five pennants in the preceding twelve seasons. Selee was a managerial wizard whose tenure with the Cubs would be short but fruitful. He started the program of acquisition that created the Cub dynasty of 1906 through 1910, when they won four pennants and two world championships. One of his own first steps was to move a young catcher already with the team, Frank Chance (who had been there since 1898), to first base. Chance would succeed Selee as manager. Both are in the Hall of Fame, Chance for his on–field leadership and exploits, Selee for his role in creating winners from the bench. Together they began a fairy tale of a team climbing the beanstalk.

In the early years of professionalism, the rowdy and boozy antics of at least some players led to a public perception, reinforced by the streak of American Puritanism especially potent in the late nineteenth century, that they were all bums unable or unwilling to earn an honest living. It was an exaggeration during the period from 1870 to 1900, and a downright untruth thereafter, as was the complementary myth that they all began as unlettered bumpkins.

Chance is a good starting point for the refutation. Born in 1877 to Scotch-English parents in Fresno, California, he was a six-foot, 190-pound youngster, nicknamed "Husk," when he entered Washington College in Irvington, now the home of a branch of the state university, at age seventeen. He appears also to have attended a dental college in San Francisco, though it is not clear whether he finished the course. There is some evidence that he briefly boxed professionally, and he once supposedly described his major qualification for being a manager as his "ability to lick any man on the ball club." Chance played catcher on his college team, and perhaps some pro ball as well, and in one of those outings he was seen by Bill Lange, a Chicago player of the nineties, who recommended that the Cubs sign him up. It was the way talent was unearthed then. "You see," one old-timer explained many years later, "in those days they didn't have an army of coaches and scouts and things of that kind. The way they got young players was by direct observation themselves. . . . Some friend of the club would tip off . . . managers, that here was a likely kid, and they would bring him up and look him over."[9] The club looked Chance over and liked what it saw, and at twenty-one he was in the majors. On May 12, 1898, he got the first of 1,272 career hits (a single). Soon afterward he stole his first base (of 401 lifetime) and acquired his first extra-base blow. By the end of the next season he was described in the *Sporting News* as "among the best backstops of the National League." In 1901 he both caught and played the outfield briefly under Tom Loftus, one of a short string of managers to succeed Anson.

It was Selee, however, who moved him to first base, because he recognized the star potential of a backup catcher already with the team, Johnny Kling. Kling, two years older than Chance, was from Kansas City, where he first learned the game in vacant lots. One of his nicknames was "Brainy Johnny." At eighteen he was already playing for a local team, the Kansas City Schmeltzers (named for owner Gus Schmeltz) as first baseman and occasional pitcher, and was the field manager. The cleverness extended beyond the field, and Kling would enjoy a long postbaseball career as a successful Kansas City businessman. After a few years as a catcher with minor-league teams in Texas, Illinois, and Missouri, he was picked up by the Cubs late in 1900 as a backup to Chance. During the next year he hit .266 in 70 regular-season games, but when Selee permanently slotted the five-foot-nine 175-pounder into the catching position, his strong arm, savvy in handling pitchers, and knack of distracting opposing hitters with chatter (they also called him "Noisy Johnny") helped propel the club to its four World Series appearances, in which he set several individual records.[10]

Selee's decision to end the competition between Chance and

Kling behind the plate by moving "Husk" to first was part of his gift for picking talent despite little playing experience of his own. It was said that he could "tell a ballplayer in his street clothes." A New Hampshire–born Yankee, forty-two years old at the start of 1902, he grew up in Melrose, Massachusetts, in the home of his father, a Methodist Episcopal minister. In 1884 he left a job with the Waltham Watch Company to make baseball his business, by raising a capital fund of $1,000 and organizing a Melrose entry in the New England League. He managed and played "some out-field," but put away his mitt forever as he proceeded to direct the fortunes of teams in Oshkosh and Omaha, for whom he won two pennants in three seasons. Then New England reclaimed him. He was hired by the Boston Beaneaters of the National League and between 1890 and 1899 he won five pennants for them as well. It was only after a three-year drought without championships from 1899 to 1901 that an an ungrateful ownership released Selee, who was then grabbed by Jim Hart of the Cubs.

Selee was a shrewd bench manager who stressed good execution of the fundamentals of a running game and signaled extensively from the bench to position his defensive players for each hitter and pitch. His hunches for what worked, and with whom, were uncanny. Over the course of his fifteen-year major-league managerial career, which resulted in a .598 winning percentage, no fewer than eleven Hall of Fame members (seven from Boston, four from Chicago) played for and learned from him. He had a "modest and retiring" disposition in a baseball world where shoving and shouting were not only tolerated but admired, and he looked more in his niche running a clothing store in Melrose during the off-season than in uniform. Yet somehow he exerted just the right amount of control to let everyone know who was boss.[11]

Selee and Hart began the rebuilding process in the 1902 season by snaring two of the three most widely known members of the 1906–10 dynasty. Joe Tinker, a contractor's son, was born in Muscodah, Kansas, but raised, like Johnny Kling, in Kansas City, whose public schools he attended and where he, too, learned his baseball. Around the time of his nineteenth birthday in 1899, he began playing semipro, and he became a full-time paid player the next year as shortstop for the Denver entry in the Western League at $75 a month. When the Cubs picked him up from Portland in the Pacific Northwest League in 1902, Selee converted him back to shortstop, where his fielding average rose, as did his salary—to $1,500 for the season. Sturdy and independent (he would later become baseball's first holdout), he was already an established Cub when, in September, he found himself with a new collaborator at second, Johnny Evers (pronounced Ee-vers), a native son of the Hudson River town of Troy, New York.

Evers's career was one of baseball's remarkable stories of totally unpredictable success. He was a beanpole who weighed a mere 108 pounds distributed over a five-foot-nine frame when he started to play ball in the spring of 1902 for the Troy club of the New York State League. (Tinker, only an inch taller, tipped the scale at 175.) Evers must have done fairly well at the plate in both senses, because he had gained some seven pounds by mid-August, when lightning struck. The Cubs' regular second baseman, Bob Lowe, was injured. Selee looked around for emergency help and got in touch with his friend Lou Bacon, the Troy manager. (There were no formal links between major and minor leagues then; farm teams were still in the future.) The unverified story goes that Bacon sent Evers to Chicago with a note: "If you keep him, you can send me $200. If not, send him back."

Evers never went back (and he never weighed more than 125 pounds). Clubhouse reminiscences report that other players resented a skinny rookie suddenly thrust among them and made him ride on the roof of the horse-drawn omnibus that took them to the parks. But Evers did not back away from confrontation; his slight frame housed a fierce Irish temper and a moody nature that got him the label of "the Crab." Lantern-jawed and determined, he took over second base and in 26 September games got 20 hits. It was on September 15, in a lightly attended game against Cincinnati at West Side Park, that reporters first recorded a grounder hit to Tinker, who whipped the ball for a force-out to Evers at second, who relayed it to Chance for two.[12]

There was no question that Evers would keep the job. He replaced Bob Lowe, and three-quarters of the championship infield was set. Tinker and Evers never were personally close and eventually stopped speaking to each other. But in a game they simply anticipated each other's moves like a pair of temperamental dancers devoted to art above all, and silently shifted positions in exactly the right way to erase two runners on one grounder with a man on first.

Selee had also induced Hart to bring over one of his Boston players, outfielder Jimmy Slagle in that 1902 season. A twenty-eight-year-old Pennsylvanian, Slagle had a high school diploma and at least some brief college experience before starting to play pro ball. He had put in several years in the minors before moving up, but there was nothing unusual about a long stay in minor-league ball. At that time it had a sustainable life of its own and did not depend on being stocked with youngsters whose contracts belonged to big-league teams and carried expiration dates and Handle with Care signs. Like Evers, he was small and a light hitter, but speed in his center-field position and on the base paths—he was nicknamed "the Rabbit" as well as "Shorty"—made him both an offensive and a defensive asset.

By the end of Selee's first year five of the eight regulars of the 1906 season were on board (though because of injury, Slagle would not appear in the Series). So were two of the pitchers who would carry them to the flag that season but not appear in October. One was Jack Taylor, a mature right-hander from Ohio—born in 1874—who, like Chance, had already been with the club for four years when Selee arrived, and who gratified the new manager by compiling a stylish 23–11 record, and a hard-to-believe ERA of 1.33. The other was Carl Lundgren, one of the earliest stars to emerge from college athletics. He had only recently graduated from the University of Illinois, where he had been not only an ace pitcher and captain of the nine that beat the snooty Ivy League's Yale, Princeton, and Pennsylvania in his senior year, but also for three years a halfback on the footballl team. Playing only from June onward, Lundgren went 9–9 with a 1.97 ERA, but he completed 17 of 18 starts, had one shutout, and walked 45 batters while striking out 66.

In 1902 Pittsburgh made a joke of the National League pennant race, finishing 27½ games ahead of second-place Brooklyn, with the Cubs back in fifth. The Pirates won again in 1903, but in that year the Cubs improved to a third-place finish, only 1½ games behind the second-place New York Giants. Selee had the running game working, helped by Chance's 67 stolen bases, which tied him with Brooklyn's Jimmy Sheckard for the league lead. Chance also had 78 walks, which often preceded a steal or sacrifice, and batted in 81 runs, only two fewer than Harry Steinfeldt of Cincinnati, whose RBI total was fifth highest in the league that year. Both Sheckard's and Steinfeldt's doings would be carefully noted in owner Hart's offices and by Selee. Chance's .327 batting average, some 50 points higher than that for the team collectively, was reinforced by more superb pitching from Taylor, who threw 33 complete games and won 21 of them. Two other Cub pitchers, Jake Weimer and Bob Wicker, added 40 victories between them.[13]

At the end of that 1903 season, the Cubs made a startling, major move when they traded the proven Taylor for the sophomore big-leaguer "Three Finger" Brown, netting them not only an ace for a decade to come but a Cub immortal. The trade, made at Selee and Chance's suggestion, testified to their power of judgment, because Brown's record in his rookie year was only 9–13. It was the second time Brown benefited from the shrewdness of someone else's appraisal of potential baseball talent. While he was working as a coal miner in his Indiana hometown a timekeeper named "Legs" O'Connell, a semipro player himself, took on Brown as a protégé and pitching pupil, telling the young man that the knob on the stump of his index finger would someday be worth a million to him, and then tutored him between shifts for a couple of years in the art of pitching. Brown later said, "If it hadn't been for Legs I would never have been anything more than a water boy or a mascot for a ball club."

In the summer of 1898 Brown, twenty-two years old, had progressed to the point of playing for Coxsville, Indiana, at $2 a day—when they played. He was a third baseman because the manager refused to believe that he could pitch. But one July afternoon the regular Coxsville pitcher was injured. O'Connell persuaded the manager to try Brown, who finished the game without yielding a hit and won it 9–2. The losers (Brazil, Indiana) promptly signed him up at $10 per game, from whence it was on to Terre Haute at $40 a month, next Omaha in 1902, and finally St. Louis.

The story dovetailed with two favorite scenarios of American pop culture: the understudy who goes on in an emergency and starts a brilliant career (luck) and the working-class kid who makes it to the top (pluck.) Brown went 15–10 in his first Cub season en route to glory and legendary duels, like those of two classic warrior-heroes, with the Giants' Christy Mathewson.[14]

The team improved to 93–60 in 1904 and a second-place finish behind the Giants, who were simply uncatchable after mid-July as they roared to 106 victories. Late in the season the Cubs picked up another building block of their 1906 team, Frank Schulte, a twenty-two-year-old outfielder playing for Syracuse in the New York State League. Schulte, like many other players of his time, had to fight his way into the game over parental objections. He came from Cohocton, New York, near Albany, where his German immigrant father, a contractor, put him to work in the office after high school graduation to learn the bookkeeper's trade and get over his baseball infatuation. The story went that he even offered the boy $1,000 to burn the uniform he wore when on the field with a nearby semipro team. Young Schulte turned him down, went on to play for various small-town industrial-league teams in New York and Pennsylvania, then moved upward to Syracuse, where Selee, on the hunt for outfield reserves, found him. In his maiden appearance in September, Schulte stood in for Jimmy Slagle in left field and got five hits in a doubleheader against Philadelphia. Convinced that they had a find, the Chicago management released outfielder Davy Jones the next year and stationed Schulte in right, moving Slagle to center.

Very late in 1904 the Cubs added outfield depth by buying Arthur Hofman for $1,500 from the minor-league Des Moines club.[15] Used as a part-time substitute, Hofman got only 26 at bats for Chicago in 1904 but hit safely in seven of them. He played in 86 games the following year. Then, toward the end of the 1906 season, Slagle was injured and Hofman substituted for him throughout the World Series.

Schulte became a fixture in right field. He was a sporty type who lived well enough to suggest that he had an independent income outside of his baseball salary. A bachelor until 1911, he kept his winter home in upstate New York and spent the off-season hunting and fishing. He was considered, according to the *Chicago Tribune,* the most "natural" batsman on the team and a better-than-fair outfielder. But he poked fun at his own defensive imperfections, claiming in later years that his right-field job was a cinch because Hofman (by then the regular center fielder) was so good. "All I have to do," he reportedly said, "is to find a shady spot in right field." When a ball came in their direction, left fielder "Sheckard would yell 'Artie, Artie, Artie,' Artie would yell 'I got it' and all I have to do is say 'Take it.' " Schulte's nickname was "Wildfire," like that of a trotting horse that he owned and raced, and named after a show in which Lillian Russell, whom he much admired, was appearing.[16]

In 1905 the team changed ownership and managers but played most of its season with six members of the 1906 World Series batting order on board—Hofman, Schulte, Chance, Tinker, Evers, and Kling—as well as pitcher Mordecai Brown. That spring the syndicate headed by Spalding and Hart offered the controllng share of the club's stock to Charles Murphy, whose career encompassed journalism, marketing, business, and politics. Murphy was a well-connected figure from Cincinnati who had worked as press

agent—an occupation rarely thought to be a doorway to power—
for the Reds and their sometime owner John T. Brush, who later
took over the Giants. In 1905 he was also doing publicity for the
Cubs. When the owning partners, who included not only Hart
and Spalding but Cap Anson, then city clerk, and Cook County
sheriff Ed Barrett, made their offer to Murphy, they realized that
he had nothing in his bank account close to the $105,000 asking
price. But they also knew that Murphy's friends in Cincinnati
were in or near high places, the highest belonging to Charles P.
Taft, the half brother of the secretary of war and future president,
William Howard Taft. Murphy gave Charles Taft his note or notes
for $100,000, which he repaid in fairly short order because the
Cubs were a live proposition, with profits of $165,000 in the year
following the sale. What possibly larger calculations underlay the
deal (which did not include West Side Park, which Spalding hung
on to) are not on the record. But the whole transaction showed
the degree to which Chicago professional baseball had become a
respectable investment, whose chief makers dined and dealt with
political heavyweights.

Murphy took charge without any change in the goal of
building a championship team as quickly as possible. It may be
that Selee welcomed the change at the top, his own relationship
with Hart possibly being problematical. Davy Jones, who played
the outfield for the Cubs from 1902 to 1904, recalled that Hart
had hired him away from the St. Louis American League team
(the future Browns) when they were in town to play the White
Sox during the bidding war between the leagues. From his office
desk, with Jones still sitting there, Hart called Selee at the ballpark.
"I've just signed a new outfielder," he said, "but I won't tell you
who he is, but take it from me, he's OK. Put him in center field
this afternoon." A Cub told Jones later that Selee's reaction was to
repeat the order to the team, looking "sort of bewildered," and to
add: "Things are getting funnier and funnier around this place."[17]

What Murphy's relationship with Selee would have been over
time cannot be known because, 90 games into the season, Selee

left Chicago to try to cure the tuberculosis that was slowly killing him. He moved to Denver, where, rather than resting in a mountaintop sanitarium, he bought a share in a minor-league club (the Pueblo Indians) and also became partner in a hotel. He lived to watch the glory years of the team he had helped to build—its three pennants and two World Series victories of 1906 through 1908—but died in July 1909, at age forty-nine.

Murphy decided to let the team elect the next manager, and the honor went to Chance, rumored to be Murphy's favorite, over "Brainy Johnny" Kling. The team finished 1905 at 92–61, only one win behind the preceding year's record. But this time it was good enough only for third place, 13 behind the league-terrifying Giants, who had again gone on a tear with 105 victories. The Cubs were also four games in back of Pittsburgh and its 96–57 record.

So the job ahead was to overtake the Giants, and Murphy began even before Selee's departure by bringing in Ed Reulbach, a six-foot-one 190-pound right-hander who, like Lundgren, had been a college star and more. Born in Detroit, he began a course leading to an electrical-engineering degree at Notre Dame, and later switched to the University of Vermont as a premed student. He finished neither program, but pitched for both schools. During summers, Reulbach also pitched for minor-league teams in Sedalia, Missouri, and Montpelier, Vermont, using aliases ("Lawson" and "Sheldon") to protect his amateur eligibility. Confused scouts, searching for three pitchers, two of them phantoms, finally ran him down. As a Cub in 1905 he was sensational. He started 29 games and completed 28, made several relief appearances, and ended with an 18–14 record and an ERA of 1.42. There were no relief specialists then, and a small corps of starters was called on to come to the rescue only when matters were getting out of hand. The Cubs' entire six-man staff wound up with a collective 2.04 ERA and 23 shutouts. Of that hot half dozen only Reulbach, Brown, and Lundgren would be on the roster at the end of 1906; the others were traded for power and more sharp pitching. As a team the Cubs had been sluggish rather than sluggers at the plate. Only Chance hit above .300 (.316). He had batted in 70 runs, with Tinker just behind at 66. But right fielder Billy Maloney, in his only season as a Cub, led the league with 59 steals, and the team as a whole was second in stolen bases and first in fielding. The Cubs approached 1906 then, with three Giant-killing weapons in hand: speed, defense, and pitching. Only more batting punch was lacking.

Getting busy in the winter, Murphy traded Jeff Pfeffer and another pitcher to Boston for cash; shelled some out to acquire Pat Moran, a backup catcher to Kling; then made a huge March trade with Cincinnati, swapping star pitcher Jake Weimer and shining third-base prospect Hans Lobert for Harry Steinfeldt. The Kentucky-born "Steinie" was nearly thirty and had apparently thought of a career on stage as a youngster. But he played hometown baseball so well that he entered the minors and climbed the ladder through the Texas League and Western Association until he attracted the attention of the Reds, who signed him in 1898 and put him at third. His 1903 average of .312 made him seem worth the loss of Weimer and Lobert, even though it had tailed off to .244 and .271 in the following two seasons. But rarely have patience and judgment been so well rewarded. In 1906 Steinfeldt would hit .327, his career best year, meantime giving the Cubs a solid anchor at third, leading the league in fielding.

Next, still on the prowl for batting strength, Murphy also traded two outfielders, a reserve third baseman, and pitcher "Buttons" Briggs, plus some cash from the ample Cub coffers, to Brooklyn for another veteran, Jimmy Sheckard. In eight years with the Superbas, as they were then known, he had hit .300 or better in three of them, and over .290 in two more. The *Tribune*'s pre-Series rundown of the position-by-position matchups in 1906 would describe him as a "scientific batsman" and "the best sacrifice hitter on the team," with great range in the outfield and a "mighty thrower."[18] Unfortunately, like many other midseason sluggers in the history of the game, he would struggle in the World Series.

Then Murphy added to the mound corps left-handed Jack Pfiester, a Cincinnatian with three years of experience pitching for a Pacific Coast League team and then Omaha, after a brief tryout with Pittsburgh. It was from Omaha that the Cubs signed him. The start of the season did not slow down Murphy's acquisitions binge. On May 8, he paid cash to the Brooklyn Superbas for backup infielder "Doc" Gessler, and on June 2 he went back to Cincinnati once more, this time with pitcher Bob Wicker and $2,000 in hand, which were accepted in exchange for Orval Overall. Overall had gone to the University of California at Berkeley and, like Lundgren at Illinois, had starred in both football and baseball. At six foot two and 208 pounds he was the physical giant of the team. He had chosen pro baseball as a career upon graduation in 1904, and starred for Tacoma (at $300 a month) for a year, winning 32 of 57 decisions there. Going to the Reds in 1905, he won 18 and pitched a sturdy 318 innings. But he had started slowly at Cincinnati in 1906, and they were ready to swap him for the more proven quantity of Wicker. Overall and Pfiester, along with Reulbach and Brown, would be the quartet who pitched the entire World Series. The path to get there was smoothed even more in the final trade of 1906, when pitcher Fred Beebe and catcher Pat Noonan, plus cash, were given to St. Louis in midseason to bring back the hardworking Jack Taylor, who added another 12 victories to the Cubs' total while losing only three. It is a sign of the 1906 Cubs' great pitching depth that neither Taylor nor Lundgren (with his 17 wins) was called on in the Series.

And so, not altogether differently from modern times but with far fewer dollars involved, a great team had been built, and as the *Tribune* had reported in its October 7 story, "These are the battles of brains which have been fought off the diamond, in the seclusion of private offices, in the short days of winter and the long hours between games"—as good a description of the work of owners and general managers today as then.

This profile of a championship baseball team in 1906 undercuts the impression that very early twentieth-century players were uneducated hicks, or for that matter cut to a different pattern than most young men of their time, except for their extraordinary skills. Jimmy Sheckard had been born on a farm, like Brown. Only Brown had almost certainly escaped a blue-collar destiny thanks to baseball. Lundgren, Overall, and apparently Chance were college graduates. Several others, like Slagle, had put in at least some college time when it was still a rarity to advance beyond high school.

The cities, big and small, were deep reservoirs of new talent. Chance and Evers were from middle-sized agricultural market centers or factory towns like Fresno and Troy. Others had fathers who were independent businessmen like Kling's and Schulte's (contractors) or Overall's, who kept a hotel in Visalia, California, and was at one time sheriff of Tulare County. Pfeister, Kling, Tinker, and Steinfeldt had been born or bred and introduced to baseball in genuine urban centers like Detroit, St. Louis, Cincinnati, Kansas City, and Fort Worth.

Professional baseball was calling to serious young men with some choices of occupation—all the more striking in the America of 1906 as the country was moving toward a society where status was conferred mainly by what one did for a living. Some players were themselves off-season businessmen. Eleven of the eighteen Cubs who saw most of the action in 1906 were married, another badge of respectability.

Physically, the players seemed to be slightly taller and heavier than the average white male American of 1906, who was smaller than his better-nourished descendants would be a century later. Almost all of the Cubs and White Sox were between five foot eight and five foot eleven and weighed on the order of 170 to 190 pounds. Skinny Evers (five foot nine and 150 pounds), and Overall, the ex-halfback (at six foot two and 214 pounds), bracketed the group. They were also, for the most part, of Scotch-Irish or English Protestant descent—but the Irish and the Germans had begun to make their inroads. No players of eastern or southern European extraction were on the team, and few, if any, were yet playing in organized ball. And of course the color line was solid, high and tight. At the major-league level there were no openly known Jewish players though there was a widespread assumption by some people that Kling was Jewish. His Jewish-born widow explained after Kling's death that her own Jewish origin was the source of the misunderstanding.[19] As the *Tribune* put it in an October 13 rundown of both teams' performances to that date:"The individual members of the two groups of renown [*sic*] ball players vary in intelligence and physical prowess quite as much as any body of men which is formed for strife upon the field of sport.... Wherever they came from and whatever their training, they have combined to make two famous groups of ball players, which have done much to bring sporting fame to Chicago."

Chance handled this aggregation with a deft combination of strategy and tough love. As a first baseman player-manager, he was in a good position to direct base runners and his pitchers; he would, on occasion, swear at Overall or Pfeister for a bad pitch. He could also sometimes steal signals from the opposition bench and relay the information to his fellow infielders. Eventually player-managers became obsolete, but in the Paleozoic age before computer printouts, Chance, like others of the breed, carried awesome amounts of information on opposition hitters in his memory.

Physically intimidating and fearless, Chance did not mind being hit by pitches—he took 36 such hits in his entire career, five of them in a single 1904 doubleheader. But he would not back off the plate, and he expected his "boys" not to do so either. Off the field he could be friendly with his team, but he never let them doubt who was in charge. He did not mind the boys playing poker in their spare hours—with a 25-cent limit—but the games had to be over by 11:00 P.M. bedtime. Nor did he object to drinking. After a game he would often take the players to a saloon across the street from West Side Park and buy the first round; but the bartender was instructed to keep an open eye and cut off anyone overindulging. He demanded thinking at the plate and fined players who swung at first pitches. And he simply hated to lose; it was said that he once came home furious after a loss, and his wife said; "Don't worry dear, you've still got me." Chance answered, "I know, but there were times this afternoon when I'd have traded you for a base hit."[20]

With Chance taking firm control of the new additions to weld them into a unit, the season began. Chance had already established the batting order that he would maintain during the entire season and in the World Series. First came the three out-fielders, center, left, and right; then Chance himself in the cleanup spot, followed by the rest of the infield, third, short, and second; then catcher Kling and the pitcher of the day.

The first few weeks of the season, which opened in mid-April, saw the Cubs floundering in fourth and fifth in the tightly bunched breakaway from the starting gate, then riding a 10-game win streak to take first, and then meeting apparent disaster in their first encounter—at home—with the Giants, whom everyone recognized as the chief contender for the National League pennant. Huge crowds mobbed the entry gates for the opener of the four-game series, and starting time was delayed an hour until special police reinforcements could be rounded up. The Cubs took the first one, 10–3, but were shellacked in the next three by John McGraw's New Yorkers, who would become their classic rivals over the next few years.

That being the case, the Cubs' first eastern trip on June 5 became the turning point of the year. In New York, as in Chicago, crowds swarmed to the park and packed it to bursting, but the hometown rooters would leave with their spirits drooping. The opening game was won by the Cubs 6–0 behind Three Finger Brown. On the next day, the pounding continued with an 8–2 win for Chicago. And on the third, an incredible 19–0 shutout, reminiscent of the huge scores of premodern baseball, was posted by the Cubs, who once more knocked out the formidable Christy Mathewson early and continued their relentless assault until the final out.

It didn't matter that the Giants won the next day's game 7–3, or that the record of the two teams against each other now stood at 4–4. The Cubs were indisputably in charge the rest of the way. According to the *Tribune*'s October 8 season summary the recruits whom Murphy had acquired for Chance "put his team so far out ahead that interest in the contest as a race was lost."

That memory was why Cub fans were not downhearted as Game Two of the Series approached.

3

Game Two and the Tools of Baseball

For those traveling to see Game Two at the White Sox park at 39th Street and Princeton Avenue, the trip was not much different from the first day's, and involved going only a few stations further on the same elevated and streetcar lines. Although the ethnicities of the neighborhood residents differed, the surroundings of both teams' grandstands were much the same—the homes, shops, and customary gathering places of working-class families constituted the urban turf that was neither slum nor snooty, the place fit to play a city game.

The weather was unluckily worse than the opening day's—a subfreezing 30 degrees at 5:00 A.M. and not expected to go more than a few degrees higher. It didn't. Some of the players, according to the *Inter-Ocean*'s writer covering the game, were complaining about what their purple and numb hands were doing to the quality of their performances. They wanted a postponement. There were murmurs among impatient advance-ticket holders that the true motive was to wait for bigger crowds on a kinder day, which would swell the players' share of the purse. True or not, the weather was likely to blame for an unusual number of errors, passed balls, and hit batsmen by both teams.

The White Sox' playing field itself looked like the home of newly arrived poor relations, which is what both the White Sox and the American League were in the eyes of the National League. The park had been opened in 1893 in time for the world's fair for a professional cricket team known as the Chicago Wanderers, who played and drew their audience from recent immigrants from the British Isles. There were not enough of these to make the Wanderers a success, however, and by 1900 the grounds were no more than a bumpy abandoned lot strewn with junk. Yet Comiskey spotted the place as a choice location. To begin with, the Cubs had been able to impose, as a condition of admitting a new team to the city, that its stadium should be located no farther north than 35th Street, and the Wanderers' field was only a convenient few blocks south of that designated boundary of the Cubs' reserved market area. Besides, it was close to public transportation, and the surrounding, heavily Irish neighborhood promised a starting fan base. Within a few blocks were St. George's Parish Church, several pubs, and a Hibernian youth club, and these made Comiskey's decision not merely wise but inspired. Generations of Chicago's Irish would enrich the labor force, the police and fire departments, the political armies of the Democratic Party, the hierarchy of the American Catholic Church, the American language, and American popular culture, most notably baseball. The South Side Irish became ardent and unshakable White Sox fans. The park stood in the territory made famous by the popular Chicago newspaper columnist of the era, Finley Peter Dunne, and his fictional philosopher-barkeep, Martin Dooley, who commented in heavy brogue and with wonderfully wry wit on current events, and eventually found a national audience. Dunne himself had done a brief stint as a baseball reporter for the city's *Daily News* in 1887. James T. Farrell, the best-known social portraitist of the area in the period around World War I and the 1920s (in the Studs Lonigan trilogy and various other successful novels) recalled living and dying by the White Sox scores in his adolescence. In time, other ethnic tribes would move in and later supplant the South Side Irish, but many of them and their writers inherited the local rough-hewn, blue-collar Sox loyalties.

In 1910 Comiskey moved the team to a larger, modern steel-and-concrete stadium that he had built at 35th and Shields, only a few blocks away from the first White Sox home. That particular Comiskey Park stood for eighty-one years until, dilapidated and unsafe, it was replaced by a newer stadium (now renamed U.S. Cellular Field) literally across the street from it. "Commie" sold the old pre-1910 park to John Schorling, a South Side tavern owner who was the president of the Chicago American Giants of the Negro League, for his team's use. The post-1919 mass migration of southern blacks to Chicago eventually changed the racial complexion of the South Side, and for years thousands flocked to see excellent black baseball played in the first and original White Sox home. The Negro League folded around 1950 as the result of the long-delayed integration of major-league baseball in 1947. Then the old place that had echoed the cheers of 1906 was torn down and replaced with low-income housing, and a chapter of the South Side's history closed.

In 1900, Comiskey's first task after cleaning up, leveling, and seeding the deserted cricket field (a job in which he sometimes joined with his own hands) was to create seating. The First National Bank of Chicago lent him the money for an enclosed wooden grandstand extending from first to third base, the roof supported by whitewashed posts. The dimensions made it a tough place for right-handed hitters: the left-field foul line was 355 feet long, left center was 400 feet from home plate, and center field was a deep 450 feet (but only when not accommodating standees). The distance to the right-field fence seems to have disappeared from available records, but given the fact that the White Sox' regular-season lineup featured four left-handed hitters (and one who batted from either side of the plate), it seems likely that it was at least as short as and possibly shorter than the left-field line. The stands could hold fewer than 5,000 spectators when the White Sox played their maiden game there in April of 1900. Two years later, a bleacher section circling the outfield was added. It is recorded (but open to doubt) that for a game on October 2, 1904, 30,084 fans were wedged in, standees included.[1]

On this second day of the World Series, only 12,595 would show up to shiver bravely. One feature of the park particularly galling to the sportswriters was the location of the press box, fully exposed on the roof of the grandstand. Unlike the audience, they could not easily muffle and glove themselves, because their hands had to be free for the keyboards of their bulky rented standard typewriters. They did not fail to make the frigid conditions a leitmotif of their stories. "More overcoats, more rugs, more blankets, [and] more flasks were apparent" among the crowd, said one reporter, "and also more chill" from "the howling northwester which swept across the bleak inclosure." The *Daily News*'s man reported that the din created by cowbells, sleigh bells, clappers, and all manner of whistles was augmented by continuous cheering from the stands because "it ws necessary to keep in motion . . . to protect one's tongue from freezing." Charles Dryden, on hand for the *Tribune,* put it in a jaunty style that had already earned him national recognition. "The little comfort that might have been abstracted from the glowing booze signs on the back fence" was lost behind a wall of standees in the top rows, "looking desperately for a ray of sunshine. A polar bear confined in the warmest part of the works would have asked for a fire for his den." Dryden also reported an "unusually heavy advance sale of third rail wienerwurst" (whatever the adjective meant), spurred by a report that neither "bottled goods" nor hot drinks would be available that day. "The redhots warmed with mustard saved many a life," he wrote. But there was plenty of now traditional ballpark fare on hand: hot dogs, peanuts, Cracker Jack (invented in 1893), ice cream, and sodas, sold by vendors already working for the king of concessionaires, Harry Stevens.

But Dryden took particular note of the plight of the journalists. "Up on the lid of Mr. Comiskey's grand stand," he recorded, "the muck rakers turned blue and purple and mottled." Despite the key role of the press in popularizing the game, baseball's owners were slow to recognize the "scribes," as they sometimes called themselves, and furnish them with decent working conditions. Some parks had no press sections at all, and some deliberately tried to exclude writers whose criticisms stung the club's management, so the open-air coop provided in South Side Park was possibly as good as accommodations got in 1906. So general were the rotten conditions that two years later, in self-defense, the *Tribune*'s Hugh Fullerton led in founding the Baseball Writers of America, a kind of proto-union. Subsequently, Comiskey and fellow owners became more aware of the need to cultivate good press relations.[2]

Fullerton was one of three bylined *Tribune* baseball reporters covering the Series, though he seems to have published no play-by-play reports. His pre-Series analysis had run on the preceding Sunday; another piece that daringly predicted a White Sox victory was supposed to have been spiked by the editors as too unlikely. The other two reporters, who filed daily stories that, taken together, provide a fine running account of the entire Series, were Charles Dryden and Irving "Sy" Sanborn. They were a distinct contrast in styles. Dryden, sometimes called "The Mark Twain of Baseball," came from Monmouth, Illinois, and did not have more than a grade-school education. He worked as an iron molder, then shipped out to sea for a while, and came to rest in San Francisco in the 1890s working for William Randolph Hearst's racy "yellow" *Examiner,* covering baseball in the Pacific Coast League. His career continued in New York for Hearst's *American* and then the *World,* owned by Hearst's major rival, Joseph Pulitzer. His racy, witty, individualistic style, spread further by syndication, brought him national fame, and in 1905 Hearst lured him to Chicago for the *Examiner,* from which, at age forty-six, he moved over to the *Tribune* a year later.[3]

Sanborn, by contrast, began his career with a strong academic orientation. Born in Vermont, he was preparing for a career as a college professor, and was graduated from Dartmouth in 1889, Phi Beta Kappa. But while waiting to take his first teaching post, he took a temporary job with the Springfield, Massachusetts, *Union* and began to cover local baseball and college football games. He liked it so well that he became a sportswriter. He worked for the *Union* for eleven years, and in the winter doubled as a theater critic. When the American League put the White Sox into Chicago in 1900, the *Tribune* reached out and hired Sanborn to complement its staff.[4]

The *Daily News* and *Record-Herald* likewise had full daily coverage, from unidentified writers, possibly Charles Hughes and James Gilruth. Both were midwestern young men, Hughes from Michigan and Gilruth from Iowa. Both were college educated; both came by stages to Chicago, the great magnet for aspiring youngsters of their kind; and both probably worked for something around the $25 a week that was the average for reporters at the time. Fullerton, an Ohioan who briefly attended the state university before entering journalism, fit that pattern.[5]

If any of the cold customers awaiting the game's first pitch looked for distraction (not already provided by the crowd's antics) in the pages of a local paper, they would have found sketches from the life of a major American city early in the new twentieth century, while the nineteenth was still a lingering presence. On that October morning the *Record-Herald* recorded the passing, at age ninety-three, of James A. Glidden at his home in DeKalb, Illinois. In the late 1860s Glidden had invented barbed wire, which made it possible to build livestock enclosures on the treeless Great Plains and so fed the explosive growth in cattle raising west of the Mississippi, which in turn helped the United States to become rich and powerful through agricultural exports. His life story was a reminder of how swiftly the saga of American growth had unfolded. He was born when the nation was barely out of its infancy and many of the Founding Fathers were still alive, when nine out of ten Americans lived on farms, when the steamboat was a novelty and the railroad nonexistent, and when there was no such thing as a "spectator sport." Now he slipped away quietly in an era of electric lights, telephones, automobiles, and even (since 1903) powered flight, on the second day of a World Series between teams of uniformed, grown men paid to play a boys' pastime and raptly followed by newspaper readers in a continentwide America with a population of over 85 million. All that change had taken place in a single lifetime. On the same note, an item two days earlier had taken note of a downstate reunion of veterans of the Mexican War, which ended in 1848. And Civil War veterans, then only in their sixties, were commonplace—some probably in the stands.

Other front-page stories were clues to the spirit of the times. The National Purity League was gamely continuing its meeting in the heart of enemy territory, the wicked big city, with the Reverend John Balcom warning that "the average department-store girl," that is, one of the thousands of women emerging from the home to the urban workplace, was "doomed morally." The city council, attempting to carry on business as usual amid the hoopla, voted to impose fines aggregating $485 on a number of violators of an ordinance hopelessly trying to restrict chimney smoke emissions. The Pennsylvania Railroad announced plans for a new terminal in the heart of the Loop, one more palatial and reverential stable for the "iron horse" that raced and snorted through old barriers of time and space. In national politics there was an upcoming New York State gubernatorial race featuring William Randolph Hearst, the chain newspaper czar, trying to parlay his fortune into a political offfice, just as his mining-millionaire father had done in getting himself elected a senator from California some years earlier. The leading foreign news report was that the U.S. secretary of war was leaving Havana after a visit to check on progress in quelling an "insurgency" against a Cuban government that was only theoretically independent. We had helped the Cubans "liberate" themselves from Spain in 1898 but reserved the right to intervene at any time to "protect" the island from "disorder."

In other national news, there was a celebrity divorce (the daughter of stage star Lillian Russell was the aggrieved wife), a New York City brokerage house failure, a strike of Wall Street telegraph messengers, and a murder-suicide in a Cleveland suburb. There, a young man rejected by a schoolteacher had shot her to death in her classroom, then killed himself. Bad news and gossip were the bread and butter of the mass-audience press, and stories involving blood, money, and sex were already likely to lead.

Pro baseball, as played in the era of President Theodore Roosevelt, existed in the midst of this mood of confidence, nervous energy, old values morphing (not without a contest) into new ones, sensation, and crowd ritual. That atmosphere did not necessarily affect the game between the foul lines, but it colored every aspect of the way it was showcased.

As game time approached, the constant hubbub of the crowd increased—some of it ragging between fans of the two teams, some of it pragmatically concerned with making and recording bets, some of it from an irrepressible beater of a large gong, and some from the previous day's cornetist, who was trying to play "Wait Till the Sun Shines, Nellie" through frozen lips. The Cubs finally arrrived, this day being their turn to dress at the Victoria Hotel and proceed to the park in open carriages. As they trotted out for their pregame warm-ups they now wore their road grays, including gray stockings and "undersweaters" beneath the jerseys that carried CHICAGO in block letters across the front and a smaller Chicago logo on the breast pocket. The White Sox had switched from their dark blue traveling outfits into whites, including solid white stockings, jerseys with a folded collar and buttons down the front, caps with blue-piped seams, and a tastefully fancy C on the left breast pocket.[6]

The uniforms were of heavy-duty flannel, and the stockings of wool, for which on this day the players, some already sweatered underneath, were undoubtedly grateful. But such uniforms must have been hell on an August afternoon with the on-field temperatures in the nineties. Being rugged, however, was part of expected male behavior, and playing baseball was publicly taken to be a "manly" exercise. Uniforms themselves carried a hint of soldierly virtues, and baseball's rulers made sure that they were not frivolous. Amateur teams could give free rein to their fancy in jersey colors, but the major leagues settled into what would be a standard mold right through the 1970s: solid or pin-striped white and gray to distinguish home standers from visitors. The look fit comfortably with the solemnity of the male bourgeois costume of the cities: solid-color suits in dark brown, gray, or navy. In 1882 Spalding had tried to get the National League to award him the exclusive contract for mandatory uniforms to be worn by all the league's teams. Each club would have a different stocking color, but players for all of them would wear identical color combinations by position—all pitchers with baby blue shirts, all catchers in scarlet, and so on through a rainbow palette. Luckily the idea was dropped after a season.[7] Not until the 1970s, when Oakland Athletics owner Charles Finley briefly arrayed his cohorts, like fruit flies, in shiny green and gold, was there a serious (and short-lived) effort to colorize the game. But after a hiatus, shirts in somewhat more subdued hues made a comeback and are now commonplace.

In any case, comfort was not one of the expected attributes of the uniforms. They were utilitarian—the outer jerseys, still collared, with half-or three-quarter-length sleeves allowing more free play to the arms, and the pants buckled under the knee over the heavy socks to protect the legs when sliding. If players lost pounds of weight on a day in which they perspired freely (and how the locker rooms smelled when daily laundering of uniforms wasn't customary is best left to the imagination), midsummer spectators could not have been terribly comfortable either. Men commonly still wore long underwear year-round, switching from wool or flannel to cotton only in the hottest weather. Over it they put long-sleeved and stiff-collared shirts and ties, then the dark woolen jackets and trousers. Light-colored linen suits were worn only in the South. Straw hats were a permitted concession to summer, but the complete outfit was mandatory for all social occasions, baseball games included. Women wore dark stockings, cotton or silk bloomers, chemises, and petticoats under long skirts and opaque shirtwaists. For adults, decorum far outranked comfort in matters of dress. Only very young children were allowed short pants and one-piece knee-length dresses.

Although the twentieth-century drift toward informality and individualism was already under way, what with jazz, ragtime, and slang becoming steadily more acceptable in music halls and newspapers, in 1906 "correct attire," strictly defined, was still expected of spectators at a public event such as a ball game, especially when ready-made clothing made it possible even for people in the 25-cent seats to "dress up" like those with higher incomes and social standing. For players, team uniforms sent a message of group identity suitable to a more highly organized society. Individual achievement was recognized, of course. Spectators cheered their particular favorites, and became especially excited when a star pitcher and an outstanding hitter were pitted against each other in the individual duel that sets a baseball play in motion. But the recognition of individuality had not yet reached the level of putting names on uniforms. That did not happen until the 1960s. In fact, in 1906 there were not even numbers on the jerseys that could be shown on the hand-operated scoreboards and matched to players listed on scorecards. Those in the stands within hearing range of the field were told by megaphone the name of each batter as he stepped into the box. Electric amplification in the form of PA systems was not introduced until 1929.

The game finally began as the White Sox "in their white stay-at-home pajamas" trotted out to their defensive positions, and the Cubs "in their gray fighting clothes" prepared to go to bat. Jones had elected left-hander Guy White, with his 18 wins and league-leading ERA of 1.52, to try to duplicate Altrock's opening-day feat. White was something special among ballplayers—a onetime practicing dentist in the District of Columbia in the off-season. He was easily recognized by his tall, skinny frame and universally referred to as "Doc." He sent his first pitch whistling down the middle for a called strike on Art Hofman. Another strike, and then the Cubs' leadoff hitter lifted a fly to Jones in center. Jimmy Sheckard bounced to first baseman Donahue, and when Rohe snared "Wildfire" Schulte's grounder at third and threw him out snappily, the crowd's cheers were especially lusty because, like Altrock, Rohe was a hero of the first game. His triple had led to the initial White Sox run that proved the margin of victory.

Reulbach now went to the hill, took his warm-up tosses, and got Sox right fielder Ed Hahn to ground out. Manager Fielder Jones stepped in next, but as he took his place at the plate, the Sox players on the bench suddenly rose and moved toward him in a body, carrying something in a large sack. It proved to be a complete silver service in a polished wooden chest, their gift to the man who had guided them to the league championship by his own work in the field and by deftly splicing, patching, and handling a lineup frequently punctured by injuries to key personnel. The crowd cheered; Jones acknowledged the tribute briefly and watched his present taken back to the bench. It was the high point of the White Sox' afternoon. Jones then also grounded out, and Isbell hit a shot straight back to Reulbach for a quick end to inning one.

It appeared that another close battle of pitchers was in the making, but the Cubs quickly put an end to that illusion. Doc White struck out Chance, which brought Steinfeldt, the Cubs' premier slugger, to the plate. Two strikes down in the count, he rifled a single to short left. Tinker followed with a perfect bunt that he beat out for an infield hit, putting Cubs on first and second with one down. Now White got little Johnny Evers to hit a weak grounder to second for a certain force-out and possible double play, but here, fate and numb fingers intervened. Isbell scooped up the ball and tried to make a backhand flip to Tannehill, covering second. The off-target throw went spinning into the outfield, and by the time it was recovered and thrown in, Steinfeldt had come around to score and Evers and Tinker were on second and third. Kling was walked to load the bases and bring the weak-hitting pitcher to bat. But Reulbach played the part of patsy at the plate too well. His roller to Isbell was so slow that by the time the White Sox second baseman had gloved it, Tinker was home with the second Cub run, Evers and Kling had each moved up a base, and the only play was to retire Reulbach at first. Hofman singled to score Evers, but the Sox snuffed out the rally when Kling, on the same play, raced homeward trying to score from first and was cut down at the plate by Donahue's perfect relay of the throw from the outfield.

In half an inning the Cubs had tripled the previous day's run production, and it would turn out to be more than Reulbach needed. From then on, the banker's son and college star, in the words of reporter Charles Dryden, "choked them off with two hits and one smokeless run." It was far from a perfect game—Reulbach walked six, hit one batsman, gave up one wild pitch, and kept Kling scrambling for several others that kicked up the dirt around the plate. Luckily for Reulbach, the batters he faced often helped by swinging at balls out of the strike zone. But wandering pitches and impatient cuts at bad ones could be blamed on the relentless frigidity. The normally solid-fielding White Sox made two errors, catcher Sullivan allowed a passed ball and their two pitchers also were guilty of a hit batter and five walks. The Cubs also had two fielding lapses, and Reulbach added another wild pitch. As the innings wound along, the cornetist referred to jovially as "Signor Cornetti," whose real name according to one reporter's account was Dan Wall,[8] kept trying, through blue lips, to cheer the crowd with hopeful repetitions of "Wait Till the Sun Shines, Nellie," but nothing helped—not even more choruses of "So Long, Murphy" from Sox rooters. It was, on the whole, a weary afternoon for White Sox supporters, who had only a few chances to cheer. The first came in the fourth, when, with nobody out, the home team got its first hit, a sizzling grounder to the right off the bat of Jones that Evers raced over to cut off but managed only to kick into the crowd along the right-field foul line as he tried to grab it. It went as a ground-rule double. Isbell's ground ball out sent Jones racing to third. Now Rohe drove an apparent sacrifice fly to Sheckard in left. But when Jones tagged up and took off, Sheckard, in one of the fielding gems that helped to offset the day's muffs and bobbles, fired a bullet to Kling that made Jones the second out in a double play, making it the turn of Cubs fans to exult.

By then, however, the White Sox were already deeper in the hole because in the top of the third the Cubs had tacked on another run on a one-out walk, a passed ball, an error, and a single. With Tinker at bat, "Steinie" tried to steal, but catcher Sullivan, whose .974 fielding average had led the American League during 1906, atoned for his previous lapse with a dead-on throw that caught him for the third out.

That did it for Doc White. He was slated to bat second in the bottom of the third, but after Tannehill grounded out Evers to Chance, Jones sent up in his place a left-handed batter,[9] reserve catcher Jay "Babe" Towne, whose .278 average put him high on the hitless wonders' list of good pinch hitters. However, Towne only flied out to center, and Reulbach put away Hahn for the second time on an infield grounder.

White had given up four runs on four hits in his three innings of work, walking two and striking out one. His replacement, Frank "Yip" Owen, was the man with the most wins on Jones's pitching staff, 22, against 13 losses, though his 2.33 ERA was only fourth, behind White's, Walsh's, and Altrock's. The opinion of the *Tribune* press corps was that he had a good mix of "speedy and slow curves" and was a good fielder at his position, and Sullivan was on record as agreeing that he threw harder than fans realized. For a while it looked as if he might save the day. He began shakily, giving up a walk and a double that confronted him with the dilemma of one out and men on second and third. But he bore down on Reulbach and Hofman, got a strikeout and a fly out, and escaped without damage. In the fifth, he set down the Cubs one–two–three.

The bottom of the fifth brought a gleam of hope for the Sox. Reulbach walked Jiggs Donahue, his first batter, got left fielder Dougherty to force out Donahue, but then threw a wild pitch that allowed Dougherty, who had safely reached first on the fielder's choice, to dash into scoring position. After Reulbach had gotten light-hitting Sox catcher Billy Sullivan to foul out, the Cubs made their second error of the inning when Tannehill's grounder went through Joe Tinker's chilled hands, and Dougherty, running full tilt, scored easily as "pandemonium broke loose among the Sox fans." Owen then stepped in and flied to Jimmy Sheckard. One lone, unearned run on one error. Still, it cut the deficit to three runs with four innings yet to play. The game seemed still to hang in the balance.

As always at a ballpark, the theater in the stands became part of the day's memories. Cops broke up a fistfight between two fans. The clanging of the rooter who had brought a giant gong tended to drown out not only rival noisemakers and the game cornet player's serenades, which now included "You're a Grand Old Flag," but also the hopeful foot stamping on the wooden stands, undertaken as much for warmth as to show support. Cub outfielders Sheckard and Hofman brought laughter with an impromptu game of tag to keep themselves warm. World Series baseball was earnest—but still fun.

Not fun was a potential tragedy when a foul ball lined into the grandstand "struck a woman who was sitting in one of the boxes full on the cheek." The crowd leaped up with a collective gasp, but the woman laughed it off, announced that she was not hurt, and even refused to be relocated from her place "just outside the wire netting" that was already used to protect spectators in the area behind home plate.

Protective gear for the players as well was reaching its modern form. When catchers Sullivan and Kling took their positions behind the plate they were wearing masks, which had first been donned in the 1880s, when a rule change said that a third strike must be taken by the catcher on the fly, not on the bounce, in order for the out to be registered. Catchers could no longer stand well behind the plate; they had to move up and crouch vulnerably behind the hitter. The rest of the catcher's body was unprotected, however, and enough bruises and broken ribs were accumulated by 1885 to inspire the wearing of an inflated rubber chest protector. The same went for the umpire. The catcher still was likely to take a hard straight-down shot off his leg, but shin guards were not part of his equipment until Roger Bresnahan, of the New York Giants, had a pair made for him in 1908, and his example was soon followed by the rest of organized baseball's receivers.

The mask was not one of today's space-age one-piece helmets. Spalding & Brothers sold equipment to amateur players by catalog, and the 1908 edition pictured what appeared to be the company's best mask, going for $4, with three transverse wires (advertised as made of "finest steel, extra-heavy black finish") below cheekbone level, and a vertical parallelogram of wire from nose to forehead. The rim was horsehair padded, but thinly so, and a ball fouled straight back to the face must have left the poor catcher's ears ringing. An elastic band held the mask to the face but allowed for it to be quickly discarded with an upward jerk from the chin when the catcher needed to ditch it quickly. One of the tricks of earlier-era catchers had been to trip up a batter starting for first by "dropping" the mask right in his path, but that was now outlawed and it had to be tossed clearly out of the playing area. Umpires had only recently stopped using long-handled brooms to clean the plate and then leaving them where they were also a hazard. Whisk brooms were the replacement.

Some of the chest protectors sold in the 1908 Spalding catalog at $8 apiece narrowed at the bottom, leaving a flap hanging down between the thighs. "Athletic supporters" were listed, but the "protective cups" of modern male athletes were not in evidence, and it is a reasonable guess that the dangling flap was intended to protect a catcher's most vulnerable area.

Catcher's mitts were no longer a novelty and, like the modern ones, had a fairly deep center pocket and separation only between the thumb and the rest of the fingers—hence, "mitts" (from mittens) rather than gloves. The first baseman, who would receive many hard throws in the course of the game, likewise wore a somewhat thinner mitt, with its edge "stiffened with sole leather," since, like the catcher, he would need to scoop an occasional low toss out of the dirt and the plentiful sharp pebbles of those early parks. The first baseman's cowhide or calfskin mitt allowed for a little more thumb separation, and its pocket was not so deep. The other fielders' gloves were thinner than the modern versions, fastened at the back of the wrist with strap and buckle, and had two leather straps joining the thumb and forefinger.

Gloves were still evolving. Not worn at all in the very early days, they were considered sissy by pioneer players, who prided themselves on how many broken fingers they had not only survived but ignored as they played through the pain. However, as hard line drives into bare hands meant more errors as well as bruised palms, common sense brought gloves into universal use. Post-1890s rule changes limited fielding gloves to no more than 14 inches in circumference and 10 ounces in weight, but first baseman's and catcher's mitts were unrestricted in size. Increasing requirements for the protection of fielders were part of a general movement toward workplace safety based on economic as well as humane considerations. A player benched by injury was not only a handicap to the team, but a skilled employee whose salary came out of the owner's pocket even though he was idle.

Bats seem to have settled into the form they would keep for a long time. They lingered in a twilight zone between handcrafted and mass-produced tools. Players who could afford it could order them tailored to taste from mass manufacturers like Hillerich and Bradby, founded in Louisville in 1883, because while bats can be turned on powered lathes from balks of ash or hickory by the thousands, it is a simple matter to stop the line and adjust the dimensions for a special request. The only limitations imposed by 1906 rules, still unchanged, were that they should be round, 2¾ inches in diameter at the thickest point, and no longer than 42 inches. Those used by the Cubs and Sox in their World Series were generally heavy—36 or more ounces—and thicker through the handle than today's. Hitters in 1906 generally separated their hands on the bat, shortened up, and tried to "place" hits out of the range of fielders rather than swing for distance.

The ball was another story. Since 1876 games had been conducted with an "Official National League" ball, neatly boxed and available to single buyers at $1.25. (The American League would follow with its own "official ball" shortly after its birth.) It consisted of a rubber center around which wool yarn was tightly wound, and the whole contrivance was held together then as now by two figure-eight-shaped pieces of leather hand-sewn together. Its dimensions were fixed at 9 to 9½ inches in circumference and 5 to 5¼ ounces in weight—where they remain.

In the Adam-and-Eve beginning days of the game, balls were homemade and uneven in quality as well as in dimensions, and it was only in 1866 that, according to the father of baseball writing, Henry Chadwick, a "small factory in New England commenced the manufacture of Base Balls as a regular article of merchandise." Other ball-making shops sprang up, and each team tried to have a local source that would produce balls that played to its strengths. It was the home team's responsibility to furnish the ball, and if it was strong on defense, "a soft dead ball would be furnished and perhaps the life pounded out of it with a mallet before the game commenced," in order to neutralize the batting power of the opponent. If the home team featured power hitters, however, "a very hard lively ball would be furnished" and, Chadwick wrote in later years, sometimes even baked just before game time "to increase its liveliness." This produced somewhat uneven results; a team on the road might score 24 runs one day and only two the next, deepening suspicions that the games were rigged. Then along came the National League, which was led, according to Chadwick (who was close to the pillars of its early establishment in their battle to give baseball respectability), by "those who had the best interest of the game at heart." So in order to "save and perpetuate Base Ball in its integrity," the league prepared specifications which required that all balls "should be made *exactly alike* and put up in sealed boxes, each ball first having been certified by a League official. This decision came at the end of 1877, bids were submitted, and although there was 'spirited competition,' the contract was awarded to A. G. Spalding & Brothers of Chicago."[10] Since the league president was Spalding's friend and mentor William Hulbert, and Spalding would eventually fill the office himself, and the story appeared in the Spalding-published annual *Official Guide to Baseball for 1907,* a little skepticism is in order about the "spirited competition," but the end result, in any event, was a boost for the fortunes of A. G. Spalding & Brothers, and an undoubted improvement in the prospects of teams on the road.

The standardization of equipment increased the possibility of accurate comparable statistics, which baseball produces and fans consume so profusely. Precise comparisons are still far from being perfect because, as Bill James and other statisticians of the Society for American Baseball Research are quick to let us know, variations in ballparks (among other things) still pose a challenge when arguing over which players had the best pitching and batting records. Such arguments, especially in the dreary winter months of baseball deprivation, are part of the mysterious allure of the game for many of its devotees.

Standardizing the sizes of bat, ball, and glove was part of that constantly ongoing balancing of defensive and offensive power and differing abilities that has made the game fascinating over its life span of a little more than a century and a half. For the batter, simply making contact is itself a heroic feat because it is so hard to hit, with a round stick, a spinning, dipping, swerving, and very small ball that flashes before him for a fraction of a second. The moment that he does hit the ball into fair territory, he rushes into a footrace on the base paths against the arm of a fielder who first has to stop a ball traveling at bulletlike speed and then whip it to the base ahead of the runner. That requires the strength of a javelin thrower combined with the accuracy of a darts champion—but not as much pinpoint accuracy as the pitcher needs to get the ball into the strike zone with "something on it." Perhaps the display of these traditional skills—hitting, intercepting, throwing, and running—once useful in the hunt and in battle stirs some buried folk memories in lovers of baseball and other athletic contests as well. Perhaps such instinctive reactions, as well as tribal loyalties and familiar ritual, brought the throngs out to stamp, yell, sing, and shiver on those October afternoons in 1906. Not all passions can be explained by items that show up in box scores.

Loyalty kept the Sox fans in the stands through the first five innings, but a trickle of exodus by the fainthearted or freezing began to flow when the Cubs widened the gap in the top of the sixth. Steinfeldt opened it with his third straight hit, a hard single to left. Tinker's overenthusiastic bunt toward the pitcher was grabbed by Owen in time for him to force Steinie at second. Chance now signaled for a hit-and-run play, which worked as neatly as a class demonstration. As Owen went into his motion to pitch to Johnny Evers at the plate, Tinker broke for second. Shortstop Tannehill ran to cover, and Evers deftly punched a single through the vacated spot, though it was retrieved quickly enough to hold Tinker at second. With Kling up, Chance once more took advantage of his club's speed and ordered a double steal. Catcher Sullivan reacted quickly and fired Owen's pitch toward third, but the too-short throw bounced over Rohe's head and into the crowd for a ground-rule double. That automatically put Evers on third and sent Tinker home with run number five for the Cubs. Owen put out the fire by retiring Kling and Reulbach, but the tall Cub pitcher now had full command of the situation when his turn on the mound came again. He walked Hahn to start the Sox sixth, but when Hahn attempted to steal, Kling gunned him down, and Jones and Isbell quickly fanned and grounded out to end the inning. More people were leaving now, and the writers, looking for color, were reduced to commenting on such irrelevancies as the presence once again of Nick Altrock's father, a former grounds-keeper for the Cincinnati Reds, whose handsome white beard, easily visible from his prominent seat, was compared to a built-in neck warmer.

There was a brief flurry of hope for the South Siders when they got their first two batters on base in their half of the seventh on a walk and a single, but Reulbach steadied and stranded them there. Then the Cubs pounded two more nails into the coffin in their eighth. Chance got an infield hit on a ball to deep short and, after being sacrificed to second, promptly showed why he had led the National League with 59 steals in 1906 by dashing to third with Tinker at bat, deftly sliding around Rohe's tag on the throw from Sullivan. Tinker cracked a single, scoring Chance. Then Tinker added to the misery of the White Sox battery by stealing second. Owen was rattled—and cold. He started to walk Kling intentionally to get to the pitcher, but his fourth ball was a wild pitch that rolled far away from Sullivan, so Kling went on past first to second while Tinker came around to score. Only then did Owen get the chance to set Reulbach down on an easy bouncer to the mound.

The score stood 7–1 with but one inning left to play, and that was anticlimactic. The Cubs got one last base runner, a lead-off walk by Hofman, whom Sheckard sacrificed to second, but he perished there as Owen managed to dispose of Schulte on a grounder and Chance on a pop foul. When the White Sox came up for their last at bat a tiny spark flickered as Reulbach hit Rohe with his first pitch. But Donahue rapped a sharp grounder that Evers fielded just as Rohe was steaming past him toward second. Johnny tagged Rohe and threw to first to double up Donahue. Sullivan sent a fly out to right, and "Circus Solly" Hofman, so named either for being a team joker or for his daring catches, cut over from center to take the ball in front of Schulte and, with a grin of victory on his face, kept on running toward the infield.

The Series was even. The Cubs ran through the crowds of clutching rooters for both sides and got into their carriages for transportation back to town, grateful for the thought of dry, warm clothes and celebratory quaffing. The White Sox made the shorter trip back to their clubhouse, accepting consolation from their fans. The player-managers stopped to give the expected statements to the reporters. Jones's comment was "Don't worry; we will bag the series." Chance bragged, "We only delayed the real start one day; that's all. We are already in the home stretch."[11] No other participants or celebrities questioned had changed their minds.

Dryden's flip game summary in the next day's *Tribune* was concise and cruel: "Over in the stockyards district, where gentle deeds and smells are rare, the Cubs dragged the Sox around their own killing beds and slaughtered them to a finish."

Game Three loomed ahead. What would it prove? Would the Cubs continue to show that Game One had simply been a bad day? Would the White Sox, who had rebounded from defeat often during the season, do it again? What pitcher would each manager choose for the test? And not unimportantly, would the weatherman be more cooperative? Meditating on these suspenseful questions, Chicagoans went to their beds. It was now the turn of the White Sox fans to renew their own courage by thinking about the club's brief but bright history and its tangible assets.

4

The White Sox and the
Business of Baseball

If the early history of the Cubs takes place in the shadow of Albert Spalding, then the beginnings of the White Sox are even more inseparable from the biography of Charles Comiskey, and what lends extra fascination to the all-Chicago World Series is that both men, who got their starts as players, were so typical of Chicago's own turbulent story. Spalding, of German ancestry, came from a small town in an area of rural Illinois founded by westward-moving Yankees. He moved to the great inland metropolis and there made his fortune, like so many other members of Chicago's business aristocracy transplanted from the countryside. Comiskey was the Chicago-born son of an immigrant Irish politician of the kind who steadily pushed their way into civic power over the spirited resistance of settlers representing "old stock" values. Two more representative Chicagoans of their time and place would have been hard to find, and though Spalding was no longer active in baseball in 1906, while Comiskey was very much so, the Spalding aura hovering over the National League gave the city Series a slight flavor of cultural clash. Baseball has a teasing power to be simultaneously a game, a business, and a symbol.

Born in 1859, "Commy" was Spalding's junior by nine years, though both were of the generation that grew up in the flush times of the post–Civil War boom. His father was "Honest John" Comiskey, alderman of the Seventh Ward, a self-made success in the lumber and shipping trades, who took enthusiastically to the clan loyalties, the bargains, the gifts and favors conferred and re-paid, of urban politics in the age of city "bosses." His son Charlie found a future in another new game that also opened hospitable arms to Irish youngsters.

Comiskey learned to watch and then play baseball with one or more of the amateur clubs that performed in the still-open spaces in and around Chicago in the 1860s and 1870s. "Diamonds girdled the city," Comiskey's early biographer noted, and on those fields, colorfully named and caparisoned teams, some commercially spon-sored—the Libertys, Actives, Mutuals, Neversweats, Aetnas, Frank-lins and Pastimes—capered and perspired for admiring crowds.[1]

Comiskey, as he told reporter George Robbins of the *Chicago Daily News* in a long autobiographical interview in 1916, be-came an enraptured onlooker. "The sandlots of Chicago were my school," he said. He watched the local heroes and dreamed day and night of doing "some of the things that they did." Honest John, however, did not encourage such airy notions. Like many of his generation, he thought of semipro baseball as something played by "town boys," to wit, bums and loafers. He packed Charlie off to St. Mary's Academy in Kansas, a private Catholic high school where an older brother was already enrolled, to cure him of base-ballitis. The idea was to apprentice him thereafter to plumber Joe Hogan. But as Comiskey recalled later in life, "Leaks didn't appeal to me a bit." Neither did "a new world . . . of books and higher thought." But baseball was played on the academy's fields by other students, including his brother Jim and a new friend and mentor, Ted Sullivan. Charlie was soon joining in and honing his skills, a husky fifteen-year-old playing almost all the positions well.[2]

When Sullivan, who had admired the kid's potential, moved on to playing semipro in Iowa, he recommended his young friend to the owner of the Dubuque Alerts. Offered a spot as pitcher–first baseman, Charlie willingly signed on for $60 a month. When the team was not playing, he padded his income by working as a "news butcher" on the railroads, working his way up and down the swaying aisles selling papers, magazines, snacks, soft drinks, and tobacco. Soon word of his ability got around and he was enticed back to Elgin, Illinois, where the celebrated watch company sponsored a team. He hesitated to leave Dubuque because love had found him. He was going with Nan Kelly, whom he would marry in another couple of years, after he had become firmly established in the questionable new world of professional sport.

The next upward step was to St. Louis, where Dubuque had played an occasional exhibition game and Comiskey had been observed by Al Spink, the editor of the *Sporting News.* In 1881 Spink wrote the twenty-two-year-old first baseman with a proposition. Would he like to play for a St. Louis team in a new alliance of clubs in process of formation, to be called the American Association? A local businessman was the owner, and was offering $75 per month. Comiskey accepted, and thereby enlisted in the first of three business wars for the control of big-city baseball as a profit-making enterprise. All three wars would find him fighting the National League. They would culminate in his becoming one of the creators of the American League, just as Spalding was instrumental in the birth of the National—one more layer of coincidence that gave special significance to the contest of the teams to which their names would always be linked.

Like all successful businessmen in that era of the trusts, the owners of baseball teams marched to a steady beat toward rationality and consolidation—toward the elimination of competition, which was so highly regarded in public discourse as a democratic and capitalist virtue, and so relentlessly stamped out by combinations in thriving industries. Chicagoan William Hulbert and his fellow team owners who created the National League aimed to put their enterprises on a solid economic footing in three ways. First, they would avoid waste by agreeing to play, on a fixed schedule, exclusively against other league members, who would be admitted only when they could guarantee good box-office returns. There would be no more waste of money by expensive travel to places that could not furnish more than peanuts at the gate, meaning that small communities need not apply. Each member club, as is still true, would have exclusive rights to its market—no new league team could be chartered in its designated city without its permission. The league's second objective was to control costs, and especially salary costs, by reducing competition for star players among the owners—hence, agreements that players who left a National League team without finishing a contract period or getting the team's okay would not be hired by any other, and would be blacklisted. And third, since Hulbert and associates wanted a sustaining base in an upscale audience, there should be a universal minimum admission price (settled at 50 cents), and no effort should be spared to cloak the game with respectability, which in 1876 meant banning alcohol sales in the parks and Sunday games. Likewise, of course, any team that was involved in any kind of cheating would be expelled, with guilt or innocence to be determined solely by a jury of the other club owners.

The new league's directorate exercised its absolute jurisdiction freely in its start-up years. The original eight members were St. Louis, Louisville, Chicago, Cincinnati, Boston, Hartford, Philadelphia, and New York. By 1880, Philadelphia, Hartford, New York, Louisville, and Cincinnati had all been dumped for one reason or another, and other teams such as Worcester, Indianapolis, Troy, and Providence had been added. All were destined to lead temporary lives as National League members. It was in revolt against such high-handed overcontrol on the part of the original league's leaders that the movement for a new "association" to challenge the budding monopoly was begun. St. Louis was one of the cities involved in the rebellion.[3]

The local businessman-owner of St. Louis's entry in the American Association turned out to be the German-born owner of a restaurant and beer garden, Christopher Von der Ahe, a figure from an era of colorful business autocrats. Mustached, bulb-nosed, sporting loud clothes, and speaking with a thick Teutonic accent, he was the image of the stage "Dutchman" beloved by comedians of the 1880s. His team, the St. Louis Brown Stockings, was the ancestor of the present-day Cardinals, not the later American League St. Louis Browns, who were to become in modern times the Baltimore Orioles, who had once been—but no, it is better not to try to follow the pea-in-the-shell game of changing team names and locales in the early days; it is a confusing distraction from the main theme of how professional baseball was made a commercial success.

Von der Ahe's business and baseball interests ran in parallel, for one of the strategies of the American Association was to make the game more working-class friendly, not only by playing on Sunday (their only day of leisure) and charging only a quarter for seats (still an hour's pay for most workers) but by selling beer to the spectators. This had special audience appeal in cities with heavy populations of immigrants whose cultures did not embrace puritanical notions about the sanctity of the Sabbath and the perils of demon rum. All six of the association's original member cities—Louisville, Cincinnati, St. Louis, Pittsburgh, Baltimore, and Philadelphia—qualified.

Von der Ahe's temperament was a combination of jolly generosity and meddlesome ignorance. His genial side was on display in ways much appreciated by the players. Shortly after Comiskey arrived and started to put up big numbers for the Browns, Von der Ahe wordlessly began putting $125 instead of $75 into his monthly pay envelope. When the team drew well, he shared the

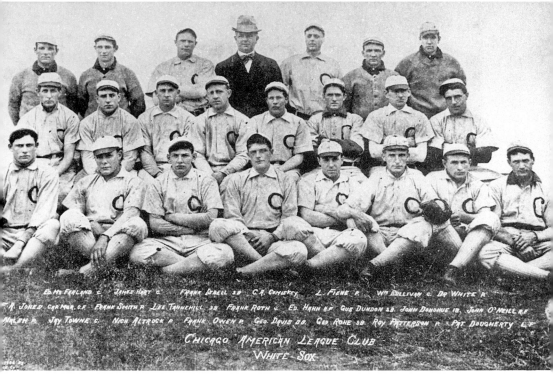

Ed. McFarland c.   James Hart c.   Frank Isbell 2b   C.A. Comiskey   L. Fiene p.   Wm Sullivan c.   Dr White p.
F.M. Jones Cap Mgr. C.F.   Frank Smith p.   Lee Tannehill 3b   Frank Roth c.   Ed. Hahn R.F   Gus Dundon 2b   John Donohue 1b   John O'Neill R.F.
Walsh p.   Jay Towne c.   Nick Altrock p.   Frank Owen p.   Geo Davis s.s.   Geo Rohe 3b   Roy Patterson p.   Pat Dougherty L.F

CHICAGO AMERICAN LEAGUE CLUB
WHITE SOX

The proud White Sox, winners of the 1906 American League pennant, pose for their conventional team shot. Not all of those shown were on the World Series roster, as is still the common practice. *Chicago Historical Society*

The refreshment vendor working the aisles was already part of the ballpark experience in 1906, but, like the spectators, he was more formally attired in jacket and hat. *Chicago Historical Society*

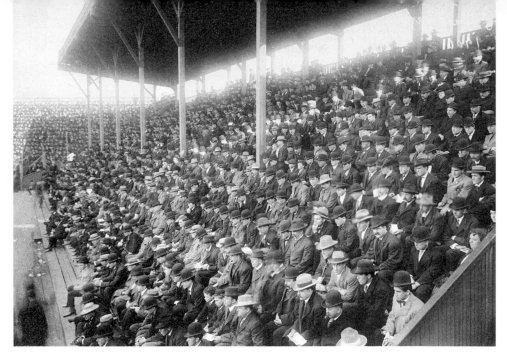

The thrills of the game were the same then as now—but Sunday best was worn in the stands, even on weekdays, adding needed respectability to leisure time at spectator sporting events. *Chicago Historical Society*

The view from the stands at South Side (White Sox) Park during a pregame warm-up that let the audience see their heroes at close range. *Chicago Historical Society*

Players sometimes posed
for "action" shots like
this one of Joe Tinker
and Johnny Evers,
which all the same
reflects the dynamic
quality of their double-
play performances.
Chicago Historical Society

Mordecai Brown, former
coal miner and future Hall
of Fame member, whose
crippled hand helped pitch
the Cubs into four World
Series and two world
championships. *Chicago
Historical Society*

The Cubs pose happily in their West Side home park. *Chicago Historical Society*

Unlucky Jack Pfiester warming up. A 20-game winner during the season, he lost two in the Series, proving the tantalizing unpredictability of baseball. *Chicago Historical Society*

Jolly Nick Altrock, the Cincinnati "Dutchman" whose clowning underscored the entertainment aspect of professional baseball but also masked the talent that handcuffed the Cubs in Game One. *Chicago Historical Society*

Baseball begins in winter thaws and ends in autumn chill, as White Sox shortstop George Davis's snugly buttoned practice sweater makes clear. *Chicago Historical Society*

Lined up for tickets at a Chicago ballpark in 1901, cheers (and shouted reports from the stands) were audible to those not yet admitted. Lucky young patrons in short pants might find a convenient knothole in the fence. *Chicago Historical Society*

Fielder Jones, White Sox player-manager, in pregame discussion with the umpires. Note that the indispensable press photographer nearby is modishly sporting a derby. *Chicago Historical Society*

Cubs skipper Frank Chance. Capless, he displays the swing that got him 1,272 career hits and the authority to be the "Peerless Leader" of his team. *Chicago Historical Society*

To bring the National Leaguers luck in Game Five—and make an appealing newspaper photograph—two genuine "cubs" from local zoos were taken on an involuntary pregame tour of the bases. *Chicago Historical Society*

Faster cameras and better reproduction techniques allowed millions of 1906 newspaper-reading fans to "see" exciting plays snapped at the moment of action. Here the waiting press photographers are lined up along the first baseline, while outfielder Jimmy Slagle, who was kept out of the Series by a late-season injury, stands nearby. *Chicago Historical Society*

Escorted women were encouraged to come to the parks, sometimes with specially reserved sections like the one shown, with chairs and narrow tables on which to deposit cloaks and other burdens— perhaps the forerunners of luxury boxes. *Chicago Historical Society*

wealth. He insisted on first-class train and hotel accommodations for his "poys" and gave unexpected presents to those who won a key game by outstanding performance. His malapropisms made him a figure of fun; he would, for example, describe a player who was frequently traded from team to team as "Dat rolling moss [who] will never catch up mit der stone." Less amusing was his innocent and wholly unfounded conviction that he understood the rules of the game. He would frequently challenge umpires or criticize his players incorrectly from his front-row seat, and he felt free to argue with his field manager.[4] That last habit was responsible for Comiskey's next upward step.[5] He had been gratified in 1883 when Von der Ahe hired his friend Ted Sullivan to manage the Browns. But the Dutchman interfered so frequently that Sullivan quit at the end of the season, and Comiskey was moved into the job. It was a big transition for him. "Responsibility taught me to become more serious, and I buckled down to study the great game as I had never studied it before."

Comiskey's promotion coincided with the temporary elevation of the American Association to big-league stature. During the 1882 season; players had followed the money, jumping back and forth between the National League and the American Association in response to competing bids just as if they lived in a free-market system instead of baseball's employer-controlled labor camp. Moreover, the new association was also threatening to outdraw the National League at the turnstiles, thanks to its triple offering to low-income patrons: cheap seats, Sunday ball, and beer. But there was still not enough of an audience for the two leagues to fight over without both of them suffering losses. Baseball operating under honest capitalist rules of competition appeared to be a losing, or at least a low-paying, proposition. So the owners did what businessmen in so many other areas were doing—they agreed to a pooling arrangement at the so-called Harmony Conference early in 1883, which also included representatives of the

tiny new Northwestern League.[6] The major understandings—
codified in the "National Agreement"—were, roughly, that the
existing leagues would confine their season schedules to games
among their own members, would honor the rights of teams in
the other leagues to "reserve" up to eleven players each (in a time
when most teams carried no more on their rosters), and would
not seek new franchises in territories served by teams of the other
leagues. With that settled, the rough outlines of "organized baseball," as its most thorough historian, Harold Seymour, notes, had
been sketched—"a galaxy of associated leagues and clubs operating under its own set of laws for the control of players and the
protection of territories."[7] With a truce in force between them,
the American Association and the National League agreed that
the winners of their respective championships should meet in a
postseason contest to determine who was king of the hill, nation-
ally speaking.

That was how Comiskey, as a player-manager, came to lead
the Browns not to a mere four consecutive championships of the
American Association from 1885 through 1888, but also to two
premodern "World Series" collisions with Cap Anson's White
Stockings, one of which he won for the "world" title. (The other
was ruled "undecided" on a technicality.)[8] It was his serious study
of strategies and his intelligent positioning and handling of fellow
infielders that brought handsome rewards. His salary of $6,000 in
1889 made him one of the game's highest-paid figures.

But the ink was barely dry on the 1883 National Agreement
when still another competitive challenge popped up. The agreement formally incorporated the "reserve clause" for the first time,
and that heated up an already simmering rebellion among the
players. Though the reserve system was presumably aimed at owners harboring foxy designs against fellow owners' chicken coops,
it was also an unabashed response to what all owners complained
of as ruinous salaries. What the clause said was simply that when
a team signed a player to his first contract, it could automatically
renew it the next year, which meant that he was untouchable by

other teams operating under the agreement except through "assignment" of the contract, that is, a trade. This froze him in place and left him no bargaining power even if the club reduced his salary, as it often did. His only choices were to accept renewal with his old team or not to play professional baseball at all.

Salaries were indeed rising to what owners called "unreasonable and ruinous proportions" in the 1880s, averaging between $1,500 and $2,500,[9] and payroll costs ate up half to two-thirds of operating expenses, leaving clubs only modest profits in the range of $20,000 to $50,000, sometimes more and sometimes depressingly (from the stockholders' viewpoint) less. Their view was that ballplayers' earnings were more than generous at a time when industrial workers' incomes for a full year (when they got to work a full year) lingered around $500. Many players did realize that they would have been earning no more than that if they hadn't been lucky enough to have the talent for big-league ball. But then as now they argued, with justice, that without them and their rare and valuable skills, there would be no quality game to draw paying crowds and so no profits at all. Unmoved, the owners in both leagues, in 1885, even adopted a salary cap—a "Limitation Agreement" of $2,000 a year—and then proceeded to violate it themselves by under-the-table payments to good players to keep them from exerting the only kind of pressure they could, holding out and refusing to play at all until they got a better deal—a costly and unpopular course that rarely worked. There is nothing new under baseball's sun.

In 1884 the disgruntled players found allies in a group of businessmen who resented being shut out of the sports market by the National Agreement, which was unmistakably a conspiracy in restraint of trade. Led by Henry V. Lucas, the St. Louis millionaire heir to a real-estate and urban-transportation fortune, they planned to organize the new Union Association of teams, which Lucas wooed players to join not only by promises of higher pay, but by vigorous denunciations of the reserve clause, which the new association promised not to employ. Lucas called it an "unjust and arbitrary rule" that free men "would no more submit to than to have rings put in their noses." The association hoped that with teams well stocked with happy free agents paid up to $5,000 a season, it could invade Baltimore, Boston, Philadelphia, Cincinnati, Chicago, and St. Louis (as well as two smaller markets, Washington, D.C., and Altoona, Pennsylvania).[10]

Unfortunately for principle, the idea was a flop, tried for only the single season of 1884. The National League and American Association fought back with tactics for which "hardball" would be far too mild a description, and "cutthroat" not excessive. They threatened to blacklist for life any players who signed on with the Union teams, and publicly branded those who did as stupid, crooked, or probably befuddled by drink. They denounced the new owners as failed businessmen trying to muscle in on the success of their betters in creating the commercial game. While they did not schedule big-league contests at times directly competitive with Union schedules, they created "reserve"—i.e., scrub—teams to play each other in the same time slots at cut-rate prices. And they found ways to circumvent their own salary cap by various kinds of secret bribes offered to especially desirable performers.

When players jumped to the new league, they were often sued for breach of contract. The Union Association won many of these battles in court, but lost the crucial one at the gates. There were still too few potential customers for too many teams—thirty-four in all among the three leagues playing in 1884 in a market heavily concentrated in a few states. (There were four leagues, if the tiny Northwestern League is included, but it vanished during the struggle.) First the least securely financed Union teams were driven off the field; then frantic schedule juggling and the hasty addition of new franchises failed to hold back a tide of red ink as team after team of the Union Association went out of business. Only five of its original eight lasted out the complete season, at the end of which the promoters surrendered and disbanded. Lucas himself approached the National League owners asking to buy a Cleveland franchise and humbly agreed to abide by all the rules, the reserve clause included.[11]

All that happened in Comiskey's first year as Browns manager. There is no evidence that he was tempted to jump the fence to the Union Association. But the next of baseball's business wars came in 1890 and was a very different matter. This time the organization of a new league came from the players themselves and called friendship and loyalty into play.

The Union Association's failure left the players more vulnerable than ever to control of the owners, who outraged them by petty harassment and cheese-paring economies like suspension of pay during injuries, charges for lost or broken equipment, and fines for various misdemeanors on and off the field.[12] These, piled atop the salary-limitation and reserve clauses, led to the formation of the Brotherhood of Professional Baseball Players in 1885—a year in which two major national labor federations, the Knights of Labor and the American Federation of Labor (both fairly recent creations), were swelling their ranks. Baseball was never far from the mainstream of American economic development.

The leader of the Brotherhood was an intriguing figure, John Montgomery Ward, who turned professional after playing ball as an undergraduate at Pennsylvania State University, becoming a star pitcher and then (after an arm injury ended his mound career) a brilliant shortstop. Eventually Ward managed both the New York Giants and the future Brooklyn Dodgers. He acquired a law degree from Columbia University while still on the Giants' active roster, and later quit the game to become a successful attorney. Ward went public with an articulate statement of player grievances and demands in 1887, listing not only the fines, salary cap, and reserve clause, but the blacklisting of holdouts and the uncomfortable truth that when a player was sold from one team to another, he got no part of the price determined by his own skills. Player objections to these conditions were crisply stated.

"We make the money," said one, and "it is only just that we ought to get a fair share of the profits." And another announced: "No man can sell my carcass unless I get at least half."[13]

The National League's answer to Ward's request for a meeting to discuss these issues was not only to stall him but to enact a further outrage in 1888, instituting a labeling scheme in which players would be classified into five groups according to their "habits, earnestness, and special qualifications" and paid a fixed salary accordingly, the worst-behaved being lowest on the scale. Translated, this meant that owners could decide what to pay players based on their evaluation of personal and private conduct, which they often reached by such means as setting detectives on the trail of suspected drunks or gamblers. Athletes were also given black marks for foul language, slovenly uniforms, and a variety of behaviors that in the opinion of their bosses were improper. The owners insisted that this part of their system of control was nonnegotiable.

Confronted with such resistance, Ward and other Brotherhood leaders organized the Players' National League of Base Ball Clubs, which would take the field in 1890 in major-league cities including Boston, New York, Brooklyn, Philadelphia, Pittsburgh, Cleveland, and Chicago. Ward found backers who would fund the experiment, and blueprinted a "democratic alliance of workers and capitalists in which both were to participate in the government and share in the profits of the enterprise."[14] A constitution was drafted under which the league would be governed by a Senate with membership equally divided among those chosen by players and by owners. There would be no salary cap, no reserve clause, and no classification system. A table of priorities for each team's distribution of its receipts was adopted. The first obligation was to expenses, the next was to salaries (guaranteed by the backers), and then came contributions to a prize fund for the winners of an annual championship contest. Further profits would go to backers, and additional surpluses would be distributed throughout the league. Contracts would be for three years, and players had the option of buying stock in their own teams.

It was a fine experiment in democratic governance of America's national game—and, like most such idealistic ventures, would require a long and costly struggle, which it faced from its opening hours. Spalding, once again heading the owners' war-plans division, used his formidable public-relations connections to denounce the Brotherhood as "an oath-bound, secret organization of strikers" in alliance with "soreheads and speculators." (Spalding, however, took Ward with him on his 1889 world tour of all-stars who played exhibitions against the White Stockings.) He also called the Players' League an organization that had "no moral foundation," and got important sportswriters like the veteran Henry Chadwick on his side. Chadwick's attitude was fairly well summed up in his reaction to a public appeal for support from members of the Brotherhood, which complained that they had been "bought, sold or exchanged, as though they were sheep instead of American citizens." To Chadwick that was a "revolutionary manifesto" and the Brotherhood itself was a conspiracy that forced players into line by "terrorism."[15] The press, with some exceptions, took the side of the owners, a typical story describing the players as "dressed in fur-lined overcoats, silk hats, and patent-leather shoes, carrying gold-headed canes . . . and smoking Rosa Perfectos or Henry Clays at twenty-five cents apiece."

When the Players' League began to recruit among the established stars, its inducements included not just bigger checks, but the opportunity to hang together with fellow players in a bid for independence. It was hard to turn friends down simply out of fear that the scheme would not work, and Comiskey, like most other outstanding performers, didn't. By the end of 1889 Ward's organization had signed up more than seventy National League players and about twenty-five from the American Association, including Comiskey. In explaining why he agreed to jump his Browns contract and become first baseman and manager for the Players' League's Chicago Pirates at $8,000 a year, Comiskey said that he did so "out of sympathy for the movement and because of my friendship for many of the men back of the venture." Looking back years later from an owner's point of view, he said that the Players' League was "bound to fail, for it wasn't constructed along the right lines."[16] But the league's framework may have had less to do with the failure than Spalding's continuing countercampaign. The public-relations attack was supplemented by the National League's strategy of enticing some of its players back with cold cash and, more strategically, getting to the capitalist bankrollers of Players' League teams with offers of a financial stake in their own, more securely established clubs, which enjoyed much greater prospects of long-term success. In the winter of 1890–91 at least two such sets of backers folded their hands, and others followed quickly enough to doom the trial venture into labor-capital partnership.

The real death blow was delivered by the bookkeepers. In 1890 all three leagues—Players' League, National League, and American Association—lost money. Both sides published questionable attendance figures, but one hard-to-verify set showed the Players' League outdrawing the National in 1890 980,887–813,768. Nevertheless, it lost between $314,000 and $385,000 during the war. The other two leagues also went into the red, to the tune of something between a quarter and a half million, but the Nationals, at least, had an ample enough treasury to withstand it. After its single season, the Players' League never took the field for another. Vague talks of merger went nowhere, and it gave up the ghost. The financial carnage had so weakened the American Association that after a brief court struggle over the reassignment of the Players' League returnees, it, too, passed out of existence as a major league, leaving the National League, reorganized in 1892 to embrace twelve teams (four of them franchises abandoned by the American Association) as the sole proprietor of the "big league" label. It had now beaten or coopted three challengers to its monopoly status in sixteen years of existence. It would shortly face another one that it could not defeat. Charlie Comiskey would not only be a participant in that rivalry. This time he would be an instigator.

★   ★   ★

Along with other Players' League performers made homeless, Comiskey returned in 1891 to the team he had left, his skills and smarts unimpaired by the year away, during which he had managed to bring in the Chicago Pirates fourth in the league's standings. Circumstances now conspired to put him, for a brief period, under the umbrella of the Nationals. He played out the season, but it was clear that the old congeniality with Von der Ahe was damaged beyond repair, and he therefore reached an agreement with his friend John T. Brush, who had recently acquired the Cincinnati NL franchise, to change the color of his stockings and be the Reds' player-manager beginning in 1892. He stayed at that job through 1894, then retired as an active player. His record on the field was more than respectable—a lifetime batting average of .264 and 1,531 hits in a total of 1,390 games—but his managerial statistics were sparkling. In eleven years of being strategist, judge of talent, and psychologist (a manager's needed assets) he won 824 games and lost 553, for a .603 mark, high on the all-time success list.

Increasingly, however, Comiskey was attracted by the business end of the game. Sometime in the 1890s, as his fortieth birthday drew closer, he decided that he wanted to become an owner. The chaotic state of the business, as he had experienced it, suggested to him that doors were still open for new entries. It was an idea that occurred to other prime players of the era as well, notably Cornelius McGillicuddy, better known as Connie Mack, who would become the longtime owner of the Philadelphia Athletics, and Clark Griffith, who would one day be the proprietor of the Washington Senators. Comiskey's inclination toward moving into a front office somewhere became more focused when, during his Cincinnati years, he became friends with the baseball writer of the *Cincinnati Commercial,* Bryon Bancroft Johnson.

Johnson was an imposing figure, a tall, heavy man who peered at the world through wire-rimmed spectacles that gave him a sober, somewhat academic appearance. He was in fact a college teacher's son. He had gone to two Ohio colleges, played baseball for both, and had some semipro experience under his belt as well before settling into his sports-covering job in Cincinnati journalism. His ambitions, like Comiskey's, who became his confidant and pal on hunting and fishing jaunts, were large, but also fueled by genuine outrage at what the National League owners were doing to the game.

"Syndicate baseball" was turning into an economic and sporting horror show. Some of its leading owners were businessmen with interests in real estate, streetcar lines, meatpacking, and other industries, with little understanding of the game's loyalties and passions. Intent on paring costs, they froze salaries at around $1,800 annually, guaranteeing a large cadre of unhappy players, who were provoked enough to try, once more, to form a union, the Protective Association of Professional Baseball Players.[17] Several of the owners either owned two teams outright or held stock in more than one—John T. Brush, for example, held shares in both the Cincinnati Reds and New York Giants—and were amenable to moving popular players from a losing to a more successful club regardless of the pleas of local fans. Seasons were shortened, and individual games were abruptly transferred from one city to another that promised better receipts on a given day. As box-office losses mounted, rosters were cut, and in 1899 four weak-sister cities—Louisville, Cleveland, Washington, and Baltimore—were simply dumped, though the league, in dog-in-the-manger style, reserved territorial rights in those towns where they did not choose to place teams. The owners could hardly have done more to make the sport unpopular if they had planned it. "What's the matter with these National League magnates?" asked the *Sporting News*. "What a shame it is that the greatest of sports should be in the hands of such a mal-odorous gang."[18]

Johnson, presumably through his acquaintance with would-be owners and backers of ball clubs—and with Charles Comiskey—succeeded in getting named in 1894 as president of the two-year-old Western League, a revival of the old Northwestern League that had died in the 1880s. Its teams came from cities in the agricultural-industrial heartland where amateur and semipro ball provided pools of potential talent, where baseball was a passion akin to the later infatuation with football and basketball, and where second-string cities could aspire to national notice through their athletic organizations. Detroit, Sioux City, Toledo, Kansas City, Indianapolis, Grand Rapids, and Minneapolis—these were existing or future homes of packinghouses, flour mills, and factories that made furniture, auto parts, and the castings and wires, batteries and dynamos, machine tools and freight cars that were the sinew of industrial production.

According to Comiskey himself, he was part of the group that had planned the league, and the timing of his own entry into it was possibly hastened by events in the winter of 1893, when he was ordered to visit the South by doctors who said he was "threatened with tuberculosis." His memoir, written in 1916, says nothing about whether Johnson had any part in the Western League's creation, possibly because by then the two men had become estranged. But Comiskey was very likely among those who put Johnson into the league presidency, and it was a fruitful move, since in a short while Johnson had made the young organization a soundly run paying proposition. The fact that "Ban," as he was universally called, found his way into the executive ranks of baseball through membership in the Cincinnati sporting press testifies to the importance of the tight connection between sports promotion and sports coverage—particularly when it is remembered that Charles Murphy followed the same route to ownership of the Cubs.

The evidence doesn't appear to sustain Comiskey's claim of playing midwife to the Western League without Johnson's assistance, nor the even more sweeping assertion by one of the White Sox owner's friends that "it was Comiskey who brought Johnson into the American League and pushed him into the leadership."[19] Johnson was no one's puppet. What is indisputable is that the two men together were anything but secretive about their intention to create a rival to the National League, and that for Comiskey a first priority was to get a team planted in Chicago, something that he boasted was "the greatest play of his life." His contract kept him in Cincinnati through 1894, but in the following year he gathered enough cash to buy the Sioux City franchise and became an owner. That was merely step one on the way "home." He led his Iowa acquisition to the Western League championship in 1895, his first year as owner-manager. For its second season he transferred it, with the official blessing of Johnson, to a more rewarding location, St. Paul. Step two!

Being an owner, Comiskey later said, "gave me a broader view of baseball, widened my vision, and made me see the interests of the game from the viewpoint of the magnate as well as the players."[20] (Later critics would have said that being an owner caused Comiskey to tighten the clasp on his pocketbook. But in fairness to him, running a franchise does teach lessons in the need for planning and prudence in the face of the unexpected. Successful business requires predictability and control, while the fun of sport lies in the uncertainty of outcome, but so long as games are commercially exhibited, the paradox will remain.)

The St. Paul club was the embryo of the Chicago White Sox. In the four seasons it played in Minnesota it never won a league pennant but came close in its first and final years, and Comiskey later grumbled that in one of them rain had beaten him out of a pennant by forcing cancellation of critical games. The opening season was one of trial and error, requiring him to "skirmish around" to put together as good a team as possible "mostly from amateur ranks."[21]

Comiskey was likewise "skirmishing around" and learning his way to maneuver through the political minefields of midwestern political conservatism. St. Paul still outlawed Sunday baseball, which was a mainstay for attracting working-class audiences. At the end of the first year, the city fathers served Comiskey with eviction papers. He pocketed them, bought a site just outside the city limits, and built a new park on his acreage—a modest but sound investment.[22] Eighteen ninety-six was described by

Comiskey as a disaster, but in 1897, the team finished third, and more important, Comiskey acquired the first of the players who would take him to the World Series. This was Frank Isbell, described by the grateful owner as one of the best and most devoted players he ever had.[23]

Certainly Isbell was the most versatile. Originally from Delavan, New York, where he was born in 1875, he had passed his young manhood in North Fork, Minnesota, working during summers in logging camps while growing up. He became so proficient in the lore and legends of Swedish lumberjacks that fellow players nicknamed him "Swede," though he was, in his peak playing years, described as a "bald, round faced Irishman."[24] He came to the St. Paul team as a right-handed pitcher, but his bat was good enough so that he occasionally was used as an outfielder. For Comiskey he became an extraordinary utility man. On the final day of the championship season of 1906, in a meaningless game against Detroit, Isbell pitched two scoreless innings. The *Tribune* noted that in 1906 alone he had played all three outfield positions as well as second base and catcher, and that this feat did not "approach Isbell's record of playing every one of the nine positions here a few years ago."[25] In the Series itself he was settled at second, with healthy results for his average. He entered it having led the team during the season with .279, and would wind up collecting eight hits in six games, four of them doubles, and with four runs driven in.

In 1900 Comiskey decided that despite "favorable surroundings and congenial friends at St. Paul . . . I had to be up and doing. Chicago, my native city, was calling." But there was more than the tug of sentiment behind the move. When the National League owners in 1899 killed off the franchises in Cleveland, Washington, Louisville, and Baltimore that were not yielding happy returns, it opened the door wider for Ban Johnson. He took an option on the Cleveland franchise and offered to move his Western League team from Grand Rapids into the baseball-bereft city and give it another chance to demonstrate a fan base. He promised the National

League directorate that he would honor the National Agreement and not tempt players away from their remaining teams, but he had some conditions, and one of them was that permission also be granted for a second team in Chicago. That one would, of course, be the St. Paul club of his friend Charlie Comiskey. The joint Comiskey-Johnson maneuver would open two metropolitan beachheads for the new league taking shape in their plans.

The "magnates" were willing to allow the invasion of what was demonstrably a city big enough for two teams, especially when they believed that the new one would remain part of a minor league. But the consent of the Colts/Orphans (twentieth-century Cubs) owner James Hart came with a modest price. The new team's stadium had to be south of 39th Street, and "Chicago" could not be part of its official title. Comiskey agreed and, of course, once settled in, simply pinched the venerable name of White Stockings (shortened two years later by headline-conscious sportswriters to White Sox), knowing that the city's name would automatically if not formally become part of the label. And so his aggregation moved 400 miles to the south. At the time he owned only two-thirds of the team, but he later bought out his Milwaukee partner.

By the end of 1900 Ban Johnson had reconfigured the Western League, which now included Detroit, Minneapolis, Milwaukee, Kansas City, and Indianapolis as well as Chicago and Cleveland, and renamed it the American League. Comiskey, still field manager as well as owner, led his transplanted club to the first AL championship.[26] But while the addition of Chicago and Cleveland to the American League had gone relatively smoothly, when Johnson made his 1901 move and declared it to be a full-blown major league, unbound by the National Agreement, it signaled the start of still another war for control of the emerging national pastime, the third in which Comiskey had been involved and which had shaped his life.

★   ★   ★

Johnson's declaration of independence for his creation included the announcement that he intended to invade the East and plant franchises in Washington, Baltimore, Philadelphia, and Buffalo, which he later changed to Boston. The immediate ramifications were a dizzying two-year upheaval during which the sun shone for players and litigators' attorneys, the latter kept busy with filings and cross-filings for restraining orders and injunctions connected with breach-of-contract suits.

To complicate the picture further, there were additional parties to the combat. One was the new union, the Protective Association of Professional Baseball Players. The union had put before the National League a set of demands such as the clubs' paying medical bills for injuries, arbitration of disputes, and release from contracts violated by the owners, and had been flatly turned down. Stung by the rebuff, the union got promises of better treatment from Johnson, and helped him to recruit National League players. Another party was a group of promoters trying to revive the American Association as a major league, who hoped to pick off some of the franchises on which Johnson had his eye.[27]

By 1902, the American League had begun to emerge as the likely winner. Baseball historians estimate that 110 former National Leaguers were on AL rosters during 1901 alone, of whom 74 were identifiable as contract jumpers. Comiskey was among those American League owners who loaded their shopping carts, his pickups including three of the future Cubs' best players (who would not, however, be with the team in 1906). More significantly, American League attendance jumped from 1,683,584 in 1901 to 2,206,457 in 1902, while in the same period National League audiences shrank from 1,920,031 to 1,683,012.[28] National League owners partly refilled their lineups by wooing players away from minor-league teams—which in those days were not "farms," but independent operations—and ignoring earlier promises under the latest version of the National Agreement to respect the minors' rights to reserve limited numbers of their own stars. The American League, not bound by any agreement at all, was equally high-handed.

The winter of 1901–2 and the subsequent season saw more byzantine maneuverings, including a proposal from two National League owners to abandon individual team ownership altogether and reorganize frankly as a National Baseball Trust, with shares of stock and appointed paid directors who would name team managers, license players, and assign them wherever they felt they would do the most good. In effect, the teams would be divisions of Baseball Inc., independently responsible for showing a year-end profit, with personnel shuffled by company headquarters. Luckily, the idea did not fly, and although major-league baseball did ultimately become a monopoly, it was at least one somewhat more consistent with the idea of sports rivalry.

There were other episodes, too, that can only be described as bizarre. At a secret National League owners' meeting in December 1901 there was an even split between factions, one—led by Brush and by Andrew Freedman, the New York Giants' owner who was generally considered contentious and corrupt—wishing to replace the league altogether with the consolidation scheme, the other opposed. This last group summoned Albert Spalding from retirement and nominated him for league president to save the organization from extinction (although Brush and Freedman claimed that the consolidation concept originated with Spalding himself). He was elected by a dubious parliamentary maneuver, was promptly served with an injunction preventing him from acting, and eventually resigned, as Harold Seymour notes, from the office he had never held. "And," in the words of "Casey at the Bat," "when the dust had lifted and men saw what had occurred," at the end of 1902 Freedman was no longer a baseball executive. John T. Brush had disposed of his Cincinnati holdings (to a group headed by the city's political boss, George Cox) and bought out Freedman's share of the Giants, thus ridding the game of his presence. In addition, a compromise president of the National League, still intact, had been named—Harry Pulliam, secretary of the Pittsburgh club.[29]

That did not complete the dizzying list of baseball follies of 1902. In July John McGraw, the hot-tempered manager of the Baltimore Orioles, then in the American League, was suspended by Ban Johnson after a number of clashes between the two strong-willed men. McGraw's response was to join with Brush in buying a majority of Orioles stock and selling it to Freedman, at that point still an owner of the Giants. Then McGraw jumped to the Giants, taking six Baltimore stars with him—nearly half the active roster—and leaving the Orioles to flounder into last place. Johnson's next move was to transfer the franchise to New York under the name of the Highlanders.[30] He had already begun that year by transferring his Milwaukee team to St. Louis, the two changes together completing his list of break-ins to cities that already had National League teams.

None of this directly affected Comiskey except to the extent that his pride and future were closely bound to the success of the American League, in whose creation he had played a part. That success was finally assured when the National League owners, financially hemorrhaging and clearly losing the fight, sued for peace. Johnson was not unwilling, and a concordat was hammered out by committees from the two leagues in Cincinnati in January 1903. The structure of organized baseball was set much as it would remain until the 1950s. The leagues agreed on who should keep or lose the players who had left their teams in the seasons of warfare. Thereafter they would recognize each other's reservations of players, cooperate on scheduling and rules, draw up a new National Agreement that would embrace the minor leagues as junior partners with decidedly limited rights, and be governed by a troika of the presidents of each league and a chairman whom they would choose. (That was replaced by a single commissioner system in 1920.) The abortive American Association had no part in these deliberations and remained a minor league, and the Protective Association of Professional Baseball Players, likewise not included among the invitees to the negotiating table, simply vanished. There would be no players' union again for many decades.

The final team alignments were set when Johnson agreed not to move in on Pittsburgh in exchange for the New York High-landers (the future Yankees) being allowed to stay where they were. (Brush and McGraw resisted to the bitter end.) Five cities—Boston, New York, Philadelphia, Chicago, and St. Louis—would be home to both a National and an American League team. The Americans would have Detroit, Cleveland, and Washington to themselves, the Nationals Pittsburgh, Cincinnati, and Brooklyn, which was considered separate from New York in theory if not in market fact. Consolidation of the clubs in the two-team cities was forbidden. This overall distribution of territories could not be changed without the consent of a majority of owners in each league, and was not until 1954.[31]

And so, twenty-seven years after the creation of the National League, organized baseball was at last assured of stability and rea-sonably steady profits. But it also became a paradox. It was the guardian of a game hailed as embracing the essence of democracy. And it was also an economic enterprise that was legally allowed to forbid the entry of new firms or the relocation of existing ones, as clear a rejection of free-market principles as could be imagined. Its employees were theoretically bound forever to the organization with which they signed their first contract. As base-ball writer Hugh Fullerton would observe in 1910, "Legally, the baseball player is a slave held in bondage, but he is the best treated, most pampered slave of history, and while there are many cases of oppression, the majority of the players receive just and equi-table treatment."[32] By then, Fullerton's writings on the game were widely known, and he was something of a semiofficial spokes-person for the collective enterprise of "major-league baseball," whose views were undoubtedly reflected in what he said. In fair-ness, however, he was no passive tool, for it was a suspicious Ful-lerton who led the charge that uncovered the 1919 "Black Sox" scandal of a rigged World Series.

Fullerton's statement was part of a long public-relations cam-paign that baseball's magnates would now launch to convince

Americans not only of the pleasures of the game but of its essential support of all-American virtues. In 1907 the select "national commission" named by Congress had "proven," contrary to all evidence, that baseball had been invented in Cooperstown, New York, and carried no stigma of non-American origins. And in his 1911 tribute to "America's National Game," Spalding asserted that baseball embodied "American Courage, Confidence, Combativeness; American Dash, Discipline, Determination; American Energy, Eagerness, and Enthusiasm," and so on through the alphabet to "American Vim, Vigor, and Vitality." This campaign to present the ballplayers themselves as heroes of unspotted manly virtue may occasionally have presented problems for the baseball writers, who in those days traveled on the same trains and stayed at the same hotels as the men they were covering, and spent time playing cards and gossiping with them in smoking cars, lobbies, restaurants, and pubs. Certainly the reporters knew which players were drinkers, which broke curfew and consorted with women of the evening, which were quarrelsome, welshed on debts, and otherwise were not cardboard cutouts of the pure athlete. By common consent that knowledge did not find its way into print, though consciously or otherwise it might have accounted for some of the sarcasm and debunking that characterized the writing of Dryden and others like him.

All of Comiskey's public pronouncements and behavior were connected with that effort to sanitize baseball's image, but his main preoccupation in the four years following the last of the baseball wars was to get his team back to the championship of the American League. In the churning of the 1901 and 1902 war seasons, and in three thereafter of canny buying and bargaining, he put together the hitless wonders after acquiring the man who would be their field leader.

The year 1901 brought Fielder Jones and Billy Sullivan into Comiskey's fold. Jones was picked up from the National League's

Brooklyn club, then named the Superbas, in the great reshuffle. He was twenty-seven years old, a native of Shinglehouse, Pennsylvania, a small town near the state's border with New York. He was the prototype of the brainy ballplayer, and had at least some post–high school education under his belt, at Alfred College. Playing for Alfred, he caught the eye of pro scouts, and in 1895 he began a short career in the minors, first with Binghamton, New York, and then with Springfield, Massachusetts. The Superbas drafted him almost immediately, and in four of the ensuing five seasons he batted over .300. He signed with Chicago six years later, but when the two leagues finally reassigned players in 1903, John McGraw insisted that Jones belonged to his New York club. After some dispute, however, the darkly handsome, curly-haired young outfielder signed with Comiskey. It was a near miss that proved profitable for Chicago. Jones (five foot eleven, 189 pounds) became a dependable player. He batted .318 in 1902, and had 24 assists, thanks to strong and accurate right-handed throws from center (though he hit left-handed). Early in 1904, Jim Callahan, who had succeeded Clark Griffith as the White Sox skipper after Griffith's departure for the New York Highlanders, quit the job after the Sox had finished seventh under his lead in 1903. Jones was named to succeed him.

It was a great move, even though the additional responsibilities may have caused a permanent drop in Jones's batting average to the neighborhood of .250. But what the team lost in batting it gained in savvy. The cigar-smoking Jones was a natural leader: quiet and low-key except when arguing decisions with umpires, "cool as a lime rickey" in a crucial situation, and a thoughtful tactician who was perfectly suited to the deadball game. "A base on balls, a sacrifice, a passed ball and a long fly was a rally," one columnist wrote some years after Jones died in 1934. He himself could hit to any field or lay down a bunt to advance runners, and he had his players use their legs and heads as well as their bats. In 1906 the White Sox stole 209 bases, Jones himself taking 26. (His high point had been 42 in 1901.) He led by smarts rather than bluster, but despite his reserved mannerisms his intensity broke through from time to time. Years later teammates would remember his happy little jig as the final Cub fly-ball out of Game One descended toward his glove.[33] In his partial season as manager, the White Sox climbed to fourth place.

Catcher Billy Sullivan was another 1901 pickup. A farm boy from southeastern Wisconsin, he seems to have gone directly into professional baseball at the age of twenty-one with Cedar Rapids, then played for various midwestern minor-league teams for three years until he advanced to the Boston National League club, the Beaneaters, in 1899. A salary of $2,400 lured him to the White Sox. Sullivan's commanding virtue was steadiness behind the plate: while his batting average of 1906, a meager .214, was also his lifetime average, he led American League catchers in fielding that season. He would catch every inning of the World Series, and get no hits. He neither smoke, drank, nor swore, leaving Jones, Comiskey, and the American League blissfully free of disciplinary problems on his account, no small blessing.[34]

Despite the poor finish, 1903 was not a complete White Sox disaster. In the first intracity postseason exhibition series between Chicago's old and new ball clubs, they had split with their stronger rivals, thanks to the pitching of two new additions of that year, Nick Altrock and Doc White. These two were among the more colorful and interesting characters who ever put on a White Sox uniform, and they also were to account for half of the victories claimed by the White Sox in the World Series of 1906.

Altrock was a Cincinnati "Dutchman," born to German immigrant parents in 1876, the same centennial year as Mordecai Brown. With a rubbery face and jug ears he was perfect for the role of a baseball clown, and that was exactly what he became in his postplaying career. But his comic mug and antics disguised genuine talent. He was taught to be a shoemaker as a boy, but like many of his city-bred contemporaries, he played semipro ball for local clubs. In 1898 he was signed by the Grand Rapids team and rewarded them with a 17–3 record. Next step up the ladder was to Louisville, then still part of the National League. But in 1899 he was sent back to the minors, where he played on both coasts before a 1902 transfer to Milwaukee, for whom he won 28 games and lost only 14. Near the season's end, the American League's Boston Pilgrims (soon to become the Red Sox) picked him up, but a slow start in 1903 persuaded the Pilgrims to sell him to Comiskey, for whom he played only a minor role at first. But he took off in 1904, going 19–14, then improving to 23–12 in 1905 and 20–6 in 1906. His weapon was a set of pitches that batters tended to beat into the ground, where he could pounce on them if they were anywhere near the mound. In winning the opening Series game he had a pitcher's record eight assists and three put-outs. In the fourth game, which he also pitched, he increased his number of errorless chances to 17.[35]

Doc White was one of the most versatile young men on a baseball diamond in the first decade of the twentieth century and, in contrast to the likes of Altrock and Brown, one who didn't need baseball as an economic ladder. He was born in April 1879 to a well-off manufacturer who owned the District of Columbia's only iron foundry. He attended Georgetown University, and in 1902 earned his dental degree (the course for which was then shorter). Doc jumped directly from semipro ball while still at school to the National League Philadelphia Phillies. He was a southpaw with a hard-to-hit sinker and pinpoint control. In his two years with Philadelphia he won 30 games against 23 losses. In the first three seasons he spent with the White Sox his highest win total was 17—twice—but his ERA was an impressive 2.13 in 1903, and it sank progressively to 1.78, then 1.76, until in 1906 it stood at a league-leading 1.52. In that year he pitched 219 innings and walked only 38 batters while striking out 95. During the close pennant race of 1904, when the White Sox finished third, he pitched five consecutive shutouts, and after that record was broken by a single, a steal, and a bloop double in the first inning of the sixth start, he held the New York Highlanders scoreless for the rest of the game.[36]

Even after retiring his dental paraphernalia, White made it clear that his horizon was not bounded by the diamond. He is said to have designed the White Sox home uniform one season, and he also enjoyed composing popular songs, one of them, "Little Puff of Smoke, Good Night," in collaboration with Ring Lardner. Like a few other baseball stars, he went onstage in vaudeville tours during the winter, and he occasionally sang some of his own compositions. Vaudeville, a set of short variety acts that usually followed a silent movie, was, like baseball, very much part of the popular-entertainment explosion of the era from 1890 onward.

The year 1903 also saw the addition to the Sox pitching staff of Frank "Yip" Owen, a Michigan native who had put in some time at the "Agricultural College" in Lansing that is now Michigan State University. He was also a rarity in baseball at that time, an army veteran who had served during the Spanish-American War. He had a brief career in the minors, sandwiched around a brief tryout with the Detroit Tigers, before Comiskey acquired him. He was to have no starts in the World Series, but relieved White in Game Two and threw six innings in the losing cause. Yet he was one of those who had put the White Sox into the Series. He won 21 games for them in 1904 and 1905, and in 1906 actually led the staff with 22, six of them shutouts. It says something about the underestimated quality of Sox pitching in the year of the hitless wonders that his 2.33 ERA was only fifth on the team, behind the ERAs of White, Walsh, Altrock, and Roy Patterson, who had been playing for Comiskey since 1899 in St. Paul.[37]

As the 1904 season approached, Comiskey continued to look for cards to deal Jones a winning hand. Unquestionably his best pick of that year was a tall and muscular (six foot one, 190 pounds) youngster, a pitcher with some potential in his fastball but little else, drafted from Newark of the Eastern League for $750. No investment of Charlie Comiskey's ever paid off so handsomely. Edward Augustine Walsh had been born in Wilkes-Barre, Pennsylvania, twenty-three years earlier, the youngest of thirteen children of an Irish coal miner. After a few years of parochial school he went to work in the mines, much like his opposite number on the Cubs, Three-Finger Brown. Playing for amateur teams of miners, he graduated to semipro ball at an occasional $50 an afternoon, and then to the organized game with Wilkes-Barre, then Meriden, Connecticut. During spring training in 1904 Walsh was taught the spitball by a roommate. He spent two undistinguished years learning to control it, winning only six games in his first season and eight in his second. But in 1906, adding the new pitch to what he already had, he notched 17 wins. His salary was $1,800. After the 1906 Series, in which he had two victories, he kept on improving—to 24 wins in 1907 and a mind-bending 40 in 1908, during which he also compiled record numbers for innings pitched, shutouts, strikeouts, and walks, and justifing Comiskey's comment years later that "he was the greatest pitcher of them all."[38]

The year 1904 also saw the return of George Davis, a slick-fielding veteran in his thirties, who had played most of the 1902 season as the Sox shortstop after twelve years in the National League, nine of them with the New York Giants, for whom he never hit less than .300. In 1903 he barely played at all, in a stubborn loner's futile rebellion against the peonage closing in on the players. He had jumped to Chicago at the end of 1901 during the interleague contract war. The peace treaty of a year later called for some players to return to the clubs they had left, and others—Davis among them—to stay with their new ones. But Davis was dissatisfied with Chicago's contract offer for 1903 and wanted to rejoin the Giants, who according to one newspaper story had offered him $6,300. In a test of whether the peace would hold up, Ban Johnson and Comiskey secured an injunction that forced Davis off the field for the Giants for all but four games. Davis refused to put his White Sox uniform back on and sat out the entire schedule. But in 1904 he gave in to reality and came back to his former spot in manager Jones's lineup. His batting average slipped into the .270 range, but in 1905 he led the league in fielding and had a respectable on-base percentage.

Davis was a native of Cohoes, New York, a suburb of Albany

that was a neighbor to Johnny Evers's Troy. When he was born in 1870, Cohoes, which had manufactured items of clothing for Union soldiers, was enjoying postwar prosperity, but not much of it seems to have trickled down to his Welsh and English immigrant parents, who already had four children and would add two more after George. Little is known of his childhood or of his postplaying career. He was someone who by choice or bad luck always tended to be the unrecognized face in the back row of the group photo. But thanks to a vigorous campaign by Cohoes and Albany sportswriters and fans (and impressive if long-overlooked lifetime stats), he is now, like Evers, in the Hall of Fame.[39]

Another 1904 roster addition was John "Jiggs" Donahue, who distributed his 178 pounds on a six-foot-one frame, the height giving him the long reach that a first baseman needs when stretching for errant throws. Aged twenty-seven in the year of the Series, he came from a large Irish family in Springfield, Ohio. He had broken in with the Dayton team of the Eastern International League, then shuttled around among other minor leagues as a left-handed catcher. He was signed by Chicago at the end of 1903. Jones and Comiskey spotted his first-base potential and put him there for most of his first season with them. It was an inspired choice, since from 1905 through 1907, playing virtually every game, he led the league in fielding average. (In 1907 it was .994.) Jiggs, married in 1904, was full of infectious enthusiasm and had what are described as "excellent habits" that were a model for his teammates. When not in uniform on the field, he was often found playing billiards, which he loved.[40]

Working hard to improve on 1904's third-place finish, Comiskey added three names to the 1905 and 1906 rolls. The first was Patsy Dougherty, another six-footer carrying 190 pounds and swinging an acceptable if not frightening left-handed bat. Dougherty would go into left field and, along with Sullivan and Donahue, give a distinctly Irish flavor to the usual starting lineup for the Sox. Dougherty came to the club by an interesting route. He hailed from rural Bolivar in southern New York, not far from

Fielder Jones's own home town of Shinglehouse, Pennsylvania. After successful big-league seasons with the Boston Pilgrims and then the New York Highlanders, Dougherty was angry when the Highlanders cut his salary, and at nearly thirty years of age simply walked out of his contract and went back to pick up his life in Bolivar, intending to leave baseball behind him as a youthful interlude. But when the White Sox came to nearby Olean for an off-day exhibition in 1906, Jones looked Dougherty up and persuaded him to return to the field in a Chicago uniform, after getting Ban Johnson's approval of the midseason switch.[41]

Flanking center fielder Jones in right was another 1906 acquisition from the Highlanders, Ed Hahn. One more of the Sox's abundant crop of left-handed hitters, and a relative lightweight at 160 pounds, Hahn was an Ohioan, apparently thirty years old (though he may have shaved some years off his recorded age). He played his first professional games, as a pitcher, for Portsmouth, Ohio, an industrial town at the mouth of the Scioto River. He spent a minor-league apprenticeship in the Southern League and was converted to an outfielder. He was signed up for the Highlanders by Clark Griffith in 1905 and had an excellent year for the New Yorkers, hitting .319 and achieving an on-base percentage of .426, earned by an ability to draw walks. But a slow start in 1906 induced Griffith to trade him to the White Sox in mid-May. His off-season occupation was unusual for a professional athlete. He had a pottery business in Portsmouth, making items of his own design.[42]

One more 1905 addition to the team proved to be of unsuspected value. This was thirty-year-old Cincinnatian George Rohe. After an off-and-on career in the minors and a "cup of coffee" interlude with the Baltimore Orioles in 1901, he was pointed out to Comiskey, who, needing a utility infielder, brought him to the White Sox for 34 games in the 1905 campaign and 77 during 1906. He played both second and third, and by the time of the World Series had improved a feeble batting average to .258.

At the start of the World Series George Davis was down with

a heavy cold. Jones plugged another Cincinnatian, Lee Tannehill, his usual third baseman, into the shortstop spot. The twenty-six-year-old journeyman infielder would probably have been dropped thanks to an anemic .186 average during the regular season, but he was credited with a strong throwing arm and smart defensive play at third. Rohe, stepping into the role, was hardly expected to be an offensive improvement. But he turned out to be the surprise understudy who brought down the house. Twice he had decisive hits that produced game-winning runs, his overall Series average of .333 tied him for team leader with Jiggs Donahue, and he also had the team in hits with seven. Two of them were triples and one was a double, and in addition he stole two bases. So much for predictability in a short series!

When Davis returned in the fourth game, poor Tannehill was benched, since Jones was not going to lose Rohe's hot bat and simply moved him to shortstop. Tannehill's name, however, stayed famous in baseball annals, since his older brother Jesse was a star pitcher for the Pirates and the Red Sox early in the new century.

This was the team that had floundered until August, then reeled off a 19-game win streak, lost the lead again, and captured the flag with two days to spare after a neck-and-neck September race with New York. It was a distinctly nonstereotypical aggregation of young men mostly in their twenties, many with college experience. Included were a former coal miner, a successful dentist, a clownish entertainer, and a couple of off-season businessmen. All were heroes in the public eye, and deservedly so in view of their skills in the nation's great game. They seemed to justify Hugh Fullerton's observation a few years later that "baseball players of the major leagues now are an intelligent, clean set of men. . . . They are being recruited from the higher levels of social and educational development. . . . Ball playing as a profession, is now regarded as an honorable means of livelihood and a field for profitable use of talents."[43]

If it occasionally appeared that the players got the larger share of honor and the owners more of the profits, that did not disturb any relationship with the public. Baseball was now comfortably embedded in Progressive Era respectability, and baseball fever was an acceptable form of enthusiasm. That enthusiasm was still high as the White Sox and Cubs, tied at one win apiece, prepared for the third meeting of the Series.

5

The Swing Games

The third and fourth games are the "swing" games of a best-of-seven Series tied at one all. If one team can win both, it has its rival pressed against the wall, a single loss spelling extinction. If, on the other hand, they split, then the World Series is down to a best-of-three set with the outcome between two evenly matched clubs a possible toss-up. Each team goes into Game Three, then, with what the flossier sportswriters of the era might have called "clenched jaws and steely-eyed determination." Such was the case as the Cubs and White Sox squared off on their first return trip to the Cubs' park. The game turned into a thriller that featured a masterful pitching performance, a moment of frightening drama, and another of literal barnyard comedy. The crowd of 13,667 that braved a day of improved but still chilly weather got its money's worth.

The maximum temperature for that Thursday, October 11, reached sometime in midafternoon, was forty-eight. It was still cold enough for the city's health commissioner to scold the transit company, in the *Chicago Tribune,* for running open streetcars that were usually reserved for summer into the Halloween season, thereby increasing the chances of colds and flu among riders. Better luck was predicted in the following day's edition, which printed a "Fair and Warmer" morning forecast alongside a cartoon showing a jolly, bearded weather maker being induced to pull the "October" lever by the proffer of a game ticket marked "Good Only in Fair Weather." As if responding to the milder climate, the entire aura of the front page on the 12th was one of easygoing mockery. There was a tongue-in-cheek story about how members of the National Purity League, which was holding its annual convention in Chicago, had made a visit to the notorious red-light district that clung to the southern outskirts of downtown, not very far from either ballpark. PURITY BAND IN THE LEVEE, the bold print advised, and tempted further reading with a subhead announcing ONE INVESTIGATOR SWOONS. There was also a love-conquers-all tale involving the son of Vice President Charles Fairbanks, who had eloped with the daughter of a Pittsburgh steelworks owner against the explicit wishes of his father. CUPID OUTWITS FAIRBANKS, the headline ran. But the story in the right-hand column of the front page carried the really big news of the day for the baseball-bemused city; the results of the third game of the Series.

In fact, Thursday's game was an almost eerie repeat of Tuesday's opener. This time the pitcher chosen to handcuff the heavily armed Cubs was not the clownish Altrock but the devastating spitball hurler, Ed Walsh. On the White Sox offensive side the firepower was supplied once more by George Rohe.

The crowds that began to collect around the entry gates on the corner of Polk and Lincoln were, like those of the first two days, small but noisy and hardy, undismayed by the continued though slightly moderating chill. As one reporter put it, "It was a day of comparative comfort for both the players and the spectators," but he added that overcoats and pocket flasks were a necessity.[1] For Charles Dryden "comparative" was not comfort enough. He groused that "shifting the seat of war from Chilblain court on the south side to Pleurisy park on the west brought small relief." A "cold and distant sun" still left the breath of the players visible, and more than half the players appeared to be suffering from flulike systems that had "bunged their heads and chests."[2] Only about a thousand more spectators had shown up than on icy Tuesday and Wednesday—13,667 in all, visiting celebrities included. Cap Anson was there again, allegedly betting with his box-seat partner against the Cubs—or perhaps the management that had fired him. So was Charles Taft, half brother of the future president and bankroller of the Cubs, who impressed the multitude by arriving in a car that honked and sputtered its slow way through the mob.

Jones's choice of Ed Walsh to pitch was a calculated risk. Only in his third major-league year, the tall ex–coal miner did flash a 1906 record of 17 wins and 13 losses and a classy 1.88 ERA.[3] But he had not yet entirely shaken the reputation that had followed him since his first recommendation by a hometown semi-pro coach: lots of speed, but "pretty wild."

Chance's countermove was to choose Jack Pfiester, the left-handed newcomer to the Cubs with a 20–8 mark. Pfiester's major weapon was what reporter Sy Sanborn called his "perfectly trained southpaw curves."[4] He had them well under control, and would walk only two batters in the entire game. And he wasted no time in getting started. As leadoff man and right fielder Ed Hahn stepped into the box, the crowd stirred in their seats under the galvanizing moment of the commencement of action. Pfiester whipped in a fastball a shade too high and the tension of waiting was snapped. The second pitch was a curve that broke too soon for ball two. The third swerved away from the left-handed hitting Hahn, catching the plate for a called strike. Back came Pfiester, undaunted, with still another curve; Hahn swung and rolled it slowly to third. One out. Pfiester's control wasn't sharp yet. Facing Jones, he went to 3–0 before getting a roundhouse hook across the plate. On the fifth pitch to the Sox captain, Jones bounced one back to the mound that Pfiester could not handle cleanly—fielding was not one of the pitcher's strong points—

and Jones beat the throw. But he handed Pfiester a gift-wrapped out one or two pitches later, with Isbell at bat, by breaking late for second on a botched steal, and getting cut down by Kling. Pfiester, meantime, had found the range; he fanned Isbell (the first of three that day for the unlucky second baseman) on a foul ball, then a called strike, and then a swing and miss. Inning over.

Now it was the turn of the Giant killers, who came charging out of the gate when their first batter, Hofman, greeted Walsh with a single up the middle. But Walsh dug in and struck out Sheckard, the first of 12 occasions that afternoon in which the Cubs, who had terrorized National League pitchers all season, would wave at the air in futility. Playing in the aggressive style that their speed allowed, the Cubs tried a steal, but Sullivan smelled it coming and, as Hofman took off for second, threw a perfect peg to Isbell for the putout. That hurt especially because Schulte followed with a bouncer into the crowd along the left-field foul line that was ruled a double and would have scored Hofman if not for the foiled theft. Instead, Schulte died at second as Chance bounced to Isbell. The Cubs, with two hits in the inning, had sent their rooters into spasms of noisy delight, but nobody realized that they would not get another for the duration of the game.

Walsh breezed through the next four innings in complete control, adding six strikeouts by the bottom of the fifth. He retired five more Cubs on grounders, and only one ball went airborne, an Evers fly to center in the second. He walked Chance in the fourth with two out, but by the time he returned to the bench at the end of the fifth, he had faced only two batters over the minimum of 15. The only threat of another hit had been a high bouncer over Rohe's head that shortstop Tannehill had snagged behind third and whipped snappily to first.

But Pfiester was fighting him on even terms. In innings two through five he too struck out six, and he got two groundouts, one deep fly ball to the edge of the crowd in center, one pop fly to the catcher, and one to shallow right on which Evers raced out to make a sensational catch. He gave up two hits. The first one, in the second, was an infield single by Jiggs Donahue that Pfiester knocked down, a pitcher's option that backfired when it slowed the ball enough for Donahue to beat Evers's throw to first. There was one out at the time, the first having occurred when Tinker brilliantly went to his right behind third, grabbed a hot smash off the bat of Rohe that eluded Steinfeldt, and threw Rohe out by a step. Pfiester then struck out Dougherty, and Donahue contributed the third out by getting caught stealing. Pfiester's other surrendered hit, however, was a solid blow in the fifth. Rohe had begun the inning with a hard shot between second and short, but Evers, who was the hero of the defense for that day ("John of Troy," one writer called him) made a great stop and nailed Rohe in time. But Donahue hit the ball high and deep, over the head of a frantically running Schulte and into the crowd in right field, allowing him to get to third with only one out. Then Pfiester drew a deep breath, expelled a cloud of vapor, and induced a pop-up to the catcher from Dougherty before making Sullivan his seventh strikeout victim of the afternoon.

It was a brilliant defensive duel of the kind that genuine lovers of the game watch with pleasure, the fans for each team realizing that a single run could be enough for victory, and that the entire game could turn on one unlucky error or one bad pitch. But for those who found defensive brilliance and five successive scoreless innings boring, there was plenty of distraction. For one thing, there was the case of the chicken in the outfield. Sometime early in the game a spectator, presumably in the crowd allowed in the outfield, managed to release a hen that he had brought into the park. That was not hard—in 1906 plenty of city people kept chickens in their backyard. One description of the bird said that it had "white stockings," whatever that meant, but which team it was supposed to represent or mock was unclear. The hen contentedly settled herself in an outfield spot, clucking and fluffing her feathers, and somehow managing to elude not only the feet of outfielders in action, but an occasional pop bottle thrown in her direction by an overstimulated spectator. Just before the sixth inning began, Nick Altrock trotted out from the first-base coaching box and shooed her off the turf.[5] The incident unfortunately left the door ajar for sportswriters to compete in labored jokes. One *Tribune* reporter said that Altrock was probably angry at the bird for all the goose eggs on the scoreboard. Charles Dryden, in his bylined piece, flailed away but never hit a smooth comic rhythm. The hen was possibly an escapee from the hospital, he suggested, a "demented creature" trying to attract the notion of Joe Tinker, who "own[ed] a chicken ranch in Kansas City" and was "known to adopt homeless and deserving hens of good character." Or perhaps she was on the field because all the good seats were taken and "she didn't have a dollar to her name." All that was missing was something about the bird's search for a good chance to catch flies, but Dryden did have what might have been the last word in referring to "a fowl in fair ground." The celebrated bird was even captured on film by one of the still photographers for the *Record-Herald*.

Another diversion was in watching the crowd react to fouls hit into the seats. A screen was in place behind home plate to protect the audience from fouls that went straight back. But the expectation of overflow audiences had led the Cubs management to put several rows of seats in front of it on a let-the-buyer-beware basis. Occasionally a line shot bounced off the screen and dropped among the risk takers, or scattered the cluster of press photographers crouched near home plate (in the days before television and telephoto lenses), ready to catch a split-second scoring play. There were also the usual pop-fly fouls that fell into the seats and tested the temperament of the audience. One spectator, "an individual of some years," dodged and let the ball bounce off the bench in front of him, a reporter noted. But another "cleverly caught a descending ball one-handed." It is unlikely, however, that he held it up in triumph as is the custom today.[6] Foul balls were supposed to be returned, but somehow the voluminous statistical records of baseball do not include any figures on the percentages successfully hidden from ushers and policemen who went after them if they were not immediately tossed back.

A special feature of this World Series was the visibility in the stands of toy bears waved frantically by the West Side supporters every time the Cubs made a good play. The bears were in high demand during the games, and as if in some prophetic anticipation of the age of tie-in promotions, stores had rushed to stock them, "big and little, fat and lean." Candy shops featured them filled with goodies. Another entrepreneur sold pottery cubs on all fours, with little indentations in their backs in which grass "fur" was planted. His stock included statuettes of Uncle Sam with "hair" of the same substance. Passersby looked with new interest at the "moth-eaten" full-grown stuffed bears that used to stand in front of furriers' and taxidermists' shops. Everyone was aware that the timing could not have been better, since it was only recently that, following a hunting trip in the Rockies by the very popular President Roosevelt, "Teddy" bears had become fashion accessories, and "at the Atlantic coast summer resorts a woman would as soon go promenading without her automobile veil as without a fuzzy toy bear under her arm."[7]

The drama on the field resumed at the start of the sixth with what proved to be the game's crucial scene. It began when Lee Tannehill faced Pfiester once again. The right-hander had enjoyed little luck at the plate up to that point. For that matter, neither had his team. In the first two games they had been held to five hits, and two of their three on this day had not gotten to the outfield. But Comiskey's men had an uncanny gift for making much out of whatever small gifts the unfathomable will of baseball's deities offered them. At this precise moment Tannehill found the swing that gave him his only hit in his nine at bats of the Series—a fast-moving roller that slipped between Steinfeldt and the third-base bag. Now Walsh was up, and the strategy clearly called for him to bunt. Pfiester was so determined not to give him anything easy to lay down that he committed the pitcher's mortal sin of walking his opposite number. As Walsh reached the base, he called for his sweater and shrugged into it while Ed Hahn walked to the plate to start the third run-through of the White Sox lineup.

Cheated of a flare hit in his last plate appearance by a great Evers catch, Hahn, batting left-handed, leaned over the plate, his bat poised. Pfiester, likewise a southpaw, let go a curveball that would normally have been expected to tail away. Instead it came inside, straight for the stocky outfielder's face. Hahn tried to pull his head back but too late—there was a thump, and he dropped to the seat of his pants, flinging the bat aside and covering his face with both hands. Blood from his broken nose streamed through his fingers as his teammates gathered around him and the murmuring crowd stood and gawked. A call went up for a doctor, and a physician visiting from Dubuque, Slattery by name, came trotting out of the stands to the fallen athlete, though he could do little except try to help stanch the bleeding. Finally, Hahn was helped to his feet, brought to the bench, and swaddled in sweaters; then he walked under his own power, along with a knot of helpers, to the Cook County Hospital, which was luckily only a block away. The hospital itself was aware of the game going on nearby as crowd cheers drifted faintly into the corridors. The *Chicago Daily News* even used its proximity as the springboard for a double plug for baseball and for itself: "The championship series is proving a material blessing from at least one standpoint. Since the games have started, physicians at the Cook county hospital have noted a change in the temperament of the usually gloomy patients. The contests have given many of them a new interest in life and they await the coming of the *Daily News* sporting extras with eagerness. Sufferers in some cases forget their pain as they attempt to rise in their beds to argue a baseball point with a neighbor."[8]

Charles Dryden, a pioneer in what came to be called the antiheroic, "Aw, nuts" school of sportswriting, was callous in his next-day report of the incident. BEATEN BY A NOSE! ran the head, and Dryden continued the theme with a description of how the "Spartan athlete" had stuck his nose into a pitch, and "the blowing away of the nose filled the bases." Dryden's tart use of the slangy rhythms coming into common speech at that time was usually much keener and more focused. His description of the first game was classically punchy: "Like the lunch hour in local chop houses, the action was fast and effective but not as clean as it might have been."

A replacement was now sent in to take the place of Hahn at first base, to which he was entitled as a hit batsman. The pinch runner was William O'Neill, listed as a utility outfielder who batted left and had come to the Sox from Milwaukee in the preceding spring. Pfiester now faced a bases-loaded, no-out situation, posing the eternal baseball question: what Houdini-like magic can a pitcher in that spot call on to escape without a score? Especially in a game where it is clear that a single run is going to be gigantic.

For a few shining moments (in the eyes of Cub fans) it looked as if he would wriggle free by the grace of luck and good fielding. He fed Jones just-off-the-plate tempters—one of which Jones got hold of and sent blazing toward right, but a foot or two ouside the foul line. With a second strike on him, Jones swung once more and lifted a low pop foul twisting toward the seats. Johnny Kling sprinted to the wire that marked off the overflow seats on the field, craned far over it with his mitt among the crowd, and pocketed the ball for the first out. Now it was Isbell's turn—he had already been struck out twice by Pfiester, and was hitless thus far in the Series. He, too, caught one of Pfiester's southpaw offerings and smashed it like a white streak to left—but again it fell inches foul. Then Pfiester got a third strike past "the Swede." And so George Rohe, the obscure substitute only a year out of the minors, who had scored the first run for the Sox on a triple into the crowd on Tuesday, came to bat. What were the mathematical odds of another hit to exactly the same area and with the same result? Enormous, and what did that matter? Sy Sanborn, who, in sharp contrast to Dryden, liked to cast his accounts in the form of epic drama, described the next forty or fifty seconds:

> The noise was deafening. White Sox backers were yelling their lungs out in the desperation of seeing appar-

ently certain victory fading from their sight. Hordes of Chance's supporters were chanting great shouts of gladness and encouragement. More than 13,000 pairs of eyes were glued upon those two men, Rohe and Pfiester, pitted against each other in a death struggle. All over the city and its vicinity, wherever details of the battle were being disseminated, other thousands of fans were hanging breathless over ticker or telegraph clicker, while batsman and pitcher eyed each other and glared defiance.

Slowly drawing back his arm Pfiester confidently shot a fast jump ball over the plate, close in. A quick step backward, a quicker swing of the bat and Rohe met that first ball pitched squarely in the middle and on the end of the bat. Quicker than that the ball started on a line over Steinfeldt's head, travelling faster and faster, it seemed, as Sheckard tore across left field to head it off. Too late he reached the spot where the ball struck earth and turned to watch it jump like some animated thing over the seats and the fringe of watchers.

At that moment, an enterprising photographer for the *Tribune* was on the roof of the stands, having climbed there during Jones's and Isbell's at bats, hoping for a good panoramic shot. Photographers, too, were a part of the game that were new in 1906, thanks to the development of high-shutter-speed and flash cameras, two more pieces of technology that widened the audience for bigtime sport from the grandstands to the newsstands. The *Tribune's* cameraman snapped Tannehill, Walsh, and O'Neill tearing around the diamond in full stride, a great action photo that spread across the inside of the front page in the next day's edition. O'Neill and Rohe pulled up at second and third, unsure whether the ball in the crowd was a ground-rule double or a triple. Umpire Johnstone waved his arm to O'Neill—"Come on home"—and the score was 3–0 Sox amid frenzy in the stands.

Tribune readers the next mornng were not the only ones who "saw" the action on the base paths through surrogate eyes. Go back to that frozen moment when the ball leaped off George Rohe's bat. Recall those thousands in the Auditorium Theater and the First Regiment Armory, whom the *Tribune,* as part of its exciting circulation war, had brought in as guests to watch the play-by-play on a "diamond" up front with counters moved from base to base and information posted as it clicked through wires from West Side Park. The paper had one of its men covering that scene, too. Like Sanborn, he gave readers their money's worth in suspense and tension:

> First half of the sixth. Three White Sox on bases. Two men out. The air yet ringing with the shouts of the Cub enthusiasts when Isbell follows Jones to the benches. The nerve tense throng at the Auditorium bends forward as the words come over the wire.
>
> "Rohe at the bat" is heard above the din. Then through the slow following silence filters the click of the telegraph instrument.
>
> The operator writes the message from the grounds quickly—too quickly to suggest to straining eyes and ears that anything has happened.
>
> The announcer leans over to read the written words. He takes up the slip of paper and a step forward, gently waving his hand for silence. . . . Every one of the 4,000 simultaneously has almost ceased to breathe.
>
> "Rohe," he begins in a low tone . . .
>
> —"It's the third out," was the common thought.
>
> "—has just made a three base hit," was the fact.
>
> Then the deluge.

"They stood on chairs and screamed and yelled," the story continued; "they threw their hats and coats into the air, they sang, they cheered, they danced in the aisles. They forgot completely that they were not in the bleachers with their eyes riveted on

Rohe cutting around the bases. They cheered Rohe, they cheered Comiskey, they cheered *The Tribune*."⁹ For the writer's employer, the last sentence was clearly the major point, and the paper itself worked to include among its 6,500 "guests"—2,500 at the armory and 4,000 in the theater—a number of "prominent citizens" like President Emil W. Ritter of the board of education (who "proved himself a real fan and cheered every play"). The media and the moguls of baseball were working together to advance their common interest, as they still do when millions gather before the television screens in their homes or in bars and restaurants.

An account of the game in the *Daily News* showed still another face of baseball reporting, the attempt to give readers the "inside dope" on what was coming to be seen as a battle of managerial wits conducted on scientific principles. That framework would also fit neatly into a popular respect for the daily evident wonders that science was delivering.

> It was the first ball pitched to him that Rohe pounded. Pfiester sent him an incurve that broke close to the inside of the plate. . . . For Rohe, a right-handed hitter, nothing better could be asked. . . . He "pulled" it to left field. Had Sheckard been aware that the ball was going on the inside he should have played more in left field, close to the line. . . . An inside ball is always "pulled" by the hitter.

It would be hard to call the remaining three and a half innings anticlimactic, but with the command that both pitchers were showing, there was a well-founded sense that the scoring for the day was probably finished, and so it proved. Unrattled by his one bad pitch, Pfiester did not yield another hit, though he got in trouble in the seventh when Tinker fumbled a grounder by Dougherty, who was sacrificed to second by catcher Sullivan. But Tannehill's deep fly was snared by Schulte in right, and though Dougherty moved to third after the catch, Pfiester struck out Walsh to end the threat. He set the Sox down in order in the eighth, but in the ninth got himself into hot water once again by the classic route of a leadoff walk to the redoubtable Rohe. Playing for an insurance run, Rohe added to his impressive record of success by stealing second. Donahue rolled a bunt toward the mound so slowly that Pfiester could do nothing but flip to Chance for the first out while Rohe sprinted to third. Now Dougherty swung and hit a ball sharply to Frank Chance, who promptly fired it back to Kling. Rohe, who had started at the crack of the bat, was already committed, and helplessly hung up between third and home. Kling, Steinfeldt, and Tinker ran him down, but Rohe, smart and speedy, kept skittering back and forth, coaxing and dodging tags, until when he was finally put out, Donahue was himself at third base on a highly unusual three-base fielder's choice. But now there were two out, and Sullivan flied out to Sheckard to end the threat.

Offensively, the Cubs had been helpless against Walsh, who mowed them down in order in the sixth through the eighth innings. Of those nine outs, four were strikeouts, four were infield grounders, and only one was a fly ball, lifted to right by Sheckard. It was, therefore, do-or-die time for the Cubs in the closing segment of inning nine, when they got a runner to third without benefit of a hit. Chance began by sending left-handed pinch hitter Doc Gessler to bat for Pfiester. Gessler was a reserve outfielder, obtained from Brooklyn early in 1906 and used in only 34 games. He rapped one to Isbell, who capped a futile day at the plate by committing an error, fumbling the ball and allowing Gessler to beat the throw to first baseman Donahue. Artie Hofman likewise hit to Isbell but was out as Gessler went to second on the fielder's choice. Walsh now unleashed a wild pitch that sent the pinch hitter to third, the only Cub hitter of the entire game to get that far. Now he was one deep infield grounder, one long fly, one more wild pitch or passed ball away from scoring. Walsh inhaled deeply, then notched strikeouts number 11 and 12 against Schulte and Sheckard. The whooping, dancing crowds of Sox fans swarmed onto the field trying to pound Walsh's back, pluck at his uniform, and bear him off on their shoulders. Game Three was history, and so was Walsh's performance. It had taken a mere two hours and ten minutes.

The postgame comments, as always, ran true to form—buoyant from the winners, and bravely smiling from the beaten. Chance was quoted as saying: "They beat us today, all right, but there are more games, and I am just as confident as ever that we will cop the series." The rival manager, however, saw it differently. "As I expected," pronounced Fielder Jones. "Now we only have two more to get, which ought to be easy under the circumstances."[10] The owners echoed their field leaders. "Two swallows don't make a summer, nor do two games a world's championship" was Charles Murphy's grin-though-it-hurts message, while Comiskey, hurrying to his auto through the mob of rooters trying to touch the hem of his garment, was majestically assured. "There's nothing to it now" was his brief answer to a reporter's shouted question.[11]

And so it appeared. But standing in the way of that easy advance to final victory was a giant with a deformed right hand, Mordecai "Three-Finger," "Centennial," "Miner" Brown. Opposing him once again was Nick Altrock, who was still in peak form after his Tuesday victory. Both men pitched masterpieces, and were so firmly in the saddle that the game moved with extraordinary speed; it was completed in one hour and thirty-five minutes. But seldom has there been an hour and a half of better baseball.

The game was played before the biggest crowd yet because the weather had finally begun to moderate. Overcoats, as one headline put it, were fed to mothballs and a mob scene in front of the South Side grounds was developing by the time the ticket office opened at noon. Fidgeting would-be patrons filled the streets curb to curb, and "among them," as Charles Dryden noted, "the gentle trolley car butted its way" while "panting autos competed with wireless messages from the stockyards, wafted along on the bosom of a southwest breeze." Dryden was overstretching the metaphor by calling a stink a "wireless message," but he may have been one of the first to record the contribution of exhaust mufflers to befouled city air.[12] All told, 18,386 people crowded into the small park—a harbinger of more to come on Sunday. The bleachers filled first, then the grandstand, and by 1:30 only the reserved boxes showed vacant seats. Six burly policemen tried to keep fans queued up in orderly fashion before the ticket windows, where clerks were frantically scooping in cash and handing out pasteboards. Meanwhile, as the players began to arrive at the field and the crowds greeted them with horns, bells, clappers, and screeches, the unlucky ones still outside the fences pushed and struggled harder, thinking that the game was already on. The greatest tumult was caused by Rohe, who got a ten-minute ovation when he came out for batting practice, but when Hahn appeared, ready to play despite a nose held in place by adhesive tape and a rubber air hose dangling from one nostril, the cheers were also loud and long. The *Daily News* claimed that Jack Pfiester had welcomed Hahn onto the field and confessed that he had worried all night about the extent of the "injury inflicted by himself."[13]

George Davis also received a hearty roar of homecoming welcome from the White Sox fans as he took up his position at short, and Lee Tannehill sat as an onlooker from the bench in order to leave Rohe and his magic bat in the lineup, at third.

Cub partisans were in full throat, knowing how badly their team needed this win. For a brief moment in the first half of the first their hopes were kindled, as Altrock handed a walk to Jimmy Sheckard and Sheckard stole second after the next batter, Schulte, had flied out. Manager Chance came up with his outfielder in scoring position and rapped a sharp grounder to third. Instead of going to first to beat the speedy Chance, Rohe alertly spied Sheckard, running with the pitch, stranded halfway to third. He turned, chased Sheckard back toward second, and caught him in a rundown that finally ended when Altrock came over to make the tag. Chance was left stranded by Steinfeldt to wipe out the scoring opportunity. But when Three-Finger picked up his glove and went to the hill, he gave the disappointed Cubs fans some consolation as he set down the first three Sox hitters on a groundout and two pop fouls to his catcher.

So it went for those swift first five innings. Steinfeldt singled to open the Cubs' second, and was sacrificed along by Tinker, Altrock pouncing on his bunt and shoveling it to first in one swift, choreographic gesture. Johnny Evers moved "Steinie" to third by his grounder to Davis. Jones now ordered an intentional walk to Kling but the catcher reached out and stung a wide pitch that traveled high and far toward right. Hahn backpedaled, hit the wire cable holding back the standees with his spine, flung his outstretched arm behind his head, and snatched the ball from the midst of the crowd for the third out. The Cub outfield matched that spectacle in the fourth when Hahn, at bat this time, skied a fly ball deep to right center that Artie Hofman ran down like a cheetah.

The Sox had put a man on in the second when Jiggs Donahue got one of Brown's two walks, but he was promptly caught stealing. In the fifth, the last of Brown's hitless frames, they got a break. George Rohe, who Cub fans would by now gladly have paid to lose his way to the ballpark, reached first when Steinfeldt bobbled his grounder and threw too high to Chance. Donahue, a .257 regular-season hitter, obligingly sacrificed him to second. Now the imposing six-foot-two figure of Patsy Dougherty stood facing Brown. He connected on one of the Cub hurler's pitches and sent a streak of lightning toward the hole between first and second. But "John of Troy" was just as speedy, diving to his left and smothering the ball. Rohe had sprinted to third, but one look at Evers, arm cocked and ready to throw, convinced him to stop there, while "the Crab" had time to throw Dougherty out. George Davis, however, could not solve Brown and plate the run. He struck out, and the inning was over.

Those first five innings of Game Four were a continuation of the dominant pitching on both sides. Altrock and Brown, in this second encounter, were consistently ahead of the hitters. But Pfiester and Reulbach for the Cubs and Walsh for the White Sox had been equally awesome. Only against Doc White and reliever Owen in the second game had the murderous Cub order been able to score much, plating seven runs. They had managed only one in the opener and been shut out in the third. The hitless wonders were predictably poorer—two in the opener, one in the second game, and three in the third—but half of those six runs were squeezed out of just one hit off the bat of Rohe.

Each side came up with a wasted hit in the sixth, but not until the seventh was home plate scuffed by a base runner's shoe. Chance led off the visitors' half with a soft looper over second. Isbell, racing out into short center, could not catch up with it, while Hahn, tearing in from right, lost it in the sun. It dropped in safely. In 1906 baseball there was never any doubt about what should be done next. Steinfeldt dropped a bunt in front of the mound, and Chance scampered to second as Altrock fielded it. Tinker now came up; the sacrifice was no longer automatic, but the shortstop bunted in his turn, hoping to fool the defense and leg it out as a hit. No soap—Altrock threw him out as well; but Chance now stood on third. Johnny Evers stood in, and cracked Altrock's first pitch into right and sent the Peerless Leader racing home with what the thousands in the stands knew in their bones, given the pitching duel in progress, would probably be the winning run.

Their bones did not mislead them. Brown set the White Sox down in order in the bottom of the seventh. In the top of the eighth, the Cubs came close to an insurance run when consecutive singles and a poor throw in from the outfield put Brown on third and Hofman on second with only one out. But Altrock steadied, got Sheckard to ground out to second, and induced Schulte, a .282 hitter during the season, to pop up to Isbell for the ex-lumberjack's second putout of the inning.

Now the bottom of the eighth, Sox with six outs left, tension mounting. A ray of light for the Sox—Dougherty slammed a hit between Chance and Evers, only the second, and the last, yielded

131

by the otherwise unyielding Brown. But George Davis hit into a force-out that erased Dougherty at second. Billy Sullivan stepped in and took two strikes. Davis broke for second on what was supposed to be a hit-and-run play. But Sullivan's furious swing missed the ball for strike three, and Johnny Kling's throw nailed Davis to complete a strike-'im-out-throw-'im-out double play. Groans from the Sox bench; pandemonium from the Cubs.

The ninth inning sustained the drama. Chance got the last hit given up by Altrock and took second base on the sacrifice by Steinfeldt. Tinker now tried, as he had in the seventh, to bunt his way on while advancing his manager 90 feet. But Altrock was waiting for that like a hawk hovering over a field mouse. He got the ball to first while Chance, underestimating Altrock's quickness, overzealously rounded third and turned on full power heading for home. "Jiggs" stepped on first base to retire Tinker, then blazed a clean strike into Sullivan's glove, and Chance was tagged out to complete the second consecutive double play to end an inning and a scoring opportunity.

Last chance for the White Sox. With two out after substitute catcher Ed McFarland (a puny .178 average in 13 regular-season games) batting for Altrock grounded to Steinfeldt and Hahn lined to Tinker, Brown tired enough to give his second walk of the game to Jones. Brown drew breath, threw a "drop ball"— nowadays called a sinker—to Kling, who dropped it. Screams from the stands—but the ball bounced against the umpire's leg before rolling away out of Kling's reach, so instead of a passed ball, it was "interference" and Jones was allowed to proceed to second but no farther. Two out, tying run in scoring position, Frank Isbell at bat. He swung, and a wicked line shot went straight for the head of Mordecai Brown, bent over in the follow-through. In self-defense Brown flung up a hand and intercepted the ball in flight. The force was strong enough to knock him off his feet as the ball rolled toward first. He rolled to his knees, scrambled after the ball, barehanded it, and flipped it to a stretched-out, waiting Frank Chance. And so the ball game ended, 1–0.

It had been a thriller, through and through. The *Chicago Daily News* reporter described it as "one of the best ever played here, and those that saw the contest will speak of it in years to come as the hardest fought and most scientifically played" they ever saw. . . .

> The tension on the rooters was at the highest and those that were on the losing side went away from the game limp and almost unable to talk for their nerves were worn out when the finish came. The joy of victory kept the supporters of the winning side going and many a frenzied rooter did not finish his war dance until midnight.[14]

Both the third and fourth games had revealed the quality of the pitching thus far. The Cubs had had 23 hits in the four, 10 of them in Game Two, with seven steals. The hitless wonders had a mere 13 hits and three steals. Yet the Cubs had only outscored their rivals 9–6—and managed to lose two of the games. The Cubs had only two extra-base hits, which was truly astonishing (though perhaps not so much in the dead-ball era), but they were both nonproductive doubles, while three of four for the Sox were triples, two by George Rohe, one of them a game winner.

And so the Series was even. "All square again and two to get," summarized one entry in a *Tribune* feature titled "Notes from the Game." Those two would tell the story. Would the surprising hitless wonders continue to rewrite the script? Or would the season-long weight of evidence be decisive and bring the Cubs back to dominance?

6

The Finale

Saturday morning found Chicago going about its usual routines, for the day before Sunday did not have the meaning in 1906 that it does now. For almost all Chicagoans, it was another morning to push aside the bedclothes early and get ready for work. The five-day workweek scarcely existed back then, though office employees had a better chance of getting let off in the afternoon than did the thousands who worked in the city's shops and factories. The weather patterns had finally shifted; the temperature predicted for the day was "continued high temperatures," and in fact the thermometer would hit 74 degrees in midafternoon. All in all, it was the start of a fine Indian summer "week-end," however anachronistic the term. It was also the harvest season, and the harvest of half a year's baseball would be gathered within the next forty-eight hours.

The improved weather, plus the slightly more relaxed work requirements of Saturday, accounted for a swelling of the crowd that brought happy smiles to both Comiskey's and Murphy's accountants, though so far as the players were concerned, their shares of the gate receipts were already locked in. All the same, there was apparently some murmuring that the turn-and-turn-about pattern of the first four games, instead of the quick knock-out by the Cubs that had been expected, hinted at a fix of some kind, possibly some under-the-table payments to the players by their bosses in gratitude for stretching the contest out. The *Inter-Ocean* indignantly rejected the idea. "It is the glorious uncertainty of baseball and the practical impossibility of corrupting a baseball team that have brought the sport to a level of popularity where in the United States today probably two-thirds of the people hang in anxiety on the outcome of the present world's championship series." The editor went on to explain that "aside from the question of any player's risking his entire future" on the possibility of exposure, it couldn't be done practically. With 15,000 to 30,000 "expert witnesses" watching each game, "could a pitcher—for instance—and he is the only man who could turn the game un-aided—pull the wool over the eyes of this crowd?" And a veteran player was quoted elsewhere as saying that as soon as a player was through with his career he would be sure to blackmail a dishonest owner by threatening to sell his story; "if the practice was general, every club would have an army of pensioners as big as the G.A.R. [the Civil War veterans' association]."[1] The words would have ironic echoes thirteen years later when several White Sox players paid by professional gamblers did throw the Series to Cincinnati, but on the other hand, alert reporters, led by Hugh Fullerton, quickly smelled something putrid in the on-field per-formance of the Chicago team and lifted the lid off the scandal, just as had been predicted.

The most eager patrons of the game began arriving as early as 6:30 A.M., half an hour after sunrise, some carrying lunch boxes and newspapers to while away the time. They could read about the college football schedule for the day and the exciting con-test between the University of Chicago and Purdue that was in store. They also read about a high school player whose neck had been broken fatally in a game the preceding day, the death of a pedestrian in New York struck by a car tearing along at 12 miles per hour, and the burning of a steamship at its dock in Hankow, China, with hundreds of casualties among the 2,000 Chinese packed aboard, though somehow, suspiciously, "all the European passengers and the crew were saved." CELESTIALS DIE IN SWARMS IN FIRE AND WATER was the *Tribune*'s grabber headline, "celestials" being one of the more popular American nicknames for the "quaint" millions who dwelled in the Celestial Kingdom, one translation of China's name for itself. There was a yellow fever epidemic in Havana. And the special tax lawyer in the city's legal department was insisting that the Pullman Company had understated its past year's earnings and owed the city nearly $42,000 in back taxes.

The crowd continued to grow—and to grow restless—as the noon hour for opening the gates approached, and a sweating and straining detachment of police could barely keep order as men jostled and crushed each other trying to get through to the ticket offices. BIG CROWDS STORM GATE was the next day's summary. By one o'clock the grandstand seats were filled and the gates were closed. Thousands of unhappy fans clamored for the few on-field seats that were still available, or offered as much as $10 for the privilege of standing in the outfield. A few made it, but others in lines that stretched for blocks in two directions either left in despair or herded themselves into a small grassy park just to the north of the ballpark that separated it from the hospital. Eventually, it was estimated, there were as many as 8,000 rooters left outside, while 23,257 "fanatics" were shoehorned into the park. The more agile and adventurous fans who failed to get in found themselves daring perches: they were "packed on adjoining roofs, clinging to telegraph poles and wires like monkeys," the *Tribune* reported, and during the game they screamed play-by-play calls to those below, adding to the general cacophony around the grounds. There were also lines waiting patiently to scramble for seats at the *Tribune*'s free remote show at the armory. By the time of the first pitch "every available square inch of floor space . . . was occupied and it was necessary to call upon the police to bar the doors to the late arrivals to prevent overcrowding of the hall and consequent violation of city ordinances." It was the "Wildest Throng Ever Seen."[2]

Pregame festivities whetted the appetite of the hordes in the stadium for the action to follow. First of all, the Cubs' bench was graced with a floral horseshoe that had been presented by "Ruby Bob" Fitzsimmons, the former world heavyweight champion, to "break the luck" of the Cubs having lost two straight on their home grounds. Chance, Murphy, and the Cubs themselves were aware of the pattern (though it applied to the White Sox as well), and their own break-the-luck gesture had been to outfit the team in their gray road uniforms this day, the afternoon's first surprise for the crowd. Also present was the white-stockinged chicken that had roamed the outfield in the third game, this time safely caged. Then there was yet another presentation ceremony as Chance and Jones were called out to receive identical gifts from the hand of George M. Cohan's stage manager: watch fobs, each bearing a diamond-shaped gold pennant studded with genuine diamonds, and inscribed "from George M. Cohan, a Lover of Baseball." Undoubtedly sincere, the gesture was good theater and good public relations, a two-bagger, so to speak, for the popular Irish American song-and-dance man and theatrical entrepreneur.

The most unusual pregame exhibition was a live animal show. Four bear cubs had been brought to the field, two by a head keeper at the Lincoln Park Zoo. Two others had been bought from a local amusement park by the board of trade, which escorted them to the park at the head of a procession of carriages carrying board members and their party of guests. Ed Heeman of the board presented them to Chance and the team at home plate. All four of the young animals were then led by their keepers—or as one account more accurately put it, dragged by chains on their "furry hams" around the bases, with no animal rights activists on hand to protest. The Lincoln Zoo pair were returned to quarters. There is no record of what became of the two who became the property of the Cubs organization.

The sun shone, jackets were shed, the roars and shouts of the "bugs" and "bugines" (Charles Dryden's names for fans of both genders) were mixed with laughter. It was a beautiful day, at last, for the start of the three-game set that would now decide the championship. Expectation was high—and it was amply fulfilled in the very first inning when, after three low-scoring games of the four already played, the lid blew off and the hitters finally thawed out. And it was the White Sox who emerged from the deep freeze first.

Hahn, whose broken nose seemed if anything to have energized him, stepped in to face Reulbach, who just seventy-two hours earlier had held the White Sox to one hit. Hahn promptly cracked a liner into center for a single. Jones routinely bunted him over in the familiar scenario. But nothing in the rest of the inning was routine. The smiling Irish "Swede," Frank Isbell, horse-collared since the opening day, took his stance and laced a double into the crowd in right, sending Hahn home with the lead run. Cleanup batter Davis rapped a grounder at Reulbach, and the six-footer snapped it up so quickly that Isbell was caught in no-man's-land between second and third. Reulbach threw to Steinfeldt, who then joined Tinker in a rundown that ended with the Cub shortstop tagging out Isbell, while Davis took first on the fielder's choice. Two out, one on, but now the pestilent, persistent Rohe was in the box, ready once more to make the Cubs' lives miserable. He connected on a Reulbach curve that did not snap as it had done on Wednesday, and sent a long fly ball into the crowd in right for a ground-rule double. Reulbach's magic had departed. He walked Donahue deliberately to set up a force at any base, then threw a sinker to Patsy Dougherty, who slammed it to the mound, where it bounced high over a leaping Reulbach's glove for what looked like a certain run-producing hit. But Evers was there when it came down, while Davis and Rohe, running with the pitch, were only steps from home. Evers made a desperate heave as the runners crossed the plate—Dougherty flung himself into a slide toward first base—and umpire "Silk" O'Loughlin signaled "Out" to erase the tallies. Runs scored before completion of a force play resulting in the third out do not count. A roar of protest rose from the Sox bench; Jones rushed in to join Dougherty in vehement argument; spectators in the top row screamed down at the crowd outside explaining the uproar; and after a moment or two of hubbub, the decision held—especially hard to argue, since O'Loughlin was an American League umpire. Thanks to sharp defense by Reulbach and Evers, a single, a sacrifice, two doubles, and a walk had netted the White Sox a mere one run.

Now it was time for the Cubs to deal with Ed Walsh, who had humiliated them on Thursday and was working on a single day's rest. The short recovery period had apparently reduced the efficiency of "Big Ed," even though in 1906 it was not at all uncommon for pitchers to work on consecutive days or even start both ends of a doubleheader. But this time Walsh had to contend with what Sy Sanborn would call "the rankest exhibition of fielding a team of champions ever gave the public."[3] He began by giving up a single to leadoff man Hofman, thus far a major Cub asset with four hits in the preceding three games. Next he faced Sheckard, who pushed a sacrifice bunt toward first that moved the Cubs' center fielder to second. Then, Schulte sent a hot shot toward third that Rohe knocked down in time to hold Hofman at second, but not quickly enough to get the out at first. Manager Chance came to the plate, and Walsh, still not quite in command of his repertoire, missed with a pair of pitches and then tried an inside curve that hit Chance's hand without damage to Chance, but darkening Walsh's own prospects with a bases-loaded, one-out situation. Walsh now bore down and got Steinfeldt, who had led the Cubs with a .327 average during the season and had four hits in the Series thus far, to slap a sure double-play ball to Isbell. But Isbell, after first neatly stepping in textbook fashion on second to force Chance, then hurled the ball out of Donahue's reach into the crowd, allowing Hofman and Schulte to score the tying and go-ahead runs and sending the Cubs rooters into refreshed frenzy. With Steinfeldt on second, Tinker tried a bunt, and again

Walsh, a fine fielder for a pitcher, grabbed the ball and lobbed it toward first, only to see Donahue drop it. By the time "Jiggs" recovered the ball, Steinfeldt, who was fast enough to have stolen 29 bases during the season, had scored the Cubs' third tally. Walsh now took matters into his own hands and, during the course of Evers's at bat, whirled and caught Tinker with too big a lead off first. He fired to Donahue, and a rundown play, with the putout going to shortstop Davis, ended the inning.

The inning had taken half an hour to play, and the fans, already hoarse, had seen four runs scored, five hits, two errors, a hit batsman, a rhubarb at first on a gem of a fielding play, a pickoff, and two rundowns. Clearly, the pitching dominance of the first part of the Series had vanished with the frosts of yesterday.

It did not seem so clear in the second, when both pitchers apparently settled in and enjoyed one-two-three innings. But in the third, lightning struck the Cubs. The no longer hitless South Side crew resumed its assault and battery on Reulbach. Isbell hit his second double of the day, showing a nice sense of symmetry—the first had been to right field, this one was to left. Switch-hitter Davis, moved into the cleanup spot and swinging left-handed, drilled another double that scored Isbell. Reulbach, Wednesday's launderer of White Sox, had now faced 11 batters, had yielded five hits and two runs, and had yet to retire a batter in the third inning. "At this juncture," reported one writer, "Manager Chance was perceived to make a cabalistic sign in the direction of the clubhouse and Jack Pfiester was seen emerging from the crowd ready to take up the White Sox burden." Readers in 1906 would quickly catch the parody of Rudyard Kipling's popular poem of 1899, calling on the civilized world to "take up the white man's burden."[4]

But the white imperialists of the day had less trouble with the "natives" than Pfiester did with the White Sox. He had pitched creditably in Game Three except for yielding Rohe's one, crushing three-run blow. It was a choice piece of unscripted drama that made Rohe the first batter he faced now, and he got a measure of revenge by striking Rohe out. But he then uncorked a pitch that hit Donahue in the back as "Jiggs" twisted to get out of its way. Dougherty stood in next, and Pfiester got him to hit a ground ball that forced "Jiggs" at second while Davis took third. Working cautiously to catcher Billy Sullivan, he took a windup a fraction too cautious—and what happened next was classic baseball as the weak-hitting Sox had played it during the season. As the pitch—a strike—headed for the catcher's mitt, Dougherty broke for second, Kling unloaded his peg to the base too late, and meanwhile veteran George Davis sprinted for the plate on his thirty-six-year-old legs and slid across as the second half of a beautiful double steal. The game was tied. Sulllivan eventually took a third strike for the final out. Pfiester had not done too badly in quenching the fire. But the worst was yet to befall him.

In the Cub half of the third another Sox error compelled Walsh to get an extra out. He struck out Sheckard, then induced a grounder to short that Davis threw into the crowd, putting the batter, Schulte, on second instead of recording out number two. Walsh gritted his teeth, got two more groundouts, then retired for a brief moment before going to the plate as the first hitter of the next inning. Pfiester opened it with the pitcher's bugaboo of walking his opposite number. Hahn bunted, but the sacrifice failed as a snappy pickup and throw by Steinfeldt forced Walsh at second. The spitballer trotted back to the bench, then blissfully watched the fireworks as the inning turned, in a *Tribune* writer's witticism, into "a glorious Fourth for the White Sox supporters."

Jones singled, and Isbell followed with his third straight double into the crowd in center, having thereby hit one to each field. That scored Hahn while moving Jones to third. Davis now arrived in the batter's box, switched to a right-handed batting position against the lefty, and doubled two more base runners home. It was a double in two senses, because it marked the second time Davis had knocked the Cub pitcher of the moment out of the game. "Pfiester flew the coop," Charles Dryden recorded, "and out came Overall" in response to Chance's emergency alarm. The young Californian right-hander, in only his sophomore year as a major leaguer, for a moment appeared to be one more sacrificial victim to the White Sox execution squad. He walked Rohe, then gave up another two-bagger, the third of the inning, to Jiggs Donahue, scoring Davis and sending Rohe to third. Now it was Dougherty's turn to join the celebration, and he sent a sinking liner into right that spelled trouble. But the celebrated Cub defense came to the rescue. Frank Schulte raced to where it was falling just in time to snag it off his shoelaces. He straightened up on the run and fired it to cutoff man Evers, who whirled in a split second and sent another bullet into Kling's glove that got Rohe at the plate as he tried to score. It was a great double play of the balletlike kind that makes baseball glow, and like Evers's great pickup in the first, it stopped the hemorrhaging. But four more runs were in for Jones's pyrotechnic experts.

Snatched from the brink, Overall was effective thereafter, giving up only one more run in the sixth. But the damage was done. "The Nationals came back desperately in every inning," Sanborn wrote, helped by the White Sox players' apparent inability to hit and to field well in the same game. In the Cub half of the fourth, Rohe threw first batter Joe Tinker's ground ball into the crowd, error number four for Comiskey's men. Walsh walked Evers, steadied enough to fan Kling, but then was unable to prevent a double steal by the two base runners that put them on second and third. Walsh put away Overall on strikes and then slipped again, letting go a wild pitch that scored Tinker. The spitballer walked Hofman but finally found enough control to strike out poor, floundering Sheckard, slumping at the wrong time of year for his club. Inning over, score 7–4 in favor of the White Sox.

Given the pattern of the day, it was still anybody's game, now in the hands of Walsh and Overall. "Orvie" got three quick outs in the fifth; Walsh sandwiched his three around a double to Chance. In the top of the sixth, after Jones struck out, Isbell hit his eye-widening fourth straight double (to right again), the 10th White Sox hit. Overall at least escaped the curse of George Davis as Cub pitcher-killer, however, getting him on a grounder to Evers, who held Isbell at third. And yet, here was the golden sub Rohe once more, singling to bring in Isbell with run number eight for the White Sox. Shaken, Overall threw a wild pitch to Donahue before getting "Jiggs" to bounce back to the mound.

Score 8–4—but the Cubs cut the lead in half in their part of the sixth inning. Walsh got two ground-ball outs, but then walked Overall and Hofman. Sheckard, still struggling, hit an apparent third-out bouncer to Rohe, who botched it for Sox error number five, filling the bases for Schulte, who already had two hits. Still hot, Schulte doubled home Overall and Hofman as Cub rooters screamed with jubilation. But Frank Chance made the third out on a shot to Isbell.

The seventh inning found Overall comfortable and getting by the bottom of the Sox order easily. In the Cubs' half the door seemed to swing ajar for another productive inning, as Steinfeldt opened with a double. Manager Jones decided that it was time to replace Walsh, and brought in Doc White. White, who had recovered from his Game Two malaise, put his formidable left arm to work and mowed down Tinker, Evers, and Kling in a row.

The eighth saw one more bit of sensational action. Overall polished off three more White Sox batters with a fly ball, a foul out, and a strikeout. The Cubs now came to bat burdened by the fact that the first man due up was the pitcher. But Chance was not going to risk giving up his now-cruising reliever for a pinch hitter. He may even have been wondering if he should not have started his young giant. Overall, as expected, went quietly. Leadoff man Hofman swung in futility at White's curves and was fanned. And once more, the Sox infield let the pitcher down, as Isbell allowed Sheckard's grounder to go past him. It was his second error (he shared the questionable honor of two with Rohe) and the White Sox' sixth and mercifully last. And it brought to the batter's box Schulte, who already had three hits for the day, creating fresh delirium in the stands, Cub pennants and toy bears bobbing and waving in circles like wind-tossed confetti. Schulte connected for a fast-moving roller into the hole between third and short that just eluded a diving Rohe's glove. Davis, swooping in behind him, managed to pick it up and throw to Donahue, but a shade too late for the out. At that instant Sheckard, who had reached second, spied the unguarded third base, put his head down, and made a mad dash for it. Rohe and Isbell (and every Sox rooter in the park) screamed for Donahue to throw the ball to Davis, who with glove outstretched was racing Sheckard toward the base. The two runners and the ball converged at almost the same instant; Davis tagged Sheckard just as their two bodies collided, and they went sprawling over the bag and lay motionless for a moment. Sheckard was out. Davis, who had risked fractured bones, had gotten his man in a thrilling play that partly redeemed a dreary afternoon of Sox fielding. The collective groans of the Cub fans and screams of Sox rooters echoed in the darkening late-afternoon sky.

And dark it was, both metaphorically for the Cubs and in reality. It was 4:30 in a fading and cooling afternoon; some houses in the vicinity were already showing lights in the windows. The Sox came up for their final turn, and Rohe, hitting after Davis's fly out to left, beat out an infield bouncer for his team's 12th and last hit and his third of the day. Donahue moved him to third on a groundout to Tinker, but Dougherty, who was truly a hitless wonder thus far, with only one hit in the five games, fanned. Reliever Overall's work was done.

And the Cubs could not make their final turn a contest. Chance flied to center; Steinfeldt grounded to Rohe. White walked Tinker—a glint of hope for a two-out rally brightened Cub fans' hearts for an instant. Chance now sent up a pinch hitter, youthful reserve catcher Pat Moran, to bat right-handed against White in place of Evers. The ball flew toward the batsman, and a sound was heard like the coup de grâce at an execution—the crack of the bat on the leather of the ball as Moran launched a grounder that Davis gobbled up and tossed to Isbell to force Tinker, although reporter Sanborn suggested that in the "gathering gloom" most of the Sox players and fans who raced ecstatically onto the field never actually saw the play completed.

It was done, and the crowd was both fulfilled and drained after what had been, score and errors aside, one of the most exciting games thus far. Dryden summed up the day plainly enough. The 23,257 spectators had looked on as "the humble people from the south side mauled the favorites in shameless fashion" and, as he put it, backed them over the dump. What the Sox had "lost in boots and bungles they made up in bingles." The "shades of night" had arrived in time to "shut out the dismal scene."

It was even more dismal for the Cubs on the following day. Simple charity should spare narration of the details. Perhaps the most dramatic moments of the day occurred before and after the action on the field. The curtain was raised in the darkness of 2:00 A.M., Sunday, when the first would-be ticket buyer showed up in front of South Side Park, according to the *Record-Herald,* which did not explain whether it had a reporter on hand to verify the time. By 7:00 A.M., two hundred hundred more were in the lines, which kept lengthening as thousands, lured by the promise of holiday good weather, converged on the grounds either to be in at the kill or to watch the Cubs pull a perils-of-Pauline escape. The gates were not scheduled to open until noon, but long before that it was evident that crowd control was going to be a problem.

Comiskey had asked for a substantial detachment of police to show up at 11:30, but a good hour before that the situation began to get out of hand as the swelling tide of new arrivals became too much for the fifty officers present to channel queues. The swarm began to push against the wooden fences lining Princeton and 39th Streets, and sometime around 10:45, with a great cracking and tearing of timbers and slats, two sections went down. A flying beam hit one of the struggling cops square in the face, and protruding nails clawed a gash, luckily missing his eye. He would not be the day's last casualty. Reinforcements arrived just in time to get inside the park and begin to push the invaders slowly back toward the gap through which they had surged, and back out into the streets. In the midst of shouts, trampling, wrestling, and shoving, some women fainted and had to be carried away to safety by policemen or cooperative civilians muscling their way to clear spaces. At least one man had his arm broken in the miniriot and was removed by ambulance A few who made it inside did so at the cost of ripped and torn clothes. Eventually, some 225 of Chicago's finest managed to restore order, guard the breach, and divert the stampede into some semblance of lines at the ticket windows, which were now thrown open in order to drain the congestion in the streets. All available seats were quickly sold out; then extra groups of clamoring would-be customers were admitted to the outfield standing room in intermittent batches until, at 12:30, no more could be allowed, though bills were being waved in the air and there were shouted offers of two, three, and four times the posted prices.

There were 19,249 officially counted spectators (in a park built to hold 5,000), but at least as many, according to direct reports from the scene, clustered around the park. They stood packed on the sidewalks; they clambered onto rooftops as distant as the Horace Mann School several blocks away (some having foresightedly brought binoculars); and, as on the day before, adventurous followers shinnied up lampposts and telephone poles and clung to cross-arms and wires and light globes. Some of these, after the two-hour-and-five-minute game, slid down to find themselves temporarily too exhausted to walk. Throughout the nine innings, beelike swarms of baseball fanatics kept up an unremittingly loud buzz. Those closest to the grandstands were helped by spectators in the top rows, some of them, it was said, placed there by Comiskey himself—who shouted down answers to their questions. Those farther away got some help from the pole sitters. One black fan on a lamppost did such a stellar play-by-play through a megaphone that those in his immediate vicinity below made up a hasty purse of $25 for him at the game's end.

The combined din of the thousands outside and in the stands was augmented by a contrivance imported into the bleachers and described in the *Record-Herald* as a "long distance siren with an unearthly sound" operated by a man with a white stocking for a hatband. Restaurant inspector Sol Van, one of the civic functionaries in the prime seats, carried a dinner gong "which he walloped with a confiscated potato masher." Easier on the ear but still strident was a band consisting of trombones, French horns, cornets, cymbals, and snare drums that between innings rendered popular favorites like "Marching Through Georgia," a northern Civil War tune. Sometimes an individual got the crowd to follow him in singing some well-known parody like "So Long, Murphy, How We Hate to See You Lose," or others on 1906 hits now long forgotten.

Aware of both the threatening impatience of the crowds and the futility of keeping the gates open for more ticket buyers, both owners agreed to ring the starting bell at 2:00 P.M., half an hour earlier than the schedule called for. The occasional spurts of applause for flashy work in fielding practice turned into a steady roar as Doc White took his warm-up tosses. Then Art Hofman strode to the plate, and in good leadoff-man fashion, shortened up and bunted the first pitch, hoping to catch the infield by surprise. But the bunt rolled foul. Hofman swung away at one of White's subsequent offerings and connected for a hit to the outfield, which took a bad hop away from Patsy Dougherty and allowed Hofman to make it to second. Sheckard, still horse-collared after 18 hitless official at bats, was spared a 19th when he obediently sacrificed Hofman to third. Schulte now brought hosannas from the Cub occupants of the stands by hitting one into the crowd in right field that brought Hofman home. A policeman—one of those whose job was to keep shooing the crowd back outside the foul lines and the designated outfield limit—retrieved the ball and tossed it back in. The Peerless Leader took his place in the box but could do nothing but bounce back to White, who tossed him out at first. Working too carefully around Steinfeldt, the "Doc" walked the Cubs' most dangerous hitter, then bore down and got Tinker to send an easy high fly to center that ended in Fielder Jones's glove. First blood to the West Side, and the warm sun shone down on a sea of Sunday hats and uncovered heads, shirtsleeves and shirtwaists, and happy Cub fans.

Then the rains came—specifically the deluge of White Sox base hits. Chance had taken a chance, sending his ace, Brown, as the back-to-the-wall stopper who would keep the team alive. Brown had given up only five hits on Tuesday, losing only because of Altrock's equally strong performance in that 2–1 opening game. On Friday he had shut out Jones's men with two hits. Now he would be pitching on one day's rest and for the third time in the same week, but that was not so unusual for great pitchers in the dead-ball era. With the Cubs' fate in his maimed right hand, Three-Finger faced the first man in the Sox order, Ed Hahn, referred to by at least one callous newspaper joker as "Beaksy." Hahn's convalescence from the broken nose of Thursday continued to improve his batting average. He had hit safely in both the fourth and fifth games, and now, after Brown had gotten a strike past him, he slammed a pitch in the direction of the mound that bounced so high that by the time it settled into Evers's glove it was too late for him to throw Hahn out. Now Jones bunted, but Johnny Kling showed why he was a star catcher by pursuing the ball and making a quick pickup and accurate throw to second in time to force Hahn and foil the attempt at a sacrifice. Isbell, however, whacked a single, moving his manager down to third, and the veteran George Davis, up next, launched a high drive toward the right-field crowd. Schulte took off in pursuit, then turned and backpedaled, reaching upward. Then he staggered, and the ball fell out of his reach for a double, sending Jones across the plate and Isbell to third. Schulte leaped to his feet and raced over to umpire Silk O'Loughlin, screaming in protest that either a policeman or a spectator had bumped him from behind just as he was about to make the catch. Artie Hofman dashed to Schulte's support. Chance hurried over from first base to join in, quickly followed by Jones and Nick Altrock (who was on the first-base coaching line) to argue the other side and defend the call. The usual scene followed—the knot of players and umpires jawing and screaming, fans standing and howling—and so did the usual result; the decision stood. Unlike the previous day's first-inning argument, this time it was the White Sox who got the benefit of the doubt. Now Rohe, the golden replacement, hit to deep short as Isbell raced for the plate at the instant of contact. But Tinker's arm was quicker than Izzy's feet, and his throw to the plate was in plenty of time for Kling to tag Isbell out. Rohe halted at first while Davis advanced to third on the play, but when Brown became intensely absorbed in meditation on what to throw to Jiggs Donahue, Rohe sprinted down to second for an unopposed steal. Brown's ultimate pitch selection was the wrong one in any case, because Donahue connected with it for a double, scoring two more Sox runs. Patsy Dougherty grounded out to end the inning, but the "Miner," who had given up six hits in 18 previous innings, now had been rocked for four, good for three runs, in one.

"Oh, those demon sox!" wrote one *Record-Herald* reporter the following day. "Wow, those 'hitless wonders.' They batted as they did in Saturday's fracas, even more so, and the cubs were helpless before the onslaught."[5] The Cubs put Evers on base in the second thanks to an error by Donahue on a bad-hop grounder, but little Johnny was promptly wiped out when Kling hit into a quick double play, on a grounder to Davis. White then struck out Brown, and the White Sox spat on their hands and got back to work.

Brown easily retired the two Sox at the bottom of the order, but when he faced the pesky Hahn for the second time, Hahn hit the second of four singles that he would get during the afternoon. Brown got two strikes on Jones and was almost out of the woods before hitting a wild streak and serving up four balls. Isbell hit a little looper over second that managed to drop between the converging Evers and Tinker, and the bases were full for Davis, who already had a run batted in. The Sox shortstop sent a wicked liner that a leaping Tinker got a glove on and managed to slow down, but by the time he scrambled back and retrieved it Hahn had crossed the plate, and Jones beat the throw to Kling. The stands shook as Sox rooters, on their feet, jumped and stamped and chanted in deafening chorus, "ONE! TWO! THREE! FOUR! FIVE!" Now Rohe hit a deep shot to short. Tinker held on to the ball long enough to freeze Isbell at third, but that allowed Rohe to make it to first and reload the bases.

Chance had seen enough. Four more hits and a walk, even though the hits were all of the "scratch" type, made it clear that the "Miner" was not at his sharpest. Chance sent him walking dejectedly back to the bench while Overall, the salvage engineer, was summoned for the second straight day. Once again it took him a couple of batters to find his groove. Donahue greeted him with a single that scored Isbell and kept the bases loaded—Davis at third, Rohe at second, and "Jiggs" himself surveying the scene from the first base that he usually occupied as a defender. It was now 6–1 Sox, Dougherty at bat. The big University of California graduate on the mound breathed deeply and decided to exert less power and more caution in aiming for the plate. But that turned out to be too much of a good thing, and he walked Dougherty, sending Davis strolling home. "FIVE! SIX! SEVEN!" the echoes boomed as Sullivan approached the batter's box. But a light hitter at best (.214 for the 1906 season and 0 for 18 thus far in the Series), he was easy pickings for Overall, who struck him out.

The inning was over. So, to all intents and purposes, were the Cubs' hopes only forty-five minutes after Brown's first pitch to Hofman. Chance's champions, who had slain the Giants and trampled the rest of the National League underfoot like a blind elephant in a domestic pet shop, could do little in the remaining hour and twenty minutes against White's left-handed assortment of inside and outside sinking curves, changes of speed, and balls that whizzed along the edges of the strike zone. He stifled their bats in the third, got them to waste a leadoff walk to Chance in the fourth, and in the fifth gave a single and a double in succession to Kling and Overall that netted the Cubs another run. He walked four, struck out two, and hit Chance on the ankle in the sixth. A single by Tinker moved "Husk" to second. With two outs, a five-run deficit, and the hour getting late, Chance gambled and tried to steal third, but was cut down by Sullivan's peg, killing the minirally. The Cubs were shut down again in the eighth.

Meanwhile, Overall was once more containing the damage so nicely that it was hard to realize that he was in only his second major-league season. After entering the game in the second, he gave up six more White Sox hits, but they were scattered widely enough to allow only one more run, in the eighth. That one, however, restored the lead to six, and nailed down the lid.

The Cubs gave one last convulsive heave and shudder in the top half of the ninth. With one out, Evers, whose play throughout the six games had been a beacon, doubled on a grounder driven into the crowd, which was pressing in closer and closer along the right-field foul line waiting for the end. Kling hit a roller to Rohe, who went for the sure out at first and allowed Evers to take third. Chance now sent up a pinch hitter for Overall, Jake Gessler, a left-handed reserve outfielder, who drew a walk. Hofman, at the top of the order, came up for a fifth at bat and got the seventh and final Cub hit, scoring Evers. In the late innings, the Sox players had begun to exult, patting one another on the back and shaking hands as they returned to the bench. Nick Altrock was joining the congratulatory chorus from his coaching box. Now, like so many teams with victory an inch away, they became a little hasty and overanxious. Sheckard—who else but haunted Sheckard?—slapped a sure-out grounder toward Rohe at third, and—Rohe fumbled it! A collective sigh of exasperation burst from the throats of thousands of White Sox lovers ready to erupt into a hallelujah chorus. Dejected Cubs fans meanwhile looked at the loaded bases, then at the scoreboard that showed their team still five runs down, but remembered that the forever blessed rule-makers of baseball had decreed in their wisdom that the clock should not dictate the result of a game, that life and hope should endure so long as there were fewer than three outs in the final frame. Schulte took his stance, left-hander against left-hander, the ace of the White Sox pitching corps against the batter whose seven hits in the Series (for 10 bases) tied him for the lead among Cub hitters. The newspapers failed to record how many pitches Doc White threw to the pride of Cohocton, New York, but on one of them Schulte swung, connected, and sent a spinning ground ball straight down the first-base line to Jiggs Donahue, who scooped it, stepped on the bag, and enjoyed the most triumphant moment a baseball player can know, making the final—and especially the final unassisted—putout of a World Series.

And then South Side Park exploded. The players knew what was coming and made a mad dash for their clubhouse, twisting and dodging their way not only through the crowd already on the field, but thousands more from the stands and likewise from those outside who now, undeterred by the police, swarmed into the park. "It resembled the rushing of a wild stream through a broken dam," recorded the *Inter-Ocean*. "In a twinkling the field was black with the throng."[6] Most of the Sox players lost their caps to the snatching hands of souvenir seekers. Charlie Comiskey himself had made a hasty exit from his box and disappeared into the team's equipment storeroom, where he kept a private office. The Cub players, too, ran a gauntlet of shouted taunts mixed with a few cries of sympathy on the way to the carriages that would get them back to the Victoria Hotel to change out of their uniforms. Inside the Sox clubhouse there was the expected jubilation. The champagne shower had yet to become a part of the winners' ritual, but "the joy of the men broke loose. Every man shook everyone else by the hand and danced with joy. It was a happy, howling band."[7]

While the howling band was getting dressed, the crowd, unwilling to let go of the moment and leave the field, surged over to where Cub owner Murphy sat in his box next to Sheriff Ed Magerstadt and a stockholder from Cincinnati. Murphy proved himself a sport and a man with a natural sense of good public relations, which had been his trade. To cries of "Speech!" he rose and announced: "The White Sox played better ball and deserved to win. I am for Chicago and will say that Chicago has the two best ball teams in the world. . . . Chicago people should be proud of both their clubs." Someone secured a White Sox pennant from a nearby box where wives and sweethearts of the Sox had been sitting, and thrust it into Murphy's hand. Gamely he waved it and called for "three cheers for the White Sox." They were given, as well as three for Murphy, which provoked him to get up again and extend his remarks with a shrewd reminder that it was the "excellent patronage which Chicago has given its two ball clubs" which enabled their managements "to go out and secure good players."[8]

Murphy escaped from the spotlight and went into the sanctum under the stands to congratulate Comiskey. By that time White Sox players, Jones included, were coming out of the clubhouse in street clothes. Jones found the owner surrounded by friends and well-wishers, but Comiskey detached himself from them to escort his field leader back into the office. Possibly giddy with the exhilaration of the moment, since he had a general reputation as a close man with a dollar, he handed Jones a check for $15,000 with instructions to divide it among the "boys." Comiskey then was driven away in an automobile. Jones, too, left by auto with his wife and son, honking and inching through the cheering crowd. But in 1906 most players not only lived near the park during the season, but went to and from their job, like ordinary mortals, by streetcar. Davis, Isbell, Rohe, and Walsh made their way, surrounded by admirers, to Wentworth Avenue, but the tracks were blocked by the happy crowds, which were slow to dissolve, and they had to make their escape on a crosstown car.

By 6:00 p.m., an hour after sunset (no daylight savings time then!), crowds in the streets were carrying on the celebration in relatively nonviolent ways. One group built a huge bonfire out of discarded crates and other combustible waste on the car tracks at 35th Street and Cottage Grove Avenue that required a hurried call to local fire stations to put it out, but there were few recorded acts of vandalism, unless that term includes the actions of some anonymous pranksters who managed to get into West Side Park after it was empty, and likewise reach the business offices of the Cubs in the Masonic Temple building, and to hang ribbons of black crepe across the doors in both places.

The only serious casualties suffered were those of four fans who were settling one of those ridiculous bets that make for lighthearted feature stories in the postgame papers. This one in Monday's *Record-Herald* was not cheerful. Pat Ryan and Henry Holland, Cubs partisans, had bet Sox fans Thomas Ryan (not described as a relative) and Ben Jacobs that the rooters for the losing nine would, with bare feet, pull the other two in a carriage, up a mile-long stretch of Milwaukee Avenue on the near North Side, and back. So Tom Ryan and Jacobs got hold of a buggy, which Pat Ryan and Holland dutifully tugged along the crowded thoroughfare, surrounded by an escort of Sox fans carrying torches and roman candles, plus a growing mob of jeering and laughing gapers attracted by the odd sight. The procession reached the northern terminus and then started back, when a southbound cable car came clanging by. The losers, whose feet by now were cold and filthy, jumped onto the back of the car, hanging on by one arm while with the other they kept hold of the buggy shafts, and began to roll along at a brisk pace. But suddenly one of the wheels dropped through the cable slot between the tracks. The buggy's shafts jerked upward, hurling the two make-believe rickshaw pullers into the street, while the buggy flipped over and also slammed its occupants to the paving stones. All four men were badly injured and carried away by ambulance from the midst of a suddenly sobered crowd. The scene could have been one of those instructive tableaux that entertained nineteenth-century parlor audiences—a moment that caught Chicago poised between two eras, the rough-and-tumble cruel pranks of frontier days, on display under the electric streetlights and traffic of an emergeing metropolis.[9]

Elsewhere the revelry continued. A happy Comiskey was holding court in the Pompeiian Room, a reception area in Adler and Sullivan's superb eight-story Auditorium Building of 1889, whose main floor housed an impressively vast and gorgeously designed theater. Wine flowed, said the *Record-Herald* writer present, as freely as the water in the decorative fountain, and Comiskey, flashing a thick roll of bills with which he was buying, allowed that there would be no sleep for him for the next twenty-four hours. Graciously he announced that he would have preferred to beat any other team than Chance's "fine lot of fellows." He wished he could find Chance, who he was certain would be "game enough to help him celebrate." Chance himself had already made the obligatory good-sport concession speech to the press, saying that the Sox had played "grand, game baseball in the series just ended and outclassed us." He added, however, that he would not concede that the White Sox were a better all-around club; "we did not play our game and that's all there is to it." Tinker and Kling, in post-Series interviews, also admitted to being outplayed, but Johnny Evers, like Chance a hard loser, made the statement that probably reflected what most Cubs and their followers were thinking: "I can't understand it, but probably I will in two or three days."[10] There was nothing much to understand—the White Sox had outpitched the Cubs' vaunted staff with a 1.50 ERA to their 3.40, and the offense, in the final two meetings, crushed them under 26 hits and 16 runs.

The sweetness of victory kept many Sox rooters away from their beds all that night. Two thousand of them, led by a party of South Side businessmen, formed an early-evening procession to visit the residences of some of the principal players. First stop was the house of Doc White, the extractor of Cub teeth, but the twirler was not in. The procession moved on along Cottage Grove Avenue toward Jones's address and bagged a catch, George Davis, who was spotted through a restaurant window eating dinner. Cries of "tell us all about it" elicited a few sidewalk remarks from the shortstop, who, his meal presumably unfinished, was borne along on the crowd's shoulders to the Jones residence a block to the west on Ellis Avenue just south of 35th Street. There they got a pleasant surprise—for the missing White was present, being joyfully entertained at the Jones family table. A speech was demanded. Jones expressed his gratitude to the team and its fans and showed them Comiskey's check. Amid the cheers, White suggested that the revelers call on George Rohe at the Hayden Hotel, only a few blocks away. No sooner said than done, and when they congregated in the street shouting his name, Rohe, with a fine sense of theater, appeared at a second-story window and threw down a stuffed white sock "fully six feet long." He also said a few gracious things, and "when last seen," the delirious crowd, flourishing the white sock, was seen heading for the White City, an amusement park near the site of the 1893 world's fair. It had a roller rink and two dance floors, and there they ragtimed, two-stepped, and drank their way through the remaining glorious hours before dawn.[11]

So the great day ended: a day that had seen yelling humanity harmlessly blowing off steam but also turning violent against restraining fences; a day that had seen simple silliness transformed into tragedy in a twinkling on Milwaukee Avenue, and fire, which had once destroyed Chicago, kindled without fear in the streets to celebrate Chicago; a day that had seen some of the lights and shadows of city life and mob emotions, inspired by the feelings that a transient sporting event aroused. That was part of the new world of 1906, linked to our own by, among other things, the persistence of baseball.

So morning dawned, with its payoffs and its letdowns. On Tuesday the *Tribune* would remind readers that Chicagoans had "spent yesterday with its head wrapped in cold towels, calling for cracked ice and more ice in an effort to recover from the effects of a week of world's pennant battles and of a night's celebration of victory or defeat." But hungover and let down or not, the business of the game was ready to be attended to. CHAMPIONS GET THEIR CHECKS AND ARE HAPPY, proclaimed the *Record-Herald*.

There was plenty of reason for happiness with this third World Series on the part of both leagues' officials, both teams' owners, and the White Sox players. Just under 100,000 people had paid to watch the contests—88,945 to be exact. The gate receipts totaled $106,550, in contrast to the preceding year's five-game set between the Giants and Athletics, which had netted only $26,774. The National Commission got 10 percent of the total, $10,655. Each club received $31,246.65. The financial success guaranteed the continuation of the two-league setup with a deciding post-season championship.[12]

The total players' share was $33,401.70, of which the winners would get 75 percent, bringing the White Sox' pot to $25,051.53. But Comiskey's added $15,000, a 60 percent increase, brought that figure to $40,951.53, which was divided among 21 eligible players. Each of those men took home $1,945.29—in some cases equal or nearly so to their entire season's salary. The Cubs split their $8,350.17 among 19 teammates, and Murphy added to the total sum $2,777.40 earned in exhibition games (the receipts split half and half between the athletes and the ownership) and a gift of $100 for each man, so that an individual share came to just under $700. Not bad for 1906, but still a considerable difference. In modern dollars, each winner probably got something between $30,000 and $40,000, and each loser $10,500 to $14,000.

The spontaneous popular celebrations were followed by the more decorous events planned by organized civic and business groups. Both teams were invited to be guests on Monday night at the Powers Theater, where Robert Edeson was playing in the last week of the run of *Strongheart,* one of the forgettable popular melodramas that predated B movies and television. Some of the players did so, but scattered themselves unobtrusively through the audience. All the same, the star came out at the end of the second act to make a brief talk on baseball that led to calls of "Jones," who was recognized as he was watching from a rear door. He turned at once and decamped, and in his haste started down a staircase to the ladies' room ("a side stairway not designated for masculine champions," as the *Tribune* put it) before recovering himself and finding another escape hatch. The same night, following the performance, there was a banquet at Rector's for the White Sox with some fifty in attendance. On Tuesday a reception and banquet were given at the Auditorium Hotel to thank the Cubs for their outstanding season. The sponsors were "thirty-third degree fans" from the board of trade, and they had gotten Mayor Dunne, Cap Anson, and a handful of other notables to promise speeches and toasts. At that banquet table John Evers, on behalf of the team, presented Chance with a four-carat diamond ring "and promised for himself and the others to work hard to qualify for another world's series next year."[13]

There was talk of parades on Saturday, October 20, for both teams, featuring floats, and more than a hundred automobiles in what would have been a spectacular procession for the time, but it never came to pass, as the teams began to disband. A number of events previously scheduled—downstate exhibition games and weekend receptions—may well have been canceled too. Sheckard left town before the Tuesday banquet because of a death in the family; Jones, Walsh, and Isbell departed at the same time, while Chance and Overall were gone by midweek. A few Cubs, at least, did not even show up on Monday to collect their checks in person. A news account suggested that "it was a wonder that any of them had been able to show up at all," though it was unclear whether the writer was referring to embarrassment or drowning of sorrows the night before as the cause.

By Wednesday morning the fever had passed, and Chicago had settled down to more mundane headlines: auto crashes, the coming local elections, the question of whether to install meters in city taxis, more unrest in Cuba, an exciting gubernatorial race in New York, a grisly murder, and a lynching. And the tides of life as captured in metropolitan journalism early in the new century closed around the week of baseball mania and flowed inexorably on.

The press paid the expected tributes to the players of both

teams and to the city itself. The *Tribune's* head editorial of Tuesday the 16th, AFTER THE BALL IS OVER, led off with this: "The *Tribune* remarked before the baseball championship games began that Chicago could not lose and it has not. It has been demonstrated that this city has the two best ball teams in the world. . . . Friendly rivalry—no fights on the field—no accusations of fraud—no whining that the best team had not won." It ended with a comforting pat on the Cubs' shoulders, reminding them that they were, after all, the National League champions. Ahead lay a new page. "The west siders must be content with the honors which have also come to them, and come justly. For the world's championship they must . . . try again and hope for 'better luck next time.' "

The *Record-Herald,* on the Monday morning after, took pains to offend neither set of fans:

> It has been a great series, furnishing excitement enough for the most exacting and making it impossible for Chicago to think much of anything but baseball. Congratulations to the sox. They have done magnificent work and it is now doubly certain that they are the stuff of which pennant winners are made. But the more they are praised, the greater is the tribute to their formidable opponents.

And then, the concluding benediction and prayer:

> *There is glory enough for both teams, and here is hoping that they may meet again for the world's championship next year.*

Ninety-nine years later, Chicago is still hoping.

7

After the Lights Go Down

The full, sad import of the Series finale was not revealed to Chicago on the morning of October 16, 1906. Both teams had shown their best faces intermittently. Both would face the 1907 season essentially unchanged thanks to the reserve clause. There would be springtimes and fresh dawns ahead.

No one knew that it was in fact over for a lifetime—that Chicago's two teams might meet again in exhibitions and, more than ninety years later, in interleague competition, but never, not even after the youngest fan in cap, knickers, and black stockings had gone to an old man's grave, never in another World Series for at least another century. Sometimes ignorance is truly bliss.

In 1907 the Cubs won the National League flag again, but the White Sox managed only a third-place finish, so it was Detroit who was the opponent in the Cubs' second World Series. This time they reversed their fortunes and beat the Tigers for the world championship. Then, in 1908, history teased with the promise of another all-Chicago meeting for the highest prize. Thrilling pennant races took place in both leagues, one of them decided in the expiring hours of the season and the other not until the day after. The Cubs and White Sox were engaged in three-way struggles that were virtually deadlocked in the final week, the Cubs with the Giants and Pittsburgh Pirates, the White Sox with Detroit and Cleveland. Late in September, the Cubs played the Giants in New York, in a game that is still celebrated and debated. What appeared to be a winning ninth-inning run for New York was nullified when their base runner on first failed to advance all the way to second as his teammate crossed the plate and a crowd immediately swarmed onto the field, halting further play. The National League ruled the game a tie that would have to be replayed if the result would affect the final standings. So it did, for at the end of the season's last day the Cubs and Giants were tied. In the October 8 playoff, Three-Finger Brown beat Christy Mathewson 4–2. But by then it was too late for the outcome to produce a repeat of the 1906 Series, because on the preceding final Sunday, Doc White had lost to Detroit.

Chicago took some comfort in the Cubs' ensuing defeat of the Tigers in the World Series for the second successive time, but was happily unaware that the 1908 world championship would be the team's last. In 1909 they slipped and lost the pennant by six and a half games to the sizzling Pittsburgh Pirates (who went on to hand the hapless Tigers their third straight postseason loss). The following year, 1910, the Cub dynasty was back in the Series, claiming the National League flag by 13 games. But this time, Connie Mack's Athletics put them away four games to one. And though it was not clear at the time, the glory years were over. From 1906 though 1910, a five-season stretch, Chance's teams had won four pennants and two world championships and never finished with fewer than 99 victories. But it was not until 1918 that the Cubs were in the Series again, this time against the Red Sox, who won 4–2—and were themselves doomed not to capture another world championship until 2004. The Cubs, however, would have it worse—their 1908 Series victory being the last through 2005, a 97-year span of finale futility that saw them in the World Series five more times without getting any closer than a 4–3 beating by Detroit in 1945. Since then more than sixty years have passed and they have never even taken the field in the ultimate deciding contest to be the best in baseball.

Thereafter the White Sox did not fare very well either. They waited eleven years for another league championship, and in the wartime autumn of 1917 defeated the Giants 4–2 in the post-season. Two years later they beat out Cleveland for the AL flag and faced the Cincinnati Reds in a World Series whose formula had been changed, for some reason, to a best five-of-nine format, where it stayed for another two years. Cincinnati beat the Sox 5–3. But in the following year came the disclosure that eight players on the Sox had been offered bribes to throw the Series, though not all of them took the money or actually participated in the fix, but simply were aware of it and did not inform the authorities. These eight men were barred from the game for life—and when average fans think about the old-time White Sox at all, thanks to the notoriety of the event (books, a movie, and an oblique reference in *The Great Gatsby*), what pops into their minds is not the hitless wonders and their against-the-odds victory in 1906, but the Black Sox and their tainted loss of 1919.

Whether punishment of the gods or some other arcane curse is responsible, the White Sox lost the winning touch for a long period thereafter. From 1919 until 2005 they appeared in only one World Series, losing to the Los Angeles Dodgers in six games in 1959. But on the eve of the centennial of their 1906 triumph, the drought was gloriously broken as they swept through two layers of playoffs and defeated the Houston Astros 4–0, sending Chicago fans into transports of bliss.

For Cub partisans, however, the century-old tale of frustrated expectations remain "the saddest of all possible words."

There may be some consolation in the fact that Chicago was not alone in deprivation nor at the bottom of the totem pole where intracity World Series are concerned. Of the five cities represented in both leagues in 1901, two—Boston and Philadelphia—never had one before they became one-team towns in the reshuffling of franchises that began in 1953. Two others—Chicago and St. Louis—achieved the experience but one time, the Cardinals and Browns contending in 1944, when so many major-league players were in military uniform that teams appeared to be recruited largely from high schools, hospitals, and retirement homes.

It is New York that skews the figures. It had the advantage of being large enough to accommodate three teams whose stadiums were linked by public transportation, so that a Dodger-versus-Yankee matchup as well as one between the Giants and Yankees qualified as a "Subway Series." The Yankees actually played the Giants in the World Series six times between 1921 and 1951, and the Dodgers seven between 1941 and 1956, the wonder years of New York baseball. The figures in those battles are lopsidedly tilted in favor of the Yankees, who took four of the six from the Giants and six of seven from the Brooklyn team. This may account for why New Yorkers are rarely neutral about the Yankees, but either love or detest them.

After the Giants and Dodgers moved to California in 1957, there was a long hiatus until the birth in 1962 of the New York Metropolitans made the Big Apple once again a two-team city. It took another thirty-eight years before the Yanks and Mets played each other in 2000 for world championship honors, giving New York in all 14 such intracity clashes. The Yanks, by subduing the Mets 4–1, ran their total of victories in them to 11.

The prospects of many more such meetings are slight. As of 2006 only Los Angeles also claims a team in each league, and that is on a debatable technicality. The Dodgers do play in Los Angeles, but the Los Angeles Angels of Anaheim, so named only recently, have their stadium in Anaheim, and the two communities are connected only by freeway drives that can stretch out long in heavy traffic. San Francisco and Oakland share the same metropolitan area and are only minutes from each other by the Bay Area Rapid Transit system and the Bay Bridge, but they are distinctly

separate cities, and disputes between their fans lack the passion of
the old neighborhood-versus-neighborhood arguments between
New York's boroughs or Chicago's North and South Sides. The
Giants and the Oakland Athletics did meet in 1989 in the only
World Series to have the distinction of being interrupted by an
earthquake. (Oakland swept in four.)

What is more, under the present system even division champions and wild-card winners must survive two rounds of hard-
to-forecast playoffs before advancing to the Series. Given those
facts, the Yanks-Mets world title meeting of 2000 was practically
a miracle.

But what of the players, the boys of summer '06? What did life
hold in store for an athlete reaching full flower in that dawn's early
light of a century? What follows when the glory has departed, the
curtain is down, and the house is dark? Begin with the bit players.
Of the 30 young men who stepped onto the grass of West Side
and South Side Parks in the great encounter—16 in White Sox
uniforms, 14 for the Cubs—five had only brief moments in the
spotlight: two pinch hitters for the Cubs, "Doc" Gessler and Pat
Moran; two for the White Sox, Ed McFarland and Babe Towne;
and one pinch runner, Bill O'Neill, who ran for Hahn when his
nose was broken, and played the remainder of the game. Each of
these had one at bat and came away without a hit, though O'Neill
scored a run on Rohe's triple. Moran hung on for another eight
seasons in the majors, Gessler played four more, and McFarland
played a final year at the top in 1908, with the Red Sox, though
for only 19 games. The big-league careers of O'Neill and Towne
seem to have ended in 1906.[1]

Of the remaining 25, three came to tragic finales. Jiggs Donahue was described as a good-natured Irishman, fond of billiards
and the clog dancing that gave him his nickname, and with a knack
for infecting teammates with enthusiasm. He played two more
seasons for the White Sox and was sold to the Senators in 1909

after only two games and played 86 for them before disappearing from the record book. He was supposedly offered a chance to return in 1912, but didn't accept. Sometime in 1914, "Jiggs" died, in an asylum, of paresis, the final stage of syphilis, which causes skin lesions, tumors of the internal organs, and eventually "progressive central nervous system involvement," producing any or all of the following symptoms: locomotor ataxia (inability of the muscles to coordinate and "irregular" movements, to wit, partial paralysis), deafness, blindness, and insanity. He was thirty-four years old.

Jiggs's teammate at the opposite corner, George Davis, had a similarly shadowed ending. At thirty-six in 1906 he was the oldest man on the field, and after a couple of subpar years, he ended his active playing career. Davis managed the Des Moines minor-league nine for a season, and then was through with pro baseball. He flitted in and out of visibility thereafter—managing a bowling alley in New York, then coaching baseball at Amherst through 1918. At that time he had twenty-two years to live. He was at one time reported to be selling automobiles in St. Louis; another report had it that he and his wife had earned their bread as professional bridge players in New York. A search by a Hall of Fame historian, Lee Allen, finally turned up a death certificate from a Philadelphia insane asylum. George Davis, too, had died of paresis.

Harry Steinfeldt, Davis's opposite number, at third base for the Cubs, was the first of their 1906 team to die. He stayed with the Cubs until 1910, when "illness began to slow him down." Given an unconditional release, he signed with the Boston Braves for 1911 but played in only 19 games before an injury forced him off the diamond for good. The Braves suspended him without pay, a decision that he challenged with a demand for an unconditional release instead so that he could look for a contract elsewhere. He won his case but never did play again. One news story reported that "his heart was broken [after the Cubs let him go] and he could not reconcile himself to Father Time's claim." A newspaper cutting of July 1911 described him as "very ill," and another said that he was in a Cincinnati hospital suffering a "complete nervous breakdown." He died of a cerebral hemorrhage in 1918. It may be that for him, having the high point of his life occur before he was thirty made the rest of it too painful to handle without a flight into madness. In any case, he is the third of the 30 to die apparently insane.

Also dying well before his time was Frank Chance himself. After leading the team to its two world championships in 1907 and 1908, and its fourth pennant in 1910, he had a final falling-out with owner Charles Murphy after numerous quarrels over Murphy's decisions about sales and trades of key players as well as other forms of interference. Murphy made a simple and blunt announcement at the end of the 1912 season: "Frank L. Chance is through as manager." By then the Peerless Leader had stopped playing regularly, appearing in only 88 games in 1910 and 31 in 1911. He was already experiencing the headaches that were the warning of worsening health troubles, stemming from asthma. He was hired as manager by the New York Yankees, but this was before their days of glory, and he could only bring them home seventh in 1913. When he was fired the following year in mid-September they were in sixth. Chance moved back to California, became part owner and manager of the Los Angeles club in the Pacific Coast League for a couple of years, then retired to private life. He could not resist the call of the Red Sox to manage in 1922, but they finished in the cellar with a mere 61 wins. The golden touch was gone, and more important, so were the golden players (including Babe Ruth) who had won the world championship four years earlier. Despite that poor showing, Charlie Comiskey stepped in with an offer of manager of the White Sox, and it was accepted, but Chance was unable to show up. He was slowly dying (of pulmonary edema and globular nephritis), and the end came in a Los Angeles hospital on September 16, 1924, six days after his forty-seventh birthday.

Some of the players who had long lives returned, willingly or not, to the obscurity from which they had come. Willingly seems to have been the case with Patsy Dougherty of the White

Sox outfield. After five more seasons with Comiskey—the last, in 1911, in which he played in 76 games with respectable numbers (including with a .289 batting average)—he announced that he had "made enough money from baseball" and simply quit. He dropped out of sight for a few years, served as president of a minor league in 1916, and then retraced his steps to his hometown, little Bolivar, New York, where he became an assistant bank cashier and worked there for twenty-nine more years until his death. One sees him as the possible local celebrity whose fame fades away as each new generation of young Bolivarians rises. (*"Mr. Dougherty was in a World Series? That old guy at the bank? No kidding!"*) A similar small-town-hero status was accorded to the lone Canadian member of the 1906 White Sox, Bill O'Neill, the Game Three substitute for the injured Ed Hahn. His obituary in the St. John, New Brunswick, newspaper noted that his name had become a "household word" in town for his baseball exploits in the "neighboring republic," and once on a visit home he was met at the station and presented with a gold watch.

Hahn himself stayed with the White Sox through the 1910 season, with steadily declining starts and averages. He then played for several years in Des Mones and Wichita back when the minors were still serving as the place where an aging player might earn a few dollars and a bit of dignity performing for small crowds and mentoring young "comers" before finally putting away the glove. When he died of high blood pressure and hardened arteries in November of 1941, age sixty-six, according to his own claim, he was working as a night watchman for the Hawkeye Cortland Cement Company's plant in Des Moines. That was the kind of slot into which old champions fit themselves for the finale back in the days before players' pensions.

Jack Pfiester, whose pitch had broken Hahn's nose, never quite regained the 20–8 heights of the world championship year, going 14–9 in 1907 and 12–10 in 1908, then rebounding to 17–6 in 1909. But in the ensuing two years he lost it, getting only 14 starts in 1910 and six in 1911, of which he won only one. Thereafter he simply vanished, except for the brief notation in *Total Baseball* that he died in Loveland, Ohio, in 1953.

Frank Owen, who relieved Doc White in the second game blowout by the Cubs, spent another couple of undistinguished years with the White Sox. From his staff high of 22 wins in 1906 he fell to single digits in the next three seasons before being released to spend five years in the minors. Like Hahn, he spent his final year or so of life as a plant security guard, at the Ford auto factory in Ypsilanti, Michigan, where he had been born, and where he died in 1942.

The Cubs' Art Hofman was another who went home again. Born in St. Louis in 1882, he died there on March 10, 1956. "Circus Solly" had several more good years with the Cubs and with other National League teams before leaving the major leagues in 1916. But he seems never to have surfaced in the press again, and the research library at the Hall of Fame, which keeps clipping files on every known professional player of the past, even when they contain no more than a single obituary, has none for him.

George Rohe, the Series hero for the White Sox, had what may have been one of the more interesting post-Series lives. At the end of the Series Comiskey exuberantly promised that he would never trade the supersub, but when Rohe's batting average sank to .213 in 1907 the owner proved to have a short memory. He put Rohe on waivers, and eventually the utility infielder played in New Orleans and other Southern League towns until 1914. Then he went to work in the steel mills of Mobile as an unnoticed laborer for seventeen years until an illness forced him to quit physically demanding work. He moved to Columbus, Ohio, and worked as a "newspaper scribe" after failing to find a job in organized baseball. He was next seen in his native Cincinnati, where he had become a commercial photographer, at which calling he worked for ten years before his retirement in 1946, shortly before turning seventy. Ten years later he was one of three guests at the annual Cincinnati Ballplayers of Yesteryear banquet at the Netherlands Plaza Hotel, the others being Jesse Tannehill and the 93-year-old "Dummy" Hoy, who had played in the earliest years of the professional game and played brilliantly in spite of being deaf and mute. Jesse Tannehill, a pitching star for the Pirates and Red Sox at one time, was an older brother of Lee Tannehill, Rohe's White Sox teammate. Lee left no footprints behind after his own retirement from active play. Rohe himself died the following year, 1957.

One other sad passing was that of Jimmy Sheckard, the Cubs outfielder who had floundered so badly at bat in October 1906 in spite of his impressive statistics in previous regular seasons. He redeemed himself somewhat in the 1907 and 1910 World Series against Detroit and Philadelphia, and continued to perform solidly for the Cubs, especially in 1911, when he scored a league-leading 121 runs and was walked 147 times, proving that pitchers still feared him and his eye had stayed sharp. In 1913 he went downhill as his talent deserted him abruptly and cruelly, the always haunting nemesis of even the best players. He was traded to the Cardinals and by them to the Reds one-third of the way through the season, at the end of which his batting average for 99 games was a mere .194. He was through in the majors. His obituary in January 1947 notes that he lost his savings in the crash of 1929, and thereafter worked variously as a laborer, milk deliveryman, and filling-station attendant. At age sixty-eight he was struck and killed by a car in Lancaster, Pennsylvania, where he had been living.

Sheckard was not the only ex-player to be financially wiped out by the Great Depression. Witness the case of Frank Isbell of the White Sox. He defies the stereotype of the has-been athlete whose money has gone to liquor and frivolity. At the end of 1909 he left the White Sox to manage the Wichita club of the Western League, having already bought an interest in its ownership. Four years later he took control of the Des Moines team in the same league, and he won the championship with it in 1915. Years later, a close friend, Fred Mankoff, informed the Hall of Fame historians that in the ensuing years, Isbell divided his time between a winter residence in Los Angeles and summers in Wichita, where he had a home on ten acres of land and $200,000 in bonds. Then he suddenly went broke in the late 1930s. Mankoff, a Wichita businessman, got Isbell a filling station to run, then put him up for a public office—county commissioner—in 1940. He was elected, but within a year died of a heart attack.

Ed Reulbach of the Cubs was the last of the group who seems to have died in economic stringency, though the record isn't entirely clear. He had a superb career in the years that he remained with the Cubs. He went on to a 17–4 year in 1907 and a 5–1, one-hit victory over the Tigers in the World's Series, then posted a 24–7 record in 1908. His arm was iron. In 1908 he pitched the full 18 innings of both games of a doubleheader against Brooklyn, and won both by shutouts. He would pitch 42 shutouts in his career. He was traded to Brooklyn in 1913, then jumped in 1915 to the short-lived Federal League, where he won 21 games against 10 losses, meanwhile serving as founding director and secretary of a proposed players' union, the Baseball Players' Fraternity, created "to better working conditions, oppose contract abuses, and advise players with grievances." Like the Federal League, it did not get very far.

Then age finally made its claim and the darkness rolled in. Reulbach retired, worked for a time for a manufacturer of pianos, and afterward ran a tire business in Maplewood, New Jersey. But the expenses of caring for a son through a long illness and final death bankrupted him. He was described in a 1932 interview as "a sad, quiet man of 50." In his last years he was "employed in the . . . equipment department" of a New York construction company, and he finally retired to Glens Falls, where he died of a heart attack at seventy-eight.

These sad stories are offset to some degree by the relative success of other Cub and White Sox veterans. On the Sox side, Fielder Jones always displayed a practical streak. He retired after the 1908 season to, as he put it, "earn some money for a change" in the lumber business in Seattle. He knew what he was about: "I intend to get out of the game before I am compelled to drift back to the minors, as is the case with most of the ballplayers who do not realize that they are going back." But he was enticed back onto the field in 1914–15 to manage the St. Louis Terriers of the Federal League. He stayed on for a couple of years after the Federal League collapsed to lead the St. Louis Browns, then quit for good to go back to the booming West Coast. He died at the age of sixty-three.

Nick Altrock turned his gift for clowning into a profitable act with Al Schacht that they performed both for the Washington Senators and in vaudeville theaters around various circuits well into the 1930s.

Catcher Billy Sullivan played until 1911, coached a few years, and made the news in 1910 as part of a stunt performed with team-mate Ed Walsh. He caught three of 39 balls that Walsh dropped from the 550-foot-high Washington Monument and declared that it was like catching an unbelievably fast pitch. He lived in Chicago for a time, and had two sons. Both played baseball in college, and Bill junior had a big-league career as a catcher, playing thirteen years between 1931 and 1947, two of them with the White Sox. The elder Sullivan bought a small filbert farm near Newberg, Oregon, to which he retired until his passing at ninety.

Ed Walsh still had his best baseball years ahead of him at the end of 1906. In 1907 he won 24 games and in 1908 an incredible 40, against 15 losses. The feat was possible because managers then were rigidly bound to pitching rotations among four or five starters, and starters also appeared, when necessary, as relievers. Walsh started 49 games and completed 42. He appeared in 66 altogether (that is, some 43 percent of the entire 154-game schedule) and was credited with six saves. Since the wins, losses, and saves total 61, there must have been five appearances in which he did not figure in the decision. He was used as needed, and in the torrid pennant race of that year, he was needed often. He appeared in 13 of the final 16 games the White Sox played. He pitched an unbelievable 464 innings, struck out 269 batters, and walked only 56. He threw 11 shutouts and his ERA was 1.42. Three years later he was still going strong, and in both 1911 and 1912 he won 27 games. But finally even that durable arm was injured, in 1913, and his greatest years were over. His lifetime ERA was 1.82, the lowest in major-league history.

Walsh coached for a time both in the minors and for the White Sox, and umpired in the American League for one year. For a while he was the baseball coach at Notre Dame, where both his sons pitched for him. Arthritis drove him to retirement in Florida in 1957 and continued to worsen. He had a special day at Comiskey Park in 1958 in which he appeared in a wheelchair to wave to the standing, applauding crowd. He died May 26, 1959, just after his seventy-eighth birthday.

Doc White, too, lived a long—and in his case healthy—life marked by intelligent management of his postbaseball career. He continued to pitch brilliantly for a couple of years in the majors; then after 1913 he left the Sox, pitched for two California teams in the Pacific Coast League (Venice and Vernon, later Hollywood), then became a part owner of Ft. Worth in the Texas League. He never went back to dental practice, but after World War I service as a physical-education instructor with an aviation unit in Texas, he managed another couple of years in Waco and Muskegon, and then went home to the District of Columbia. There he became a physical-education instructor at his old high school, coached two sports at Wilson Junior College, and died just before his ninetieth birthday in 1969. His record of five straight shutouts stood until Don Drysdale of the Dodgers broke it in June 1968—at which time White sent him a gracious telegram of congratulations. He also played the violin and was an avid gardener, who won prizes with his rose exhibits.

White and Jones, to take only two examples, were both intelligent middle-class businessmen who found in baseball a profession that earned them money in youth, which they put to prudent business use in their postbaseball lives.

It was the same with a few of the Cubs. Three-Finger Brown, after another few sensational years with the Cubs (and memorable duels with Christy Mathewson) managed for a time (he handled the St. Louis Federal League club just before Jones took over) and then returned to Indiana to work in public relations for oil and gas companies. Johnny Kling, who so often caught Brown, likewise was a shrewd businessman. He sat out the entire 1909 season when owner Murphy would not give him the raise he demanded, and lived on the income from a billiard parlor that he operated in Kansas City. He became one of its leading citizens, owned the minor-league Kansas City Blues from 1933 to 1937, invested widely in real estate, and raised Angus cattle on a 100-acre ranch. He died of a heart attack in 1947.

Orvie Overall, the strapping Californian who had done so well in relief in the Cub losses of Games Five and Six, continued an illustrious career with the Cubs. In the 1907 World Series he won two games against Detroit. He won 15 in 1908, and 20 in 1909 with 205 strikeouts, which put him at the top of the league, and nine shutouts. But arm trouble made its always threatening appearance in 1912, and after a pair of up-and-down seasons he quit, became a citrus farmer briefly, and then completed a trouble-free transition from baseball to finance. At the time of his death in 1947 he was vice president of the Fresno branch of a Los Angeles bank.

Johnny Evers passed on in the same year, the sixth member of the 1906 Cubs to go. After his playing days he managed the Braves, Cubs, and White Sox for various intervals, then went back to Troy and ran a sporting goods store there, superintended a stadium and sports center in Albany, and maintained a part owner-ship in its minor-league team at the time of his passing on. The other half of the second base–shortstop combination, Joe Tinker, also stayed in baseball for a while after ending his active career in 1912. He managed the Reds briefly, then jumped to the Federal League and took its Chicago entry, the Whales, to first place in 1915. After the league folded he stayed in Chicago to manage the 1916 Cubs and got them to fifth. He continued to scout for them during the 1920s, while he took over the presidency and management of Columbus in the American Association, and in time he managed Buffalo's and Jersey City's minor-league clubs. He also ran a saloon on Chicago's West Side and acted a bit in vaudeville. By 1929 he had accumulated a nice little stake, including a controlling interest in a franchise in Orlando, Florida. He invested in Florida real estate during the Florida land boom of the 1920s and lost heavily in its collapse. He retired to the Sunshine State, but life turned sour for him when his health failed. Diabetes cost him a leg, amputated in the mid-1930s, and he was disabled and bedridden when he finally died on his sixty-eighth birthday, in 1948.

He was in that respect like poor "Wildfire" Schulte, who also managed both minor-league teams and his money well, and owned a Georgia peach farm of some 16,000 acres from 1913 on in addition to other assets, presumably including the trotting horse that furnished his nickname. But when he died in 1949 he was described as having been "an invalid for many years."

And so of the 25 who played for more than an inning or two or a single at bat, 11 died in relative obscurity, three tragically young. Twelve passed on reasonably well fixed, and these included seven who had spent a number of years in baseball after they stopped playing. For those, their years on the field were not only a separate segment of their lifelong careers, but a gateway to long-term success. For all of them, so far as can be judged, it was part of the sunshine of youth that warms the recollections of age.

> I returned, and saw under the sun, that the race is not to the swift, nor the battle to the strong, neither yet bread to the wise, nor yet riches to men of understanding, nor yet favor to men of skill; but time and chance happeneth to them all. (Eccles. 9:11)

They were swift, strong, and men of skill, but as the scripture notes in one challenge-proof verse, time and chance did indeed bring them by one path or another to the inevitable event. But baseball survives them, as it has survived a tidal wave of cultural change in the United States over more than a century and a half—not without changes, but in the basic form that it took on a June day in 1846 when the New York Knickerbockers engaged in a match against the New York Base Ball Club on a field in Hoboken, New Jersey.

There is an entire flowery literature dedicated to the proposition that baseball will always be with us so long as there are springtime and youth and dreams and hope and a generous number of other ennobling human qualities in our collective life. But baseball sentimentalists are not always of the same breed as baseball lovers and historians. Perhaps yes, perhaps no. Institutions are no more immune than individuals to the reach of time and chance. Nothing lasts forever.

But baseball memories are unusually enduring. Few other sports devote such obsessive attention to amassing and compiling detailed records for ongoing reconsideration and debate. Few others seem to have fans who share in continued recall of key historical moments. This is especially true for World Series games, especially after the advent of photography, moving pictures, television, and videotape, which have preserved the images of those decisive plays forever. The camera has given immortality to Bobby Thomson's "shot heard 'round the world" that put the Giants into the Series of 1951, Willie Mays's over-the-shoulder catch of Vic Wertz's 425-foot drive to the Polo Grounds' center field in 1954, and Carlton Fisk waving his arms toward fair territory as his Series-tying home run of 1975 settled into the stands. It has also given virtually eternal life to unlucky goats, too—to Mickey Owen dropping the third strike in 1941, or poor Bill Buckner making an error on Mookie Wilson's grounder of 1986. In this treasure house of memories, players gain a share of the game's endurance over generations. While the 1906 World Series produced no single spectacular freeze-frame moment comparable to those just mentioned, its overall vitality and especially its unexpected underdog's victory created solid and heartwarming memories in which Chicago's champions of 1906, winners and losers alike, no matter what differing ends fate dealt them afterward, will survive—if not forever, then at least for part or all of a second century since the event, and perhaps longer.

Afterword

When the city of Chicago's eighty-eight-year drought of baseball world championships was finally brought to an end in 2005, it seemed almost miraculous to faithful fans. That may be stretching things too far—but there was certainly a fairy-tale quality to the amazing triumph of the White Sox. The story had elements of "Cinderella" and "The Ugly Duckling," plus unexpected reverses, last-minute rescues, and surprise heroes.

At the season's start, they were a team undergoing a deliberate revamping. They had finished the preceding two seasons with high home-run totals but second-place finishes in the American League's Central Division, so owner Jerry Reinsdorf and general manager Ken Williams had agreed to focus more on speed and defense. Over the winter they traded or let get away two of their most powerful hitters, Magglio Ordonez and Carlos Lee, putting more of the runs-batted-in burden on outfielders Aaron Rowand

and Paul Konerko, as well as Frank Thomas, with whom Konerko alternated at first base and designated hitter. Thomas was a proven star, but his health was questionable and in fact he would miss most of the season due to injury. The White Sox added two new outfielders, speedy Scott Podsednik and Jermaine Dye whose on-base percentage was respectable, plus experienced catcher A. J. Pierzynski. They acquired a newcomer from Japanese baseball, Tadahito Iguchi, as their new second baseman. They bolstered an inconsistent pitching staff with the pick-up of Orlando "El Duque" Hernandez and another Japanese player, reliever Shingo Takatsu (in 2004). All of these changes meant facing 2005 with a team unaccustomed to playing together under manager Ozzie Guillen, only in his second year on the job, and dedicated to a new strategy. Guillen said in an interview that he respected home runs, but what he hoped the nightly television highlights would show more often would be "my team turning a double play with the bases loaded in the ninth to win the game."

Greatness was not expected by the supposed media experts. The annual baseball preview of *Sports Illustrated,* in a thumbnail summary of the team's prospects, sniffed: "Last World Series win was 1917. Is next division title in 2017?" And the Chicago sports press was equally skeptical. Four of the six *Tribune* baseball writers making predictions about the AL Central picked Minnesota to win, another chose Cleveland, and only one chose the White Sox. Given the fact that the White Sox would play most of their April games against Central Division rivals, a forecaster wrote, "the new version of the Go-Go Sox could be all but gone from postseason contention by mid-May."

The team proceeded immediately to dismantle these assumptions. In a foretaste of things to come, they won their opener 1–0 behind a shutout by Mark Buehrle. Three weeks later, on April 25, they were 16–4. By the end of June they had won 35 games, lost only 17, and were five games ahead of Minnesota. A starting rotation of Buehrle, Freddy Garcia, Jon Garland, Jose Contreras, and Hernandez was keeping opposition scores low, there was plenty of slugging from Thomas, Konerko, Rowand, Dye, and Carl Everett, in addition to timely hits that won close games. The White Sox would capture 35 one-run victories before the season's end, and by its midpoint Podsednik had already stolen 37 bases of the 59 he would rack up altogether. The bullpen was also staying abreast, and when Takatsu lost his early-season effectiveness, other hurlers like Damaso Marte and Dustin Hermanson took up the slack. July 15 saw the White Sox still with a .667 winning percentage (58–29) and a division lead now fattened to 10 games—it would soon reach a peak of 15—and with four of their players on the American League All-Star team. The doubters who had been saying for weeks that the team could not long continue winning two out of every three games it played were apparently silenced.

But then came the dreaded slump to add the torment of suspense to the saga. The White Sox began to sputter in the second half of July, and during August they lost 15 games while winning 12. By the 7th of September they had added just 29 victories to their July 15 total and 22 to the loss column. Those were not entirely discreditable numbers in themselves, but meanwhile the Cleveland Indians had begun a white-hot second-half run, playing .750 baseball—they were 33–11 in the final six weeks—and, leaping over Minnesota, were steadily cutting into the White Sox lead. By the end of the third week of September, with 11 left to play, that lead had dwindled to a game an a half. Haunting the minds of all Chicagoans were earlier collapses by teams on the brink of victory, especially that of the Cubs who had, in 1969, blown a 12-game August lead over the pursuing New York Mets. Would fortune once again cruelly manhandle the Windy City?

Not if the White Sox could help it! Pulling themselves together at the last minute, they won six of their next eight games, while the Indians stumbled—and on Thursday the 29th clinched the pennant with a victory over Detroit. The three games left with the Indians were now meaningless. The White Sox swept them to end the season with 99 victories, including the final five games in a row, and without ever having relinquished first place from the starting gun.

Now came a playoff run that still reads like fiction. The White

Sox squared off in the first round against Boston, the AL wild card winner, which had only a year earlier broken its "curse" with a miraculous run of eight straight wins that began when they were down to the Yankees 3–0 in the American League championship series. But now the magic deserted to their opposition. In the opener, the White Sox exploded for 14 runs, while Red Sox sluggers were held to a mere two. Three of the White Sox tallies came on a three-run homer (one of four for the White Sox that night) off the bat of Podsednik who had not hit a single round-tripper during the entire season. It was an omen. The next night, in a contest tightly pitched in early innings, the White Sox fell behind 4–2, but Iguchi came up in the fifth and delivered a three-run blast. Rookie reliever Bobby Jenks, who had joined the team in midsummer, held on to the lead, retiring six of the last eight batters he faced. It was another one-run victory to add to the Sox's impressive season total.

In Game Three, with the White Sox hanging on to a 4–2 lead in the bottom of the sixth, the Red Sox loaded the bases against Damaso Marte with nobody out. "El Duque" Hernandez then came in from the pen to retire the side without permitting a score, and the White Sox added another in the ninth to sweep the series with a 5–3 win and advance to the championship round against the Los Angeles Angels.

The opening contest on October 11 went to the California team, 3–2, proving that the White Sox were at least humanly vulnerable. On the following night, Buehrle pitched nine strong innings, giving up only a single run in the fifth. But four Angels pitchers had matched that performance, and the White Sox came up in the bottom of the ninth in a 1–1 tie. A. J. Pierzynski, at bat with two out, swung at a third strike. The umpire's hand went up in the fateful signal, but Pierzynski heard no "out" call, and moreover thought that he had heard the ball hit the dirt before it smacked into catcher Josh Paul's glove, so he took off for first because on a third strike not cleanly caught by the catcher, the runner must be tagged out or thrown out to complete the play. Many catchers routinely tag the batter when there is any doubt, but Paul rolled the ball back to the mound and walked toward the dugout. Faced with a decision as to which player had made the right judgment, the umpire ruled that in fact Paul had only trapped the pitch, leaving the ball in play and Pierzynski entitled to the base. Minutes later, Joe Crede doubled home pinch runner Pablo Ozuna, who had stolen second, with the winning run. "I'd rather be lucky than good," said Guillen in the postgame interview, but a more balanced view was that his team had been both lucky *and* good to escape leaving Chicago two games behind.

In the balmier California climate, the White Sox pitchers and hitters became even more unbeatable. Garland followed Buehrle's complete game with another, a four-hit performance yielding only two runs, which the White Sox topped with five of their own. Then it was Freddy Garcia's turn to go a full nine innings and limit the Angels to two runs, while the White Sox, helped by homers from Pierzynski and Konerko, piled on with eight of their own. The fifth and final meeting of the teams saw a fourth straight complete game from White Sox pitchers—this one from Contreras, that buried the Angels, 6–3. It was a feat unequalled in postseason play since Yankee pitchers had recorded five complete games against the Brooklyn Dodgers in the 1956 World Series, four of them for victories—including a perfect game by Don Larsen.

It had been forty-six years since the White Sox were in a World Series. Their 4–2 loss to the Dodgers (now transferred to Los Angeles) in 1959 was personally recalled in 2005 only by middle-aged and older fans. The job that confronted them was beating a Houston Astros team that had recovered from a miserable start to finish with 89 victories plus playoff wins over tough Atlanta and St. Louis. On the opening night they would go up against guaranteed future Hall of Fame pitcher Roger Clemens, who, aging or not, was finishing off a spectacularly good season. But in the first two innings, Clemens, not at his best because of a sore hamstring, was assaulted by three runs and left the game. Houston pulled even in the top of the third, but Contreras then steadied through the eighth and turned the game over to middle reliever Neal Cotts in the eighth, while the White Sox added two go-ahead runs, their total of five including homers from Crede and Dye. The Astros threatened in the ninth, and Jenks was called in once again. The six-foot-three, 270-pound young giant struck out the final two Astro batters to put Chicago up by a game. Final score, 5–3.

Game Two, played in Chicago on a cold and rainy October 23, seemed to push the limits of credibility. Andy Pettitte, another Astros pitching star, faced Buehrle, and the two teams stood tied at two runs each in the fifth, when the Astros pushed across two more to take the lead. In the bottom of the seventh, however, Pettitte yielded a double to Uribe. Dan Wheeler relieved him and walked Iguchi, then hit Jermaine Dye. It was another controversial call that went the Sox way, as all the breaks seemed to be doing. The Astros insisted that the ball had first hit Dye's bat (which Dye himself later said he thought to be the case) but lost the argument. With the bases loaded, Astros manager Phil Garner sent right-hander Chad Qualls in to face the White Sox first baseman and Konerko drove his first offering high and deep into the stands for a grand slam. The Astros were shaken but not crushed. They fought back in the top of the ninth with two runs off a crestfallen Jenks, and the game was tied. In the bottom of the ninth, Scott Podsednik came to bat against the formidable Astros closer, Brad Lidge, already credited with 42 regular-season saves. Podsednik launched a Lidge pitch into the stands for a walk-off game winner, circling the bases amid fireworks from U.S. Cellular Field's exploding scoreboard and ecstatic screams from some 41,000 delirious fans celebrating the familiar scenario of a last-minute, one-run Chicago victory. Final score, 7–6.

The scene shifted to Houston for Game Three. This time the mound matchups were Garland and 20-game winner Roy Oswalt, another of the Houston pitchers who had carried the team brilliantly in its great stretch run. The Astros got him four runs off Garland in the first four innings, but in the top of the fifth, the White Sox answered with five of their own. Once more, however, the White Sox bullpen, which had enjoyed a long rest during the

Angels series and several days of waiting for Houston to complete its playoff, could not hold the lead through the final frames. Cliff Politte, Cotts, and Hermanson all labored in the eighth to hold off a Houston rally, but were not able to keep the Astros from tying the game. Orlando Hernandez took over in the ninth, followed by Marte, and the struggle continued through four extra innings without a run. And then, in the top of the fourteenth, a relatively obscure pinch hitter, Geoff Blum, who had appeared in only 31 games for the White Sox all year—and was a former Astro now pitted against old teammates—hit a two-run homer, making Marte the winning pitcher and putting the White Sox one game away from the ultimate triumph.

That was achieved in another brilliant game that seemed to sum up the entire history of the 2005 White Sox. Superlative pitching by Freddy Garcia and Brandon Backe for the Astros kept both teams scoreless through seven innings. Lidge was brought in for the eighth—an early entry for a closer, but Houston manager Phil Garner had no choice at this point but to lead with his ace. Ozzie Guillen countered with pinch hitter Willie Harris, and Harris, with a two-strike count on him, singled. Podsednik, the newly emerged home-run hitter, now played small ball and sacrificed Harris to second. A groundout by Carl Everett moved the runner to third, and a two-out single by Dye brought him across the plate. The next White Sox batter ended the inning, and it was now up to the pitching staff to get the last six outs. In the bottom of the eighth, Houston showed just how hard that was going to be. Politte, in relief, hit Willy Taveras, then walked Lance Berkman to put two men on base with one out. He retired Morgan Ensberg on a fly to the outfield, then was replaced by Guillen with Neal Cotts, who put away Jose Vizcaino on an infield grounder. A scoreless White Sox top half of the ninth followed, and it was now the moment for acute anxiety.

Jenks, coming on to close, gave up a looping single to pinch hitter Jason Lane. Brad Ausmus sacrificed Lane to second. With the tying run in scoring position, one out, and millions of fans in the stands and in front of TV screens throughout America holding their breath, Garner sent up another pinch hitter, Chris Burke. Burke lifted a high, twisting foul ball toward third base that Juan Uribe, running hard from his shortstop position, grabbed for the out as he tumbled into the stands. Orlando Palmeiro, the Astros' last hope, connected with a pitch and sent a grounder streaking toward the gap in the center of the infield, an almost certain base hit. Uribe, like a streak of lightning, raced toward the ball, scooped it up, and fired it to Konerko a split second before Palmeiro's foot could touch the bag. The White Sox were champions of the world, winning their third straight playoff series while on the road. And their last game of 2005 had been an exact duplicate of the one played on Opening Day, a 1–0 shutout. Ozzie Guillen had said that he wanted the highlight shows to feature a game-ending double play for a victory, and Uribe's fielding gem came close to fulfilling that wish as the White Sox players rushed together on the field to join in a wild, war-whooping dance of exultation.

The White Sox won 16 of their final 17 games. Of the 11 in the postseason, four had been by one run (as had also been the single loss to the Angels). The pitching staff had held the opposition to 34 runs throughout all three series, and managed one shutout. The defense had been almost flawless, and in the final four games the White Sox had stolen five bases and recorded a team batting average of .289 and a slugging average of .493.

After such glories came the final victory parade that wound through Chicago's South Side and ended under a rain of shredded paper in the financial district. It was witnessed by an estimated 700,000 spectators in the jammed streets and countless more on TV. It was a coronation fit for kings, which the White Sox had proven themselves to be. On the verge of the hundredth anniversary of their first world championship, they could look forward to possibly adding a fourth in 2006. Only time would tell. But their 2005 heroics would remain fixed in baseball's record books and memories so long as the game itself would last.

Appendices

National League Team Stats and Standings, 1906

Offense

TEAM	G	W	L	PCT	GB	R	OR	HR	AVG	SB
CHI	155	116	36	.763		705	381	20	.262	283
NY	153	96	56	.632	20	625	510	15	.255	288
PIT	154	93	60	.608	23.5	623	470	12	.261	162
PHI	154	71	82	.464	45.5	528	564	12	.241	180
BRO	153	66	86	.434	50	496	625	25	.236	175
CIN	155	64	87	.424	51.5	533	582	16	.238	170
STL	154	52	98	.347	63	470	607	10	.235	110
BOS	152	49	102	.325	66.5	408	649	16	.226	93

Pitching and Defense

TEAM	CG	SH	SV	HRA	BB	SO	ERA	FA	E	DP
CHI	125	30	10	12	446	702	1.75	.969	194	100
NY	105	19	18	13	394	639	2.49	.963	233	84

TEAM	CG	SH	SV	HRA	BB	SO	ERA	FA	E	DP
PIT	116	27	2	13	309	532	2.21	.964	228	109
PHI	108	21	5	18	436	500	2.58	.956	271	83
BRO	119	22	11	15	453	476	3.13	.955	283	73
CIN	126	12	5	14	470	567	2.69	.959	262	97
STL	118	4	2	17	479	559	3.04	.957	272	92
BOS	137	10	0	24	436	562	3.14	.947	337	102

AMERICAN LEAGUE TEAM STATS AND STANDINGS, 1906

Offense

TEAM	G	W	L	PCT	GB	R	OR	HR	AVG	SB
CHI	154	93	58	.616		570	460	7	.230	214
NY	155	90	61	.596	3	644	543	17	.266	192
CLE	157	89	64	.582	5	663	482	12	.279	203
PHI	149	78	67	.538	12	561	543	32	.247	165
STL	154	76	73	.510	16	558	498	20	.247	221
DET	151	71	78	.477	21	518	599	10	.242	206
WAS	151	55	95	.367	37.5	518	664	26	.238	233
BOS	155	49	105	.318	45.5	463	706	13	.237	99

Pitching and Defense

TEAM	CG	SH	SV	HRA	BB	SO	ERA	FA	E	DP
CHI	117	32	3	11	255	543	2.13	.963	243	80
NY	99	18	5	21	351	605	2.78	.957	272	69
CLE	133	27	4	16	365	530	2.09	.967	216	111
PHI	107	19	4	16	425	749	2.60	.956	267	86
STL	133	17	5	14	314	558	2.23	.954	290	80
DET	128	7	4	14	389	469	3.06	.959	260	86
WAS	115	13	1	15	451	558	3.25	.955	279	78
BOS	124	6	6	37	285	549	3.41	.949	335	84

CUBS 1906 REGULAR SEASON RECORDS

Hitting:	G	AB	R	H	2B	3B	HR	RBI	BB	AVG	OBP	SLG	SB
Frank Chance, 1b BR/TR, 6', 190 lbs.	136	474	103	151	24	10	3	71	70	.319	.406	.430	57
John Evers, 2b BL/TR, 5'9", 125 lbs.	154	533	65	136	17	6	1	51	36	.255	.302	.315	49
Joe Tinker, ss BR/TR, 5'9", 175 lbs.	148	523	75	122	18	4	1	64	43	.233	.292	.289	30
Harry Steinfeldt, 3b BR/TR, 5'9.5", 180 lbs.	151	539	81	176	27	10	3	83	47	.327	.381	.430	29

Hitting:

	G	AB	R	H	2B	3B	HR	RBI	BB	AVG	OBP	SLG	SB
Frank Schulte, lf BL/TR, 5'11", 170 lbs.	146	563	77	158	18	13	7	60	31	.281	.318	.396	25
Solly Hofman, cf BR/TR, 6', 160 lbs.	64	195	30	50	2	3	2	20	20	.256	.326	.328	13
Jim Sheckard, rf BL/TR, 5'9", 175 lbs.	149	549	90	144	27	10	1	45	67	.262.	.343	.353	30
John King, c BR/TR, 5'9.5", 160 lbs.	107	343	45	107	15	8	2	46	23	.312	.355	.420	14
Mordecai Brown, p	36	98	11	20	1	0	0	4	6	.204	.250	.214	0
Jack Pfiester, p	31	84	5	4	0	0	0	1	3	.048	.091	.048	0
Ed Reulbach, p	34	83	4	13	0	0	0	4	2	.157	.176	.157	0
Orval Overall, p	31	84	10	15	3	0	0	4	2	.179	.198	.214	1

Pitching:

	W	L	PCT	G	GS	CG	SH	SV	IP	H	HR	BB	SO	ERA
Mordecai Brown, p BB/TR, 5'10", 175 lbs.	26	6	.813	36	32	27	9	3	277	198	1	61	144	1.04
Jack Pfiester, p BR/TL,5'11", 180 lbs.	20	8	.714	31	29	20	4	0	242	173	3	63	153	1.56
Ed Reulbach, p BR/TR, 6'1", 190 lbs.	19	4	.826	33	24	20	6	3	218	129	2	92	94	1.65
Orval Overall, p BB/TR, 6'2", 214 lbs.	16	8	.667	31	24	19	2	1	226	193	2	97	127	2.75

CUBS 1906 WORLD SERIES RECORDS

Hitting:	G	AB	R	H	2B	3B	HR	RBI	BB	SO	AVG	SB
Frank Chance, 1b BR/TR, 6', 190 lbs.	6	21	3	5	1	0	0	0	2	1	.238	2
John Evers, 2b BL/TR, 5'9", 125 lbs.	6	20	2	3	1	0	0	1	1	3	.150	2
Joe Tinker, ss BR/TR, 5'9", 175 lbs.	6	18	4	3	0	0	0	1	2	2	.167	3
Harry Steinfeldt, 3b BR/TR 5'9.5", 180 lbs.	6	20	2	5	1	0	0	2	1	0	.250	0
Frank Schulte, lf BL/TR,5'11", 170 lbs.	6	26	1	7	3	0	0	3	1	3	.269	0
Solly Hofman, cf BR/TR, 6', 160 lbs.	6	23	3	7	1	0	0	2	3	5	.304	1
Jim Sheckard, rf BL/TR, 5'9", 175 lbs.	6	21	0	0	0	0	0	1	2	4	.000	1
John Kling, c BR/TR, 5'9.5", 160 lbs.	6	17	2	3	1	0	0	0	4	3	.176	0

Pitching:	G	GS	CG	SV	SHO	W	L	ERA	IP	H	ER	BB	SO
Mordecai Brown, p BB/TR, 5'10", 175 lbs.	3	3	2	0	1	1	2	3.20	19.2	14	7	4	12

Pitching:

	W	L	ERA	G	GS	CG	SV	SHO	IP	H	ER	BB	SO
Jack Pfiester, p BR/TL, 5'11", 180 lbs.	0	2	6.10	2	1	1	0	0	10.1	7	7	3	11
Ed Reulbach, p BR/TR, 6'1", 190 lbs.	1	0	2.45	2	2	1	0	0	11	6	3	8	4
Orval Overall, p BB/TR, 6'2", 214 lbs.	0	0	2.25	2	0	0	0	0	12	10	3	3	8

White Sox 1906 Regular Season Records

Hitting:

	G	AB	R	H	2B	3B	HR	RBI	BB	AVG	OBP	SLG	SB
"Jiggs" Donahue, 1b BL/TL, 6'1", 178 lbs.	154	556	70	143	17	7	1	57	48	.257	.316	.316	36
Frank Isbell, 2b BL/TR, 5'11", 190 lbs.	143	549	71	153	18	11	0	57	30	.279	.316	.352	37
Lee Tannehill, 3b/ss BR/TR, 5'11", 170 lbs.	116	378	26	69	8	3	0	33	31	.183	.244	.220	7
George Davis, ss BB/TR, 5'9", 180 lbs.	133	484	63	134	26	6	0	80	41	.277	.333	.355	27
George Rohe, 3b BR/TR, 5'9", 165 lbs.	77	225	14	58	5	1	0	25	16	.258	.307	.289	8
Patsy Dougherty, lf BL/TR, 6'2", 190 lbs.	87	305	33	69	11	4	1	31	19	.226	.272	.298	11

Batting													
Fielder Jones, cf BL/TR, 5'11", 180 lbs.	144	496	77	114	22	4	2	34	83	.230	.340	.302	26
Ed Hahn, rf BB/TR, 5'9", 180 lbs.	141	506	82	112	8	5	0	28	72	.221	.318	.257	21
Billy Sullivan, c BR/TR, 5'9", 155 lbs.	116	387	37	83	18	4	2	33	22	.214	.262	.297	10
Doc White, p	29	85	11	12	1	1	0	3	13	.185	.321	.231	3
Nick Altrock, p	38	100	4	16	2	0	0	3	8	.160	.222	.180	2
Ed Walsh, p	42	99	12	14	3	2	0	4	3	.141	.175	.212	0
Frank Owen, p	42	103	7	14	4	0	0	7	8	.136	.205	.175	0

Pitching:

	W	L	PCT	G	GS	CG	SH	SV	IP	H	HR	BB	SO	ERA
Doc White, p BL/TL, 6'1", 150 lbs.	18	6	.750	28	24	20	7	0	219	160	2	38	95	1.52
Nick Altrock, p BB/TL, 5'10", 197 lbs.	20	13	.606	38	30	25	4	0	288	269	0	42	99	2.06
Ed Walsh, p BR/TR, 6'1", 193 lbs.	17	13	.567	41	31	24	10	1	278	215	1	58	171	1.88
Frank Owen, p BB/TR, 5'11", 160 lbs.	22	13	.629	42	36	27	7	0	293	289	4	54	66	2.33

WHITE SOX 1906 WORLD SERIES RECORDS

Hitting:	G	AB	R	H	2B	3B	HR	RBI	BB	SO	AVG	SB
"Jiggs" Donahue, 1b BL/TL, 6'1", 178 lbs.	6	18	0	6	2	1	0	4	3	3	.333	0
Frank Isbell, 2b BL/TR, 5'11", 190 lbs.	6	26	4	8	4	0	0	4	0	6	.308	1
Lee Tannehill, 3b/ss BR/TR, 5'11", 170 lbs.	3	9	1	1	0	0	0	0	0	2	.111	0
George Davis, ss BB/TR, 5'9", 180 lbs.	3	13	4	4	3	0	0	6	0	1	.308	1
George Rohe, 3b BR/TR, 5'9", 165 lbs.	6	21	2	7	1	2	0	4	3	1	.333	2
Patsy Dougherty, lf BL/TR, 6'2", 190 lbs.	6	20	1	2	0	0	0	1	3	4	.100	2
Fielder Jones, cf BL/TR, 5'11", 180 lbs.	6	21	4	2	0	0	0	0	3	3	.095	0
Ed Hahn, rf BB/TR, 5'9", 180 lbs.	6	22	4	6	0	0	0	0	1	1	.273	0
Billy Sullivan, c BR/TR, 5'9", 155 lbs.	6	21	0	0	0	0	0	0	0	9	.000	0

Pitching:	W	L	ERA	G	GS	CG	SV	SHO	IP	H	ER	BB	SO
Doc White, p BL/TL, 6'1", 150 lbs.	1	1	1.80	3	2	1	1	0	15	12	3	7	4
Nick Altrock, p BB/TL, 5'10", 197 lbs.	1	1	1.00	2	2	2	0	0	18	11	2	2	5
Ed Walsh, p BR/T, 6'1", 193 lbs.	2	0	1.20	2	2	1	0	1	15	7	2	6	17
Frank Owen, p BB/TR, 5'11", 160 lbs.	0	0	3.00	1	0	0	0	0	6	6	2	3	2

OVERALL SERIES STATS
CHICAGO WHITE SOX (AL), 4;
CHICAGO CUBS (NL), 2

CHI (A)

PLAYER/POS	AVG	G	AB	R	H	2B	3B	HR	RB	BB	SO	SB
Nick Altrock, p	.250	2	4	0	1	0	0	0	0	1	1	0
George Davis, ss	.308	3	13	4	4	3	0	0	6	0	1	1
Jiggs Donahue, 1b	.333	6	18	0	6	2	1	0	4	3	3	0
Patsy Dougherty, of	.100	6	20	1	2	0	0	0	1	3	4	2
Eddie Hahn, cf	.273	6	22	4	6	0	0	0	0	1	1	0
Frank Isbell, 2b	.308	6	26	4	8	4	0	0	4	0	6	1
Fielder Jones, of	.095	6	21	4	2	0	0	0	0	3	3	0
Ed McFarland, ph	.000	1	1	0	0	0	0	0	0	0	0	0

PLAYER/POS	AVG	G	AB	R	H	2B	3B	HR	RB	BB	SO	SB
Bill O'Neill, of	.000	1	1	1	0	0	0	0	0	0	0	0
Frank Owen, p	.000	1	2	0	0	0	0	0	0	0	1	0
George Rohe, 3b	.333	6	21	2	7	1	2	0	4	3	1	2
Billy Sullivan, c	.000	6	21	0	0	0	0	0	0	0	9	0
Lee Tannehill, ss	.111	3	9	1	1	0	0	0	0	0	2	0
Babe Towne, ph	.000	1	1	0	0	0	0	0	0	0	0	0
Ed Walsh, p	.000	2	4	1	0	0	0	0	0	3	3	0
Doc White, p	.000	3	3	0	0	0	0	0	0	1	0	0
TOTAL	.198		187	22	37	10	3	0	19	18	35	6

PITCHER	W	L	ERA	G	GS	CG	SV	SHO	IP	H	ER	BB	SO
Nick Altrock	1	1	1.00	2	2	2	0	0	18	11	2	2	5
Frank Owen	0	0	3.00	1	0	0	0	0	6	5	2	3	2
Ed Walsh	2	0	1.20	2	2	1	0	1	15	7	2	6	17
Doc White	1	1	1.80	3	2	1	1	0	15	12	3	7	4
TOTAL	4	2	1.50	8	6	4	1	1	54	36	9	18	28

CHI (N)

PLAYER/POS	AVG	G	AB	R	H	2B	3B	HR	RB	BB	SO	SB
Mordecai Brown, p	.333	3	6	0	2	0	0	0	0	0	4	0
Frank Chance, 1b	.238	6	21	3	5	1	0	0	0	2	1	2

Johnny Evers, 2b	.150	6	20	2	3	1	0	0	1	0	1	3	2
Doc Gassler, ph	.000	2	1	0	0	0	0	0	0	0	1	0	0
Solly Holman, of	.304	6	23	3	7	1	1	0	2	0	3	5	1
Johnny Kling, c	.176	6	17	2	3	1	1	0	0	0	4	3	0
Pal Moran, ph	.000	2	2	0	0	0	0	0	0	0	0	0	0
Orval Overall, p	.250	2	4	1	1	1	1	0	0	0	1	1	0
Jack Pfiester, p	.000	2	2	0	0	0	0	0	0	0	0	1	0
Ed Reulbach, p	.000	2	3	0	0	0	0	0	1	0	0	1	0
Frank Schulte, of	.269	8	26	1	7	3	0	0	3	0	1	3	0
Jimmy Sheckard, of	.000	6	21	0	0	0	0	0	1	0	2	4	1
Harry Steinfeldt, 3b	.250	6	20	2	5	1	1	0	2	0	1	0	0
Joe Tinker, ss	.167	8	18	4	3	0	0	0	1	0	2	2	3
TOTAL	.198		184	18	36	9	9	0	11	0	18	28	9

PITCHER	W	L	ERA	G	GS	CG	SV	SHO	IP	H	ER	BB	SO
Mordecai Brown	1	2	3.20	3	3	2	0	1	18.2	14	7	4	12
Orval Overall	0	0	2.25	2	0	0	0	0	12	10	3	3	8
Jack Pfiester	0	2	6.10	2	1	1	0	0	10.1	7	7	3	11
Ed Reulbach	1	0	2.45	2	2	1	0	0	11	6	3	8	3
TOTAL	2	4	3.40	9	6	4	0	1	53	37	20	18	35

GAME ONE

White Sox

	AB	R	H	BI	BB	PO	A	E
Hahn, rf	3	0	0	0	0	1	0	0
Jones, cf	4	1	1	0	0	3	0	0
Isbell, 2b	4	0	1	1	0	0	1	1
Rohe, 3b	4	1	1	0	0	1	2	0
Donahue, 3b	4	0	0	0	0	12	2	0
Dougherty, lf	3	0	0	0	0	1	0	0
Sullivan, c	3	0	0	0	0	5	1	0
Tannehill, ss	3	0	0	0	0	1	4	0
Altrock, p	2	0	1	0	1	3	4	0
Totals	30	2	4	1	1	27	14	1

Cubs

	AB	R	H	BI	BB	PO	A	E
Hofman, cf	3	0	0	0	0	1	1	0
Sheckard, lf	3	0	0	0	0	1	0	0
*Moran	1	0	0	0	0	0	0	0
Schulte, rf	4	0	1	0	1	1	0	0
Chance, 1b	4	0	1	0	0	13	0	0
Steinfeldt, 3b	4	0	0	0	0	0	2	0
Tinker, ss	3	0	0	0	0	2	3	0
Evers, 2b	3	0	0	0	0	1	3	0
Kling, c	2	0	1	0	0	8	1	1
Reulbach, p								
Totals	29	1	4	0	1	27	14	2

* batted for Sheckard in 9th

										R	H	E
White Sox	0	0	0	0	1	1	0	0	0	2	4	1
Cubs	0	0	0	0	1	0	0	0	0	1	4	2

WP Altrock

LP Brown

Three base hits—Rohe. Struck out—by Brown: Hahn, Isbell, Donahue (3), Tannehill, Altrock; by Altrock: Brown, Hofman, Evers. Stolen bases—Isbell, Schulte; Dougherty. Sac—Hahn, Hofman, Brown. Left on base—White Sox 3, Cubs 4. Wild pitches—Altrock (Kling scoring), Brown. Passed balls—Kling (2), Rohe scoring on Kling error in 5th. Time—1:45. Umpires—Johnstone and O'Loughlin. Attendance—12,693.

GAME TWO

Cubs

	AB	R	H	BI	BB	PO	A	E
Hofman, cf	4	0	1	1	1	2	0	0
Sheckard, lf	4	0	0	0	0	3	1	0
Schulte, rf	4	0	1	0	1	1	0	0
Chance, 1b	5	2	1	0	0	12	0	0
Steinfeldt, 3b	3	1	3	1	0	0	2	0
Tinker, ss	3	3	2	1	1	0	3	1
Evers, 2b	4	1	1	0	2	4	6	0
Kling, c	2	0	1	0	0	5	1	0
Reulbach, p	3	0	0	1	0	0	2	0
Totals	32	7	10	4	5	27	15	1

White Sox

	AB	R	H	BI	BB	PO	A	E
Hahn, rf	3	0	0	0	1	0	0	0
Jones, cf	3	0	1	0	1	1	0	0
Isbell, 2b	4	0	0	0	0	5	2	1
Rohe, 3b	2	0	0	0	1	0	3	0
Donahue, 1b	3	0	1	0	1	11	1	0
Dougherty, rf	2	1	0	0	2	1	0	0
Sullivan, c	4	0	0	0	0	7	2	2
Tannehill, ss	3	0	0	0	0	1	3	0
White, p	0	0	0	0	0	0	1	0
*Towne	1	0	0	0	0	0	0	0
Owen, p	2	0	0	0	0	1	4	0
Totals	27	1	2	0	6	27	16	3

* batted for White in 3d

										R	H	E
Cubs	0	3	1	0	0	1	0	2	0	7	10	1
White Sox	0	0	1	0	0	0	0	0	0	1	2	3

WP Brown

LP White (3), Owen

Two base hits—Kling, Jones. Struck out—by Reulbach: Sullivan, Owen, Jones; by White: Chance; by Owen: Reulbach, Kling. Bases on balls—off White, 2; off Owen, 3; off Reulbach, 6. Double plays—Sheckard-Kling; Evers-Chance. Stolen bases—Chance (2), Tinker (2), Evers. Sac—Sheckard, Reulbach. Hit by Pitcher—Rohe. Wild pitches—Owen, Reulbach. Steinfeld scored on Isbell error in 6th, Tinker scored on Sullivan error in 5th, Tinker scored in 3d, Dougherty scored on Tinker error in 3d, Evers scored on wild pitch in 8th. Left on base—Cubs 6, White Sox 6. Time—1:58. Umpires—O'Loughlin and Johnstone. Attendance—12,595.

Game Three

White Sox

	AB	R	H	BI	BB	PO	A	E
Hahn, rf	2	0	0	0	0	0	0	0
O'Neill, rf	1	1	0	0	0	1	0	0
Jones, cf	4	0	1	0	0	1	0	0
Isbell, 2b	4	0	0	0	0	1	4	1
Rohe, 3b	3	0	1	3	1	0	1	0
Donahue, 1b	3	0	2	0	0	14	0	0
Dougherty, lf	4	0	0	0	0	0	0	0
Sullivan, c	3	0	0	0	0	10	3	0
Tannehill, ss	3	1	1	0	0	0	4	0
Walsh, p	2	1	0	0	1	0	3	0
Totals	29	3	5	3	2	27	15	1

Cubs

	AB	R	H	BI	BB	PO	A	E
Hofman, cf	4	0	1	0	0	1	0	0
Sheckard, lf	4	0	0	0	0	2	0	0
Schulte, rf	4	0	1	0	0	1	0	0
Chance, 1b	2	0	0	0	1	7	2	0
Steinfeldt, 3b	3	0	0	0	0	1	2	1
Tinker, ss	3	0	0	0	0	3	2	0
Evers, 2b	3	0	0	0	0	1	2	0
Kling, c	3	0	0	0	0	11	3	0
Pfiester, p	2	0	0	0	0	0	2	0
*Gessler	1	0	0	0	0	0	0	0
Totals	29	0	2	0	1	27	11	1

* batted for Pfiester in 9th

										R	H	E
White Sox	0	0	0	0	0	3	0	0	0	3	5	1
Cubs	0	0	0	0	0	0	0	0	0	0	2	1

WP Walsh
LP Pfiester

Two base hits—Schulte. Three base hits—Donahue, Rohe. Struck out—by Pfiester: Isbell (3), Dougherty, Sullivan (2), Tannehill Jones, Walsh; by Walsh: Sheckard (2), Tinker (2), Kling, Pfiester, Schulte (3), Evers (2), Hofman. Sac—Donahue, Sullivan. Stolen base—Rohe. Left on base—White Sox 4, Cubs 3. Hit by pitcher—Hahn. Wild pitch—Walsh. Time—2:10. Umpires—Johnstone and O'Loughlin. Attendance—13,667.

GAME FOUR

Cubs

	AB	R	H	BI	BB	PO	A	E
Hofman, cf	4	0	2	0	0	1	0	0
Sheckard, lf	3	0	0	0	1	1	0	0
Schulte, rf	4	0	0	0	0	1	0	0
Chance, 1b	4	1	2	0	0	12	1	0
Steinfeldt, 3b	2	0	1	0	0	1	1	1
Tinker, ss	1	0	0	1	0	2	3	0
Evers, 2b	3	0	1	0	0	2	4	0
Kling, c	3	0	0	0	0	6	3	0
Brown, p	3	0	1	0	0	1	4	0
Totals	27	1	7	1	1	27	16	1

White Sox

	AB	R	H	BI	BB	PO	A	E
Hahn, rf	4	0	1	0	0	1	0	0
Jones, cf	3	0	0	0	1	0	0	0
Isbell, 2b	4	0	0	0	0	1	4	0
Rohe, 3b	3	0	0	0	0	0	4	0
Donahue, 1b	1	0	0	0	1	13	2	0
Dougherty, lf	3	0	1	0	0	2	0	0
Davis, ss	3	0	0	0	0	4	1	1
Sullivan, c	3	0	0	0	0	3	1	0
Altrock, p	2	0	0	0	0	3	8	0
*McFarland	1	0	0	0	0	0	0	0
Totals	27	0	2	0	2	27	20	1

* batted for Altrock in 9th

										R	H	E
Cubs	0	0	0	1	0	0	0	0	0	1	7	1
White Sox	0	0	0	0	0	0	0	0	0	0	2	1

WP Brown

LP Altrock

Struck out—by Brown: Dougherty, Sullivan (2), Davis, Isbell; by Altrock: Brown (2). Double plays—Kling-Evers; Altrock-Donahue-Sullivan. Sac—Steinfeldt (2), Tinker (3). Stolen base—Sheckard. Left on base—White Sox 3, Cubs 5. Passed ball—Kling. Time—1:35. Umpires—O'Loughlin and Johnstone. Attendance—18,384.

Game Five

White Sox

	AB	R	H	BI	BB	PO	A	E
Hahn, rf	5	2	1	0	0	1	0	0
Jones, cf	4	1	1	0	0	1	0	0
Isbell, 2b	5	3	4	2	0	2	2	2
Davis, ss	5	2	2	3	0	2	8	1
Rohe, 3b	4	0	3	1	1	0	2	2
Donahue, 1b	3	0	1	1	1	15	0	1
Dougherty, lf	5	0	0	0	0	0	0	0
Sullivan, c	4	0	0	0	0	6	2	0
Walsh, p	2	0	0	0	2	0	3	0
White, p	0	0	0	0	0	0	0	0
Totals	37	8	12	7	4	27	19	6

Cubs

	AB	R	H	BI	BB	PO	A	E
Hofman, cf	3	2	1	0	2	2	0	0
Sheckard, lf	4	0	0	0	0	1	0	0
Schulte, rf	5	1	3	2	0	2	1	0
Chance, 1b	4	0	1	0	0	8	0	0
Steinfeldt, 3b	5	1	1	0	0	1	2	0
Tinker, ss	4	1	0	0	1	2	2	0
Evers, 2b	3	0	0	0	1	2	5	0
*Moran	1	0	0	0	0	0	0	0
Kling, c	3	0	0	0	1	9	0	0
Reulbach, p	0	0	0	0	0	0	0	0
Pfiester, p	0	0	0	0	0	0	0	0
Overall, p	2	1	0	0	1	0	2	0
Totals	34	6	6	2	6	27	13	0

* batted for Evers in 6th

										R	H	E
White Sox	1	0	2	4	0	1	0	0	0	8	12	6
Cubs	3	0	0	0	0	2	0	0	1	6	6	6

WP Walsh, White (7)

Reulbach, Pfiester (3-LP), Overall (4)

Two base hits—Isbell (4), Davis (2), Rohe, Donahue, Schulte, Steinfeldt, Chance. Struck out—by Reulbach: Sullivan; by Pfiester: Rohe, Sullivan; by Overall: Walsh (2), Jones, Isbell, Dougherty; by Walsh: Hofman, Sheckard (2), Kling, Overall. Bases on balls—off Reulbach, 21; off Overall, 2; off White, 5; off Walsh, 1. Stolen bases—Rohe, Dougherty; Tinker, Evers. Sac—Jones; Sheckard, Reulbach. Hits—off Reulbach, 5 in 2⅓ innings; off Pfiester, 3 in 1 inning; off Overall, 4 in 5⅔ innings; off Walsh, 5 in 6⅓ innings; off White, 1 in 2⅔ innings. Left on base—White Sox 8, Cubs 10. Hit by pitcher—by Pfiester: Donahue; by Walsh: Chance. Wild pitch—Overall; Walsh. Time—2:40. Umpires—Johnstone and O'Loughlin. Attendance—23,257.

GAME SIX

White Sox

	AB	R	H	BI	BB	PO	A	E
Hahn, rf	5	2	4	0	0	1	0	0
Jones, cf	3	2	0	0	1	3	0	0
Isbell, 2b	5	1	3	1	0	1	4	0
Davis, ss	5	1	2	3	0	1	4	0
Rohe, 3b	5	1	2	0	0	3	4	1
Donahue, 1b	4	0	2	3	0	14	1	1
Dougherty, lf	3	0	1	1	1	0	0	1
Sullivan, c	4	0	0	0	0	3	1	0
White, p	3	0	0	0	1	1	2	0
Totals	37	8	14	8	3	27	16	3

Cubs

	AB	R	H	BI	BB	PO	A	E
Hofman, cf	5	1	2	1	0	3	0	0
Sheckard, lf	3	0	0	1	1	2	0	0
Schulte, rf	5	0	1	1	0	0	0	0
Chance, 1b	2	0	0	0	1	10	0	0
Steinfeldt, 3b	3	0	0	0	1	0	1	0
Tinker, ss	4	0	1	0	0	2	6	0
Evers, 2b	4	1	1	0	0	1	1	0
Kling, c	4	1	1	0	0	6	2	0
Brown, p	1	0	0	0	0	0	0	0
Overall, p	2	0	1	0	0	0	1	0
★Gessler	0	0	0	0	1	0	0	0
Totals	33	3	7	3	4	24	11	0

★ batted for Overall in 9th

									R	H	E
Cubs	1	0	0	0	1	0	0	0	1	3	7	0
White Sox	3	4	0	0	0	0	1	X		8	14	3

LP Brown (2), Overall
WP White

Two base hits—Davis, Donahue, Schulte, Overall, Evers. Struck out—by Overall: Sullivan(2), Donahue; by White: Brown, Hofman. Bases on balls—off Brown, 1; off Overall, 2; off White, 4. Hits—off Brown, 8 in 1⅓ innings; off Overall, 6 in 6⅔ innings. Double play—Davis-Donahue. Sac—Jones; Sheckard. Stolen base—Rohe. Left on base—White Sox 8, Cubs 9. Hit by pitcher—by White: Chance. Time—2:00. Umpires—O'Loughlin and Johnstone. Attendance—19,249.

Notes

CHAPTER 1: OPENING DAY

1. *Chicago Tribune,* Oct. 4, 1906.
2. James Grossman, Ann Keating and Janice Rieff, eds. *Encyclopedia of Chicago* (Chicago: University of Chicago Press, 2004), 568–69.
3. Figures vary depending on methods of computation—see two websites, www.cjr.org/tools/inflation and www.eh.net/hmit for examples. Wage data can be found in the Bureau of the Census volumes (various years) entitled *Historical Statistics of the U.S.*
4. Steven Riess, *Touching Base: Professional Baseball and American Culture in the Progressive Era,* rev. ed. (Urbana and Chicago: University of Illinois Press, 1999); *City Games: The Evolution of American Urban Society and the Rise of Sports* (Urbana: University of Illinois Press, 1989).
5. Robert G. Spinney, *City of Big Shoulders: A History of Chicago* (DeKalb: Northern Illinois University Press, 2000), 57–62.
6. Ibid., 68.
7. Ibid.
8. The figure on horses is from Perry Duis, *Challenging Chicago: Coping with Everyday Life, 1837–1920* (Urbana: University of Illinois Press, 1998), 61. That on automobile licensing is from Bessie Louise Pierce Papers, Special Collections Research Center, University of Chicago Library, Box 23, Folder 1, 62. All of the color material on Game One itself, except where otherwise specified, is from the *Chicago Tribune,*

Record-Herald, Inter-Ocean, and *Daily News* for October 9 and 10, 1906. Chicago readers may want to know that the lines referred to were the Douglas and Garfield branches of the El, and the streetcar lines on Twelfth, Harrison, Ogden, and Van Buren, and on Paulina and Robey.

9. Pierce Papers, Box 23, Folder 1, 37.

10. There are some elisions in the headlines, which took up almost a third of a page.

11. *Tribune,* Oct. 8.

12. Pierce Papers, Box 23, Folder 1, 37; Spinney, 126–27; *Chicago: Historic City* (Chicago Department of Development and Planning, 1976), 43.

13. Pierce Papers, Box 23, Folder 1, 37.

14. Spinney, 63–65; see also Riess, 39.

15. Reiss, 31, and elsewhere in his opening chapter.

16. Society for American Baseball Research, "A Fan's Eye View," *Baseball in Chicago: A Celebration of the 80th Anniversary of the 1906 World's Championship Series* (Cooperstown, NY: 1986), 5–10.

17. Figures on the 1906 Cubs are from two sources: Peter Golenbeck, *Wrigleyville: A Magical History Tour of the Chicago Cubs* (New York: St. Martin's Press, 1999), 111–19; and a long article by Sy Sanborn in the *Chicago Tribune* of October 7, 1906, which is also the source of the data on the White Sox performance in 1906. The statistics are not always totally reliable or consistent, partly because record-keeping was sometimes inaccurately transcribed from reporters' notes, reporters and official scorers did not always check their own copy carefully, and changes in scoring rules sometimes led to disagreement and confusion over what constituted a win, a loss, a hit, a sacrifice, and so on through the columns of the box scores. I checked the newspaper reports against two encyclopedias—John Thorn, Pete Palmer, Michael Gershman, and David Pietrusza, eds. *Total Baseball,* 5th ed. (New York: Viking, 1997) and *The Baseball Encyclopedia: The Complete and Official Guide to Major League Baseball,* 9th ed. (New York: Macmillan, 1993). Where both encyclopedias agree, I take that figure as definitive; where they disagree (which is rare) I note the discrepancy. Thus, *Total Baseball* gives Frank Owen's 1906 W–L record as 22–13 as opposed to the *Baseball Encylopedia's* 22–12. Likewise, *TB* awards Ed Reulbach a 19–4 mark but the *BE* says 19–6. And again, *TB* gives Nick Altrock a 20–13 mark, while *BE* allows only 20.

18. *Record-Herald,* Oct. 6.

19. Ibid., Oct. 7.

20. Text furnished by my friend Ms. Vera Chatz, who recalled obligatory singing of it in Chicago's schools as late as the 1940s.

21. *Record-Herald,* Oct. 4.

22. *Tribune,* Oct. 10

CHAPTER 2: THE CUBS AND THE FOUNDATIONS OF BASEBALL

1. Albert G. Spalding, *America's National Game: Historic Facts Concerning the Beginning, Evolution, Development and Popularity of Base Ball, with Personal Reminiscences of Its Vicissitudes, Its Victories and Its Votaries* (New York: American Sports Publishing Co., 1911), 207–8.
2. Andrew Carnegie, *Triumphant Democracy; or Fifty Years' March of the Republic* (New York: Scribner, 1886), 1.
3. Quoted in Peter Levine, *A.G. Spalding and the Rise of Baseball* (New York: Oxford, 1985), 90.
4. Jerome Holtzman and George Vass, *The Chicago Cubs Encyclopedia* (Philadelphia: Temple University Press, 1997), 257.
5. John Thorn, Pete Palmer, Michael Gershman, and David Pietrusza, eds., *Total Baseball,* 5th ed. (New York: Viking, 1997), 434; Harold Seymour, *Baseball: The Early Years* (New York: Oxford, 1960), 334.
6. The statistics are from the Major LeagueBaseball website(http://mlb. com/NASApp/mlb/mlb/playersindex.jsp). Earlier almanacs and encyclopedias may give different calculations. See note 17, chapter 1.
7. Levine, *Spalding,* 72. Data on the ballparks is from Holtzman and Vass, *Cubs Encyclopedia,* 325–28.
8. Quoted in John Thorn's essay, "Our Game," in *Total Baseball,* 5.
9. Lawrence Ritter, *The Glory of Their Times: The Story of the Early Days of Baseball Told by the Men Who Played It,* Enlarged Edition (New York: Perennial Books, 2002), 92–93.
10. Kling file, A. Bartlett Giammati Research Center, National Baseball Hall of Fame, Cooperstown, New York, hereafter referred to as BGRC. These files contain not only newspaper clippings, but often photocopies of entries from David L. Porter, ed., *Biographical Dictionary of American Sports: Baseball* (New York: Greenwood Press, 1987), hereafter referred to as *BDAS.* I cite to that source only when I have gone to it directly; where copies are included in a BGRC file, I have not cited them, just as I have not cited separate clippings in those files.
11. *BDAS.* Selee himself was voted into the Hall of Fame by the Veterans Committee in 1999.
12. Evers file, BGRC.
13. *Total Baseball* provides slightly different numbers: 20–8 for Weimer, 19–10 for Wicker. Where such conflicts occur, I try to furnish both sets of figures.
14. Brown file, BGRC. There are minor discrepancies in stories in the file. Brown says, in an interview with a Terre Haute paper in 1919, that he got $60 a month with the Terre Haute club, not $40, and that he did not replace the Coxsville pitcher because of an injury but because he showed up drunk.

15. Again, a discrepancy—the *Cubs Encyclopedia* gives this information; *Total Baseball* has him coming from Pittsburgh, where he had only three appearances in 1903. The *Chicago Tribune* seems to solve the discrepancy by saying that he was secured by Pittsburgh in the fall of 1903 but played only two weeks. Left open is who paid the $1,500 and to whom.
16. Schulte file, BGRC.
17. Ritter, 39–40.
18. *Chicago Tribune.* Oct. 7.
19. Kling file, BGRC.
20. Peter Golenbeck, *Wrigleyville: A Magical History Tour of the Chicago Cubs* (New York: St. Martin's Press, 1996), 110.

Chapter 3: Game Two and the Tools of Baseball

1. Richard C. Lindberg, *The White Sox Encyclopedia* (Philadephia: Temple University Press, 1997), 337–38. The figure seems especially suspect in view of the fact that in the final game of the Series, when the White Sox park was crammed with a crowd that literally broke down fences to get in, the official paid attendance was just under 20,000. See chapter 7.
2. Robin F. Bachin, *Building the South Side: Urban Space and Civic Culture in Chicago, 1890–1919* (Chicago: University of Chicago Press, 2004), 231–32.
3. Richard Orodenker, *The Writers' Game: Baseball Writing in America* (New York: Twayne Publishers, 1996), 35.
4. Obituary, *Chicago Tribune,* July 19, 1934.
5. Clippings from the Chicago Press Veterans Association mss, Chicago Historical Society; obituary of Fullerton at A. Bartlett Giammati Research Center, Cooperstown, New York; Norman Green, Stephen Lacy, and Jean Folkerts, "Chicago Journalists at the Turn of the Century: Bohemians All?" *Journalism Quarterly* 66, no. 4 (1989) 873.
6. Marc Okkonen, *Baseball Uniforms of the Twentieth Century* (New York: Sterling Publishing Co., 1991), 20, 25.
7. Levine, 78.
8. *Chicago Record-Herald,* Oct. 11.
9. A lefty according to the *Chicago Tribune*'s pre-Series (Oct. 7) article, though *Total Baseball* lists him as both batting and throwing right-handed.
10. Spalding's *Official Baseball Guide,* 1907.
11. *Chicago Tribune,* Oct. 11.

Chapter 4: The White Sox and the Business of Baseball

1. G. W. Axelson, *"Commy": The Life Story of Charles A. Comiskey* (Chicago: Reilly & Lee, 1919), 19.

2. *Chicago Daily News,* April 15–26, 1916.
3. Harold Seymour, *Baseball: The Early Years* (Nw York: Oxford, 1960), 75–85, 135–47.
4. *Chicago Daily News;* Seymour, 175.
5. Seymour, 61–62.
6. Ibid., 145.
7. Ibid., 143.
8. The Browns won three of the five games completed, one ended in a tie, and one was declared forfeited to Chicago when Comiskey pulled his team off the field in protest against an umpire's call. Ibid., 186.
9. Ibid., 117–18.
10. Ibid., 148–49.
11. Ibid., 149–61.
12. Ibid., 131–36.
13. Ibid., 222, 225.
14. Ibid., 228.
15. Ibid., 230, 232.
16. George S. Robbins, "First Story of Life Told by Comiskey," *Chicago Daily News,* April 16–26, 1916. This was a ten-part series of articles written by a *News* sportswriter based on interviews with Comiskey. The articles were identified in the text as the first, second, and so on, and I have cited them by number in this fashion under the label CDN Series.
17. Seymour, 310–11.
18. Ibid., 304; David G. Voigt, *American Baseball: From Gentleman's Sport to the Commissioner System* (Norman: University of Oklahoma Press, 1966), 227.
19. CDN Series, no. 7.
20. Ibid.
21. Ibid.
22. Richard Lindberg, *Who's on 3d? The Chicago White Sox Story* (South Bend, IN: Icarus Press, 1983), 21.
23. That date is Comiskey's recollection. Other biographical sources put Isbell's debut at 1896.
24. BGRC file.
25. *Chicago Tribune,* Oct. 7.
26. CDN Series, no. 8; Lindberg, 21–23; Seymour, 307.
27. Seymour, 310–13.
28. Ibid., 314.
29. Ibid., 317–21.
30. Ibid., 319–21.
31. Ibid., 322–23.
32. Hugh Fullerton and John Evers, *Touching Second* (Chicago: Reilly & Britton, 1910), 45.

33. BGRC file.
34. Ibid.
35. Ibid.
36. Lindberg, 27.
37. BGRC files on Owen and Patterson. *Total Baseball* gives Owen's birth year as 1879, but the BGRC file includes an obituary says his death certificate lists the year as 1881.
38. BGRC file; Porter, 586.
39. BGRC file including clip from *Albany Times Union,* July 26, 1998.
40. BGRC file.
41. Ibid.
42. Ibid.
43. Fullerton and Evers, 41.

<h3 style="text-align:center">CHAPTER 5: THE SWING GAMES</h3>

1. *Chicago Inter-Ocean,* Oct. 12.
2. *Chicago Tribune,* Oct. 12.
3. "Walsh's Start in Baseball," ibid.
4. Ibid., 1.
5. Ibid., 2.
6. *Chicago Record-Herald,* Oct. 12.
7. *Chicago Daily News,* Sporting Extra, Oct. 11.
8. Ibid.
9. "Fans Guest of *Tribune," Chicago Tribune,* Oct. 12, 2.
10. *Chicago Record-Herald,* Oct. 12.
11. *Chicago Tribune,* Oct. 12.
12. "Back to the Coop with Hoodoo Hen," *Chicago Tribune,* Oct. 13.
13. *Chicago Daily News,* Sporting Extra, Oct. 12.
14. *Chicago Daily News,* Oct. 13.

<h3 style="text-align:center">CHAPTER 6: THE FINALE</h3>

1. *Chicago Inter-Ocean,* Oct. 14; *Chicago Tribune,* Oct. 14.
2. *Chicago Tribune,* Oct. 14.
3. Ibid.
4. *Chicago Inter-Ocean,* Oct. 14.
5. *Chicago Record-Herald,* Oct. 15
6. *Chicago Inter-Ocean,* Oct. 15
7. Ibid.
8. *Chicago Record-Herald,* Oct. 15.
9. Ibid.
10. Ibid.
11. Ibid.

12. The *Tribune* and *Record-Herald* for Oct. 16 reported very slightly differ-ent numbers as did the *New York Times* of the same date. The *Daily News* had the correct figure for the gate receipts, which it put at $106,550.
13. *Chicago Tribune,* Oct. 16.

CHAPTER 7: AFTER THE LIGHTS GO DOWN

1. All information for the remainder of this chapter comes from three sources: (Thorn; et. al, *Total Baseball* Porter, ed., *BDAS;* and most of all, the extensive clipping files of the A. Bartlett Giammati Research Center in Cooperstown. I have not cited specific newspaper clippings or letters within the files, as some are undated and unmarked.

Index